A BACKGROUND OF
PHYSICAL GEOGRAPHY

+A BACKGROUND OF
PHYSICAL GEOGRAPHY

BY

GEORGE P. KELLAWAY, B.Sc., F.R.G.S.

PROFESSIONAL ASSISTANT IN THE COUNTY BOROUGH OF WIGAN EDUCATION DEPARTMENT
FORMERLY HEAD OF THE DEPARTMENT OF EDUCATION IN THE NIGERIAN COLLEGE OF ARTS,
SCIENCE AND TECHNOLOGY
SOMETIME PRINCIPAL OF THE WEYMOUTH TRAINING COLLEGE

MACMILLAN
London · Melbourne · Toronto

ST MARTIN'S PRESS
New York
1966

First Edition 1945
Reprinted 1947, 1948, 1950, 1953, 1955, 1957, 1960
Reprinted with photographs 1966

MACMILLAN AND COMPANY LIMITED
Little Essex Street London WC 2
also Bombay Calcutta Madras Melbourne

THE MACMILLAN COMPANY OF CANADA LIMITED
70 Bond Street Toronto 2

ST MARTIN'S PRESS INC
175 Fifth Avenue New York NY 10010

PRINTED IN GREAT BRITAIN

PREFACE TO THE REPRINT, 1966

THE need to reprint has provided an opportunity to include a selection of photographs illustrative of different regions, and a number of questions based on the photographs to give students practice in the interpretation of photographs.

I am indebted to my daughter, Susan, for some of these photographs.

1966.   G. P. K.

PREFACE TO THE FIRST EDITION

THE chief aim of this book is to provide a comprehensive foundation in Physical Geography for students in the Advanced Courses of schools and colleges, particularly those preparing for the " higher " examinations (General Certificate of Education at Advanced and Scholarship levels, Intermediate Degree, etc.). In such limited capacity it cannot, of course, claim to be self-sufficient for this purpose, but, at least, it provides a sound minimum on which further reading can be based.

It frequently happens that students with very little elementary knowledge of Geography discover an interest in the subject, and then find that the more advanced reading is beyond their grasp. For this reason sufficient elementary foundation has been included to enable such students to undertake the more advanced reading without undue difficulty. This feature of the book may possibly appeal to a considerably larger section of the community than that for which it is primarily intended.

The numerous diagrams which have been included at every stage should facilitate a more thorough understanding of the essential principles involved, and should be of especial service to those whose geographical background is somewhat meagre.

Throughout, every effort has been made to keep the work accurate and up to date, and although much generalisation has been inevitable, it is hoped that this has not been at the expense of sound geographical principles.

v

I have to thank the Controller, H.M. Stationery Office, for permission to reproduce the two synoptic charts on p. 180, and the following examining bodies for permission to reproduce selected questions: University of Bristol, University of Cambridge, University of London, University of Oxford, Joint Matriculation Board, Oxford and Cambridge Schools Examination Board, Central Welsh Board. The sources of individual questions are acknowledged in the section beginning on p. 227.

To my former colleague, Mr. F. J. Campbell, I wish to pay a very special tribute for his invaluable help and inspiration at all times during our association. To link his name with this book, however, would be in no sense fair to him, for he has been kept in ignorance of its preparation, and I can only hope that I have violated none of the principles which set his scholarship and teaching on such a high plane.

To my wife, also, I owe more than conventional thanks; sometimes my enthusiastic collaborator, sometimes my severe critic, she has never failed in her encouragement.

Finally, to Mr. A. J. V. Gale, who has edited the work with the utmost skill and in the spirit of full co-operation, I wish to extend my warmest thanks; ours has indeed been a happy partnership.

1944.   G. P. KELLAWAY.

CONTENTS

LIST OF PHOTOGRAPHS

(between pages 222 and 223)

BIBLIOGRAPHY

EXCEPT in the matter of treatment and presentation, this book makes no other claim to originality, and the author readily acknowledges his indebtedness to a host of published works.

Students are strongly advised to amplify their reading of this volume by making frequent reference to the appropriate sections in the many standard works which are available. The following list is by no means exhaustive, but it provides a good, representative selection:

Brooks, C. E. P. *Climate in Everyday Life* (Benn, 1950).
Brunt, Sir D. *Weather Study* (Nelson, 1942).
Holmes, A. *Principles of Physical Geology* (Nelson, 1944).
Johnstone, J. *Introduction to Oceanography* (Hodder & Stoughton).
Kendrew, W. G. *Climatology* (2nd ed., O.U.P., 1957).
—*The Climates of the Continents* (5th ed., O.U.P., 1961).
Lake, P. *Physical Geography* (4th ed., C.U.P., 1958).
Martonne, E. de. *Traité de Géographie Physique* (Colin, Paris). Also the shorter translation in English by Laborde.
Miller, A. A. *Climatology* (Methuen, 1953).
The Observer's Handbook (Meteorological Office: H.M.S.O., 1956).
Wooldridge, S. W., and Morgan, R. S. *Physical Basis of Geography* (Longmans, 1937).

G. P. K.

CHAPTER I

THE EARTH AS A PLANET

WHEN man, by reason of his intellectual superiority over the animals, eventually won for himself some degree of leisure and freedom from his ever-exacting struggle for existence, it is scarcely surprising that he began to think about the earth on which he lived, about the sun which gave him light and warmth by day, and about the moon and stars which gave him a lesser light by night. In time, learned men in the then great centres of civilisation began to formulate theories to account for what they observed. Many of these theories, it is true, seem quite fantastic to us today, but theories they were, nevertheless. They showed the mind of man at work on the problems of the universe ; they were the stepping-stones to present-day knowledge.

To the Greeks of three thousand years ago the earth was represented as a flat elliptical disc bounded by an ocean river, and it was not until the seventh century B.C. that the spherical shape appears to have been considered. Then, we read, Thales, a Greek philosopher, definitely advocated the sphere, and this view was still held by Aristotle in the fourth century B.C. In the following century Aristarchus of Samos, a Greek astronomer, taught his followers that the earth revolves round the sun, while Eratosthenes, a Greek mathematician who lived at about the same time, calculated the size of the earth with fair accuracy.

The great Roman writers, notably Strabo and Pliny in the first century A.D. and Ptolemy in the second century A.D., appear to have stressed descriptive geography rather than the mathematical aspect of the subject, with the result that a fairly complete record of the known world was compiled.

The Middle Ages thrust Geography, no less than the other sciences, back into obscurity, but fortunately many of the more valuable works lived on in the great libraries. They were recovered during the revival of interest which accompanied the great wave of exploration which followed the journeys of Marco Polo in the thirteenth century A.D.

Perhaps the grandest period in the whole history of geographical discovery occurred about the close of the fifteenth and the beginning of the sixteenth centuries. In 1486 Diaz discovered the Cape of Good Hope ; in 1492 Columbus made his famous voyage across the Atlantic to discover America ; in 1497 Vasco da Gama reached India via the

1

Cape ; in 1520 Magellan passed through the strait which bears his name and set out across the Pacific Ocean to meet his death in the Philippines, but one of his ships continued and was the first to sail right round the world.

Since then, geographical discovery has progressed enormously with the advance of science and our knowledge of the earth has become increasingly thorough, although it is still by no means complete.

SHAPE OF THE EARTH

A land-dweller, with no previously acquired knowledge of the earth, can tell very little from his own observations about its shape and movements ; mountains and valleys do not seem to conform to any particular shape. A dweller by the sea might guess rather more, for he would notice, always assuming the visibility to be perfect, that the higher he climbed above the surface of the sea the farther would be his range of vision, and that at each level there would be a definite limit to this range ; he could say that the surface of the sea appeared to be curved rather like an upturned bowl.

Fortunately, we are not dependent on our own individual observations for our knowledge of the earth's shape ; we have at our disposal all the evidence which has been accumulated throughout the ages.

The earth approximates to a sphere of radius nearly 4,000 miles, but the exact shape can only be determined after a careful study of astronomy and with the help of instruments of great precision.

After establishing the general roundness of the earth, it was discovered that the polar diameter (that is, the line passing through the earth from one pole to the other) was 26 miles shorter than the equatorial diameter (that is, a line passing through the centre of the earth and terminating at the equator). It was then held that the earth was slightly flattened at each of the two poles (due, possibly, to its rotation) and the earth was referred to as an oblate spheroid. But even this is not a satisfactory description for all purposes, for whereas the North Polar area appears to be slightly flattened, the South Polar area appears to bulge slightly. The flattening, however, is rather more pronounced than the bulging. In view of this it is now usual to speak of the earth as a geoid—a word which conveys little since it simply means earth-shaped. This departure from the spherical shape, however, must not be over-emphasised ; to liken the earth to a pear is as misleading as to liken it to an orange. Nor must we be unduly impressed with the heights of mountains and the depths of oceans. A few simple calculations will make this clear.

Suppose that the earth has been reduced to the size of a football of, say, 8 in. diameter. The shortening of the polar axis would then be represented by about *one fortieth of an inch*, while the highest mountains and deepest oceans would be represented by about *one two-hundredth of an inch*. The best of footballs, sensibly spherical, would be a much less perfect sphere than this.

Yet, in spite of the relative insignificance of these irregularities on the earth's surface, we must understand what is meant by the true earth surface. Generally we can say that free fluids will give such a surface, for their shape is controlled by gravitational force. We shall look for the shape of the earth, therefore, not over the land, but over the oceans and other large bodies of water.

Evidence for an approximately spherical shape. (*a*) One of the most striking pieces of evidence must surely be that historic voyage (since repeated many times) by one of the ships in Magellan's company. Setting out from Spain and maintaining a generally westerly course, this small vessel sailed right round the earth before returning to her home port.

(*b*) If the earth were flat the sun would rise (and set) over its whole surface at the same time, and at any particular moment the angle of incidence of the sun's rays would be uniform over the entire surface. (The sun is about 93 million miles from the earth, and as the earth is relatively small—8 thousand miles in diameter—the rays from the sun reaching the earth are practically parallel.) The accompanying diagrams show that the angle of incidence cannot be the same over the whole of a curved earth.

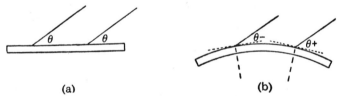

(a)   (b)

(*c*) The shadow of the earth on the moon during eclipses always has a circular outline. Of all rotating bodies, the sphere is the only one which gives a circular shadow in all positions.

(*d*) From the deck of a ship the horizon, in good visibility, always appears as a circle, described about the ship as centre; from the " crow's-nest " the horizon is a larger circle.

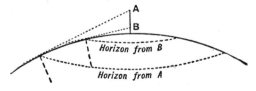

(*e*) When a ship "comes over the horizon", it is the slender mast which appears first, not the massive hull. The hull remains hidden behind the convex surface after the taller masts or funnels have appeared above it.

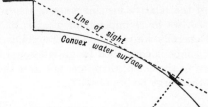

(*f*) The classic demonstration by Alfred Russel Wallace in 1870 on the Bedford Level, a continuous water surface in the Fens, showed the actual curvature of the earth very vividly. Three signals, aligned at intervals of three miles, were adjusted until they were all the same height above the surface of the water. It was then found that the middle signal protruded very nearly *six feet* above the " line of sight " joining the end pair. The " line of sight " was a straight line, but the signals conformed to the curvature of the earth. This is illustrated, in exaggerated form, in the diagram.

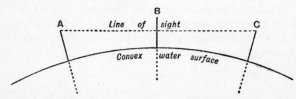

From observations of this kind it is possible to calculate the size of the earth. Let *d* miles be the distance from the middle signal to either of the terminal signals ; let *h* miles be the amount the middle signal protrudes above the line of sight joining the other two ; let *r* miles be the radius of the earth. Then $d^2 = 2rh$ (very nearly).

(*g*) Other bodies in the universe (the sun, the moon and the planets) are seen as spheres whenever, and from whatever angle, they are observed. It is reasonable to conclude that the earth, too, conforms to this seemingly universal law.

IMPORTANT DEFINITIONS

Axis. The earth rotates about an *axis* (that is, a line corresponding to an imaginary axle).

North Pole and South Pole. The points at which the axis " cuts " the earth's surface are the poles. The North Pole is the one which is directed towards the Pole Star.

Direction. Direction *over the earth's surface* is made quite simply by reference to four " cardinal points ", North, South, East and West. A north-south line is the shortest distance between the two poles ; an east-west line maintains constant distance from the poles.

In practice, the *compass* is often used to determine direction, but the **North Magnetic Pole** is by no means coincident with the *North Pole.* Over most of the globe, therefore, *magnetic north* differs from *true north*, but the difference (angle of declination) can be readily measured.

Equator. The equator is equidistant between the two poles, and is clearly a circle which divides the earth-sphere into two hemispheres (northern and southern).

Parallels of Latitude. Parallels of latitude run *parallel* to the equator, and are numbered, both northwards and southwards, according to the angle subtended at the centre of the earth by a north-south arc of surface which is bounded by the equator and the particular parallel of latitude.

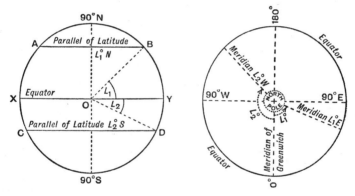

Meridians of Longitude. Meridians of longitude are *north-south lines* (that is, lines running from the North Pole to the South Pole). That which passes through Greenwich (London) is known as the **Prime Meridian**, and is numbered 0°. Other meridians are numbered from the Prime Meridian, both eastwards and westwards, according to the angle subtended at the axis by the arc of a parallel of latitude which is bounded by the Prime Meridian and the particular meridian of longitude.

The meridian opposite that of Greenwich is said to be in longitude 180° East if we approach it by travelling eastwards from Greenwich, but in longitude 180° West if we approach it by travelling westwards from Greenwich. Thus the meridians 180° E. and 180° W. are identical. Together the Prime Meridian and the meridian 180° make a complete circle ; similarly any other pair of opposite meridians makes a circle.

Position of points on the earth's surface. Latitude and longitude together enable the position of any point on the earth's surface to be defined precisely ; but it is necessary to describe the latitude and longitude *completely*.

Thus latitude $\phi°$ refers to one of two circles, and longitude $\theta°$ refers to one of two semi-circles. These intersect in *four* points, and ambiguity results. But latitude $\phi°$ N. refers to only one circle, and longitude $\theta°$ W. refers to only one semi-circle. These can only intersect in *one* point, and there is no ambiguity.

Great Circles. If we imagine a plane to pass through the centre of the earth, it will " cut " the surface of the earth in a circle (very nearly) no matter what the inclination of the plane. Such a circle is known as a **Great Circle.** The equator is clearly a Great Circle ; other parallels of latitude are not Great Circles. Any pair of opposite meridians are Great Circles.

Great Circles provide the shortest distance between two points on the surface of a sphere ; hence the value of Great Circles in navigation, both by air and sea. Great Circle routes between any specified places may be illustrated quite simply on a globe by drawing a piece of thread taut between the places.

THE GLOBE AND THE MAP

Even in comparatively primitive civilisations, men have attempted to represent by crude charts and other devices those features of the earth's surface which were of the greatest importance to them. Some such method was obviously necessary for recording ownership of land, grazing rights, the positions of neighbouring settlements, and the many other aspects of everyday life. To-day, in our highly organised society, the map is not only a kind of " shorthand " for describing the earth's features, but an almost indispensable part of the intricate machinery which has gradually been built into the lives of men. The administrator, the town-planner, the surveyor, the engineer, are but a few of the people who use maps frequently.

The only *true map* of the earth is, of course, the globe ; but the globe, though very useful, is bulky and not easy to handle, with the result that its use is restricted.

A very small part of the globe is, however, sensibly flat, and therefore can be represented on a flat sheet of paper with very little error. But when we attempt to represent the whole earth, or even a large part of it, on a flat map, we are confronted with a very different problem. First we must decide exactly what purpose the map is to serve, and we must then keep that purpose ever in mind. On a flat map we cannot possibly preserve everything exactly as it is on the globe ; at best the map will be no more than a compromise.

To help in drawing a suitable map, various **projections** have been devised. These are mathematical devices, designed so as to embody some definite principle.

Thus, if we wish to represent the whole world so that *areas* are strictly comparable over the entire surface of the map, we have a choice of several projections which will fulfil the requirements. Each will adopt its own particular method (that is, the spacing of the parallels and meridians will differ from one projection to another), but the final result will be the same—areas will be strictly comparable. But while preserving area we have ignored *shape*, *distance* and *direction* ; shape will, therefore, probably be very distorted, while distance will not only be inaccurate, but also variable from one part of the map to another.

A good atlas usually contains maps drawn on most of the common projections. An examination of different projections, used for the same earth-region, will reveal how *area*, *shape*, *distance* and *direction* all differ. It is imperative, therefore, that the underlying principle of any particular projection should be understood before a map is used to show characteristics of the earth's surface.

ROTATION OF THE EARTH

In very early days, when man first began to observe the relative movements of the earth and sun, it is not surprising that he regarded the sun as moving round a stationary earth. He was not conscious of any movement of the earth, but he was conscious of the " apparent " movement of the sun. He did not realise that the " apparent " movement of the sun from east to west could be equally well explained by a rotation of the earth from west to east and a stationary sun.

A globe may be used to illustrate some of the more important consequences of the earth's rotation, particularly if a darkened room and a parallel beam of light are available.

First, it will be noticed that exactly one half of the globe is in light and one half in darkness, and that a well-defined "shadow-line" separates the two halves. This is precisely the explanation of **day and night.**

If, now, the globe is slowly rotated from west to east (for example, so that America moves into the light as Asia moves into darkness), it will be noticed that fringes in the west move into the light as fringes in the east move into darkness. **Sunrise** begins earlier in the east, and becomes progressively later as we move to the west.

Next, let the globe complete one rotation ; the earth completes a similar rotation in one day. A person standing at either of the two Poles would merely turn completely round in a day. (We are, of course, considering only the effects of rotation.) A person standing at the equator, on the other hand, would travel about 25,000 miles through

B

space in one day (that is, at the rate of about 1,040 miles an hour). A person in the north of Scotland (latitude 60° N.) would travel at the rate of rather more than 500 miles an hour. (The length of the parallel 60° N. is one-half the length of the equator.) Yet we are not conscious of these great speeds ; everything which goes to make up the earth (land, water, atmosphere) moves as a whole. Conditions may cause relative movement within the atmosphere ; then we are conscious of a wind.   Or, again, the pilot of an aeroplane, or the driver of a motor-car, will be conscious of movement through the atmosphere because he is moving relatively to the atmosphere ; he then experiences air resistance, a very important factor in high speeds.

Longitude and Time.   Between two successive risings of the sun at any one place, 24 hours must elapse. (This statement will be modified later, but it serves the present purpose.) In that 24 hours the earth has rotated through an angle of 360°.

Thus, 360° of rotation cause a difference in time of 24 hours.
  1° of rotation causes a difference of 4 minutes.
  15° of rotation cause a difference of 1 hour.

For every 15° of longitude we move *east* from the meridian of Greenwich, the local time (that is, as determined by local observations of the sun) will be 1 hour *in advance* of Greenwich time.

For every 15° of longitude we move *west* from the meridian of Greenwich, the *local time* will be 1 hour *behind* Greenwich time.

When, at any particular place on the earth's surface, the sun reaches its highest altitude, it is noon at that place. Moreover, when it is noon at one place it is also noon at all places along the same line of longitude. (That is the reason for the name " meridian ", from the Latin *meridies*, meaning " mid-day ".) From this it follows that if we calculated *local time* from the *local noon*, each meridian would have its own *local time*. This would inevitably lead to confusion, particularly in these days when the life of even the smallest village is inseparable from the life of the country as a whole.

To eliminate the confusion which many different local times would necessarily cause, Standard Time Belts have been introduced. These belts, drawn quite arbitrarily, are zones of approximately 15° of longitude. (Latitude is of no consequence in this respect.) Over the whole belt one standard time is kept, based on the local time of one particular meridian within the belt. The standard time of one belt will then differ by an hour from the standard time of the neighbouring belt.   In Britain the standard time is based on the Meridian of Greenwich, but Eire uses its own standard. Countries such as Australia, Canada, the U.S.A., and the U.S.S.R., which have a great extent from east to west, make use of several time belts. A person travelling across such a country would therefore alter his watch by one hour on passing from one belt to the next. The same general principle applies at sea, but clocks and watches are then adjusted daily to a local time based on the position of the ship ; that time is observed throughout the day.

International Date Line. Consider first a problem which, though simple, often causes much misunderstanding. Solely as a result of the earth's rotation, a point on the equator travels about 25,000 miles through space in 24 hours, or at the rate of about 1,040 miles an hour. Now assume that an aeroplane takes off at sunrise from the point where the Meridian of Greenwich crosses the equator, and that it flies due east, just above the surface of the earth, at a speed of 260 miles an hour relative to the earth's surface. Thus, it actually has a speed of 1,040 miles an hour due to the earth's rotation, and an *additional* speed of 260 miles an hour due to the power developed by its own engines. For the present purpose it may therefore be said that the aeroplane's *base* (fixed to the earth) is travelling through space at 1,040 miles an hour, and that the *aeroplane* is travelling at 1,300 miles an hour.

Sunrise will occur again at the base 24 hours after the aeroplane took off (that is, after the base has travelled 25,000 miles). But travelling at 1,300 miles an hour, the *pilot of the aeroplane* will next see the sunrise after a little more than 19 hours (that is, after he, too, has travelled 25,000 miles, and returned to his starting-point with reference to space). This interval of 19 hours the pilot calls a *day*—the interval between two successive sunrises. Similarly his second *day* will be one of 19 hours ; and his third ; and so on.

But flying at 260 miles an hour relative to the ground, the aeroplane will again reach its base after about 96 hours' flying. Those who have remained at the base will call this period *four days*, for their *days* have each been of 24 hours. The pilot, on the other hand, will call this length of time *five days*, for his " days " have each been of about 19 hours. This difference of a day is clearly due to the fact that the pilot has ignored his own movement relative to the earth ; while the base has rotated *four* times, he has actually rotated *five* times.

Now assume that he takes off as before, and flies west instead of east. His speed through space will be 780 miles an hour ; that of the base will still be 1,040 miles an hour. The pilot's " day " will now be one of about 32 hours, and he will say that he has taken only *three days* to complete the circuit, while those who have remained at the base will still say that he has taken *four days*. Again there is a difference of a day ; the pilot has actually rotated only *three* times, whereas the base has rotated *four* times.

When moving eastwards, therefore, the effect is to *shorten the length of the apparent day* ; when moving westwards the effect is to *lengthen the apparent day*.

This same problem can be examined in another way. Again assume that the pilot takes off from the point where the Meridian of Greenwich crosses the equator, and let him fly due east. But on this circuit he will carry with him an accurate chronometer, synchronised to Greenwich Time. In longitude 15° E. he will find that the *local time* there is 1 hour *in advance of* his chronometer, and in longitude 180°E. the *local time* will be 12 hours *in advance of* his chronometer. As he continues to fly east, during the return half of the circuit, the local time will continue to *gain* on his chronometer, and when he returns to his base there will be a difference of 24 hours—a whole *day*.

If he makes the circuit flying westwards, local time will be 1 hour *behind* his chronometer in longitude 15°W., and 12 hours *behind* in longitude 180°W. As he continues to fly west, during the return half of the circuit, the local time will continue to *lose* on his chronometer, and when he returns to his base there will again be a difference of 24 hours.

Suppose, now, that the pilot, when flying westwards, suddenly *advances local time* by 24 hours when he crosses the 180th meridian (that is, he misses one whole day); he will start the return half of the circuit with local time 12 hours *in advance of* his chronometer, and he will arrive back at his base with local time synchronised to his chronometer again.

Similarly, when flying eastwards, let him suddenly *put local time back* by 24 hours when he crosses the 180th meridian (that is, let him start to count the past 24 hours all over again). He will therefore begin

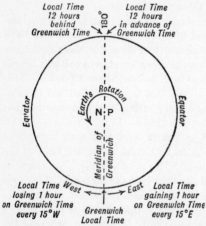

the return half of the circuit with local time 12 hours *behind* his chronometer, and he will arrive back at his base with local time synchronised to his chronometer.

This principle is, in fact, adopted at the International Date Line. On the two sides of the "line" there is a difference of one whole day in the local times. Thus, when crossing the "line" from *east* to *west* a whole day is missed; for example, the time would suddenly change from, say, 9 p.m. on April 5 to 9 p.m. on April 6. When crossing the "line" from *west* to *east* the past 24 hours must be counted afresh; for example, the time would suddenly change from 9 p.m. on April 5 to 9 p.m. on April 4.

In general the International Date Line follows the 180th meridian, for here there is almost uninterrupted ocean. The 180th meridian, however, does cross some land, and passes through certain island groups. For this reason the Date Line zig-zags, where necessary, to avoid land and to leave island groups wholly on the same side of the line. It passes between Alaska and Siberia (through the Bering Strait), and then swings away to the west to leave the whole of the Aleutian Group on the same side as Alaska. The 180th meridian is then followed to about 30°N. latitude, where another loop to the west is necessary to leave the whole of the Hawaiian Group on the east of the line. South of the equator another big bend is made, this time to the east, to leave the whole of the Fiji and Tonga Groups, together with Kermadec and the Chatham Islands, on the same side as New Zealand.

THE EARTH'S REVOLUTION

Seasons. The earth revolves round the sun once in approximately $365\frac{1}{4}$ days ; the orbit is an ellipse which lies wholly in one plane, the plane of the ecliptic. Throughout the revolution, the earth's axis is inclined at an angle of $66\frac{1}{2}°$ to the plane of the orbit. The inclination of the axis is such that the North Pole always points towards the Pole Star—at least, for the present purpose, this assumption is quite permissible. In other words, since the Pole Star may be considered as being at an infinite distance from the earth, the axis of the earth always moves parallel to itself.

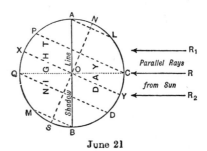

June 21

Because of the inclination of the axis, the revolution of the earth round the sun is the cause of the change of seasons through the year. The diagram shows the position of the earth in relation to the sun's rays on June 21 ; it represents a projection of the earth on the plane of the axis.

With centre O, and a suitable radius, describe a circle to represent this projection of the earth. Let the sun's rays be R, R_1, R_2, etc., and let the ray R be such that, if produced, it would pass through the centre of the earth ; then R is vertical at C ; the sun is "overhead" at C ; it is *noon* at C (and at all points along the same meridian as C). The "shadow-line" will clearly be a line at right angles to RCO, and passing through O.

Direct observation shows that the noon sun is "vertically overhead" at the Tropic of Cancer (latitude $23\frac{1}{2}°$ N.) on June 21. The point C must therefore lie on the Tropic of Cancer.

Direct observation also shows that the sun does not " sink " below the horizon at the Arctic Circle (latitude $66\frac{1}{2}°$ N.) ; nor does it " rise " above the horizon at the Antarctic Circle (latitude $66\frac{1}{2}°$ S.) on this date. The " shadow-line " will thus be inclined at an angle of $23\frac{1}{2}°$ to the axis in the diagram. The axis, NOS, may therefore be drawn ($\angle AON = 23\frac{1}{2}°$).

The equator may now be drawn, through O, at right angles to NOS. The Tropic of Cancer may also be drawn, through C, parallel to the equator. (Join CO and produce it to cut the circle at Q). The Tropic of Capricorn may be drawn, through Q, parallel to the equator. The Arctic and Antarctic Circles, also parallel to the equator, are drawn through A and B respectively. (COQ is at right angles to AOB ; XOY is at right angles to NOS. Therefore $\angle COY = \angle QOX = \angle AON = 23\frac{1}{2}°$. Therefore the " Tropics " are correctly spaced in relation to the equator. Also $\angle YOB = \angle XOA = \angle (XON - AON) = 66\frac{1}{2}°$. Therefore the " Circles " are correctly spaced in relation to the equator.)

As the earth rotates about its axis NOS, no point within the area ANL (that is, within the Arctic Circle) can possibly rotate into *night*, and no point within the area BSM (that is, within the Antarctic Circle) can possibly rotate into *day*. The equator, however, is " bi-sected " by the " shadow-line ", and will therefore experience equal day and night.

On June 21, therefore, we pass from 24 hours' continuous daylight for every point within the Arctic Circle, to 12 hours of daylight and 12 hours of night at the equator, and to 24 hours' continuous night for every point within the Antarctic Circle. In the Northern Hemisphere days are longer than nights ; in the Southern Hemisphere nights are longer than days. The north of Scotland (60° N.) has a longer period of daylight than the south of England (50° N.) *at this date.*

By varying the position of the " overhead sun ", the diagram can be modified to illustrate conditions throughout the whole of the northern summer season. Thus, on May 21 (or July 21) the sun will be " overhead " in about latitude 16° N. (*C* will therefore be in latitude 16° N., and $\angle YOC = \angle AON = 16°$.)

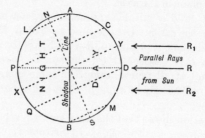

December 21

The position of the earth in relation to the sun's rays on December 21 is shown in the diagram (p. 12). Now the sun is " overhead " at the Tropic of Capricorn ; every point within the Arctic Circle is in continuous night for 24 hours ; the equator still experiences 12 hours of daylight and 12 hours of night ; every point within the Antarctic Circle is in continuous daylight for 24 hours. In the Northern Hemisphere nights are now longer than days ; in the Southern Hemisphere *days* are longer than *nights*. The length of daylight will be greater in the south of England than in the north of Scotland.

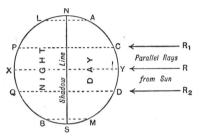

March 21 and September 22

The diagram shows the position of the earth in relation to the sun's rays on March 21 (and September 22). Now the sun is " overhead " at the equator, and in the diagram the " shadow-line " becomes coincident with the axis. Every parallel of latitude is therefore " bisected " by the " shadow-line ", and every point on the globe will experience 12 hours of daylight and 12 hours of night.

Thus, between March and September the " overhead " noon sun *appears* to approach the Tropic of Cancer, remain stationary for a day, and then withdraw towards the equator. This day—June 21—when the overhead sun *appears to stand still* over the Tropic of Cancer, is known as the **Northern Summer Solstice** (from the Latin *sol*, meaning " sun ', and *stare*, meaning " to stand "). Similarly, December 21, when the noon sun is vertical over the Tropic of Capricorn, is known as the **Northern Winter Solstice.**

The two days, March 21 and September 22, when the noon sun is " overhead " at the equator, are known as the **Equinoxes** (from the Latin *aequus*, meaning " equal ", and *nox*, meaning " night "), that is, the times of " equal nights " over the whole globe. March 21 is called the **Spring (or Vernal) Equinox** ; September 22 (or 23) the **Autumnal Equinox.**

The different " seasonal positions " of the earth may all be shown on one diagram. Here, however, several difficulties arise. First, there is the question of scale. On an ordinary piece of paper it is impossible to represent the size and distance of the sun correctly, even if the earth

is made very small. Secondly, there are the difficulties which arise
when we attempt to represent in two dimensions something which
actually occurs in three.

In the accompanying diagram we are to imagine the four circles as
standing up on the plane of the paper. They are placed round an
ellipse, at the centre of which is the sun. (Actually the sun is not

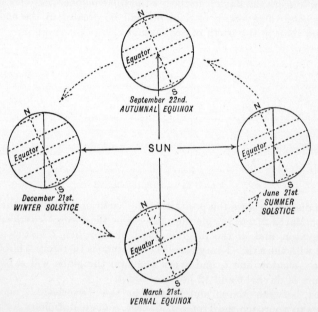

quite at the centre of the earth's orbit, but for the present purpose we
may assume that it is.)

Now suppose that we are looking *across* this ellipse from a point well
outside the ellipse and above the plane of the ellipse. Of the nearest
circle we shall see only that half which is in darkness. (The face turned
away from us will be in the light.) Of the farthest circle we shall see
only that half which is in the light. (The face turned away from us
will be in darkness.) Of the two circles to our left and right we shall
see one half in light (nearer the sun) and one half in darkness. (The
faces which are turned away from us will be similarly divided.) Thus,
in all four positions, we may imagine the " two-faced " circles as half
in day and half in night.

When showing several positions of the earth on one diagram the
axes must all be parallel in the several positions.

To show the actual point of incidence of the " overhead ray " two
different methods are used. In the case of the June and December

positions, the method of the diagram on p. 11 is followed, but in the March and September positions the point of incidence is shown on the equator, at the centre of the circle. Both methods may be considered correct ; the choice is merely one of convenience and suitability.

Other effects of the Earth's Revolution. The varying lengths of day and night are clearly an important aspect of " season ". Thus, in the British Isles there are long hours of daylight in summer, and equally long nights in winter.

Another important aspect of " season " is the altitude (or angle of elevation) of the noon sun.

The diagram, which represents conditions on June 21, shows the altitude of the noon sun in latitude 50° N. The angle of elevation of the noon sun is the angle between the ray RL and the tangent at L (LGT) ; but

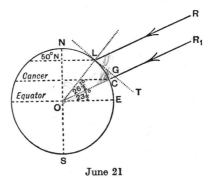

June 21

$\angle RLT = \angle LGO = 90° - (\angle LOE$
$- \angle COE) = (90 - 26\frac{1}{2})° = 63\frac{1}{2}°.$

In the south of England, therefore, the noon elevation of the sun on June 21 is $63\frac{1}{2}°$, and this is the highest elevation ever attained in that latitude.

In the north of Scotland (latitude 60° N.) the noon elevation on June 21 is $53\frac{1}{2}°$.

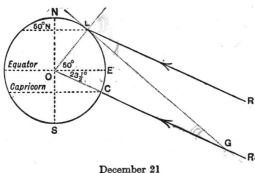

December 21

The conditions on December 21, showing the noon elevation in latitude 50° N., are represented in the diagram.

Now $\angle RLG = \angle LGO = 90° - (\angle LOE + \angle EOC) = (90 - 73\frac{1}{2})° = 16\frac{1}{2}°.$

In the south of England, therefore, the noon elevation of the sun on December 21 is $16\frac{1}{2}°$; in the north of Scotland it is only $6\frac{1}{2}°$.

The noon elevation of the sun may be expressed generally as follows :

June 21.

$90° - (L° - 23\frac{1}{2}°)$, where $L°$ is any given latitude between $23\frac{1}{2}°$ N. and $90°$ N.

$90° + (L° - 23\frac{1}{2}°)$, where $L°$ is any given latitude between the equator and $23\frac{1}{2}°$ N.

December 21.

$90° - (23\frac{1}{2}° + L°)$, where $L°$ is any given latitude between the equator and $66\frac{1}{2}°$ N.

The sun does not rise above the horizon in latitudes north of $66\frac{1}{2}°$ N.

March 21 and September 22.

$(90° - L°)$, where $L°$ is any given latitude (north or south).

The angle of elevation of the sun is an important factor in determining the amount of solar energy incident upon unit area of the outer spherical surface of the atmosphere.

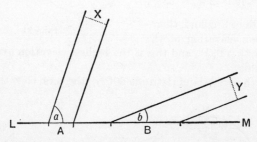

Let X and Y be two equal beams of " solar energy " (that is, they include both heat and light, and all other rays emitted by the sun) incident on a surface LM. Let the angle of incidence of X be a, and the angle of incidence of Y be b, and let the areas " covered " by the beams be A and B respectively.

Since the beams X and Y are of equal cross-sectional area and have passed only through space, there is no reason for supposing that one should possess more solar energy than the other. But the diagram makes it clear that, if the angles of incidence are different, the areas on the surface LM, " covered " by the beams, will be different. Thus if $\angle a$ is greater than $\angle b$, then area A is less than area B, and the intensity of the energy on A greater than that on B.

In other words, the solar energy will be more *concentrated* if the area is smaller ; the greater the angle of incidence, the greater the potential heating effect of the sun's rays.

The angle of incidence also has another effect. The diagram represents, in very exaggerated form, the "shell" of atmosphere which surrounds the land and water surfaces of the earth.

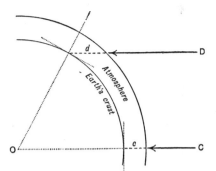

When solar energy passes through the atmosphere, some of the energy is given up to the atmosphere, not so much to the air itself as to the numerous impurities—countless millions of particles of dust, smoke, etc., minute droplets of water, and water vapour.

When the angle of elevation of the sun *decreases*, the distance which the rays have to travel to cross the " shell " of atmosphere increases. (The distance *d* is clearly greater than the distance *c*.) Further, it is reasonable to assume that the farther a ray has to travel through the atmosphere, the greater will be the amount of solar energy given up to the atmosphere, and the less will be the amount available for heating the land and water surfaces. (Most of the energy given up to the atmosphere is transformed into heat which is distributed through the atmosphere. Gradually this heat is dissipated into space, and so lost to the earth before it has produced any appreciable effect.)

The energy which ultimately reaches the land and water surfaces is transformed into heat on those surfaces. Such heated surfaces, in turn, heat the lower layers of the atmosphere (that is, those layers of the atmosphere in which we live our normal lives). This heat, too, is gradually dissipated into space, but not until we have experienced its effects. The land masses and large bodies of water thus become the *effective* source of the heat which warms the atmosphere. In fact, the earth may be regarded as a *dark radiator*, transmitting afresh the energy which it has received from the sun, which is a *bright radiator*.

In general we may say, therefore, that the greater the angle of elevation of the sun's rays, the more " concentrated " the solar energy which is incident on the outer surface of the atmosphere, and the greater the proportion of the total which actually reaches the land and water surfaces.

The heating effect will, clearly, be at a maximum when the rays are vertical upon the surface. In equatorial regions the angle of incidence, during a large part of the day, is always fairly large, with the result that equatorial regions are always warm, and usually hot.

In polar regions the angle of incidence is never large, and for long periods the sun does not rise above the horizon, with the result that polar regions are usually cold, and never more than warm.   In Britain the marked difference between the summer and winter elevations gives rise to the warmer summer temperatures.

Thus, the inclination of the earth's axis, together with the earth's revolution round the sun, is the cause of the various factors which go to distinguish one season from another :

(a) the varying lengths of daylight and darkness,

(b) the angle of elevation of the noon sun,

(c) the amount of " solar energy " which actually reaches any particular part of the earth's surface.

From what has been said it will be apparent that (c) is, in effect, the direct result of a combination of (a) and (b), for the total amount of solar energy which reaches the earth's surface at any particular place in one day will depend, *partly* on the duration of daylight, and *partly* on the rate at which the energy is being given up to the earth. (A *longer* day with slightly *lower* temperatures may well be as useful for agriculture, for example, as a rather *shorter* day with slightly *higher* temperatures.   This principle has, in fact, been demonstrated in Canada.)

It must be understood, however, that in this discussion we have been concerned only with the effects due to rotation.   We have completely ignored such other important factors as " cloud cover ", which will exert a powerful modifying influence.

Apparent Course of the Sun across the Sky in the different seasons. Suppose we are standing in the south of England, facing due south :

At the Equinoxes the sun would rise due east (that is, to our left), travel across the sky in front of us so that, at noon, its elevation would be about 40°, and set due west.

At the Summer Solstice the sun would rise in the north-east (that is, rather behind us, to our left), travel across the sky to reach its maximum elevation of about 63½° at noon, and set in the north-west (that is, rather behind us, to our right).

At the Winter Solstice the sun would rise in the south-east (that is, rather in front of us, to our left), travel low across the sky to reach its greatest elevation of 16½° at noon, and set in the south-west (that is, rather in front of us, to our right).

At the Summer Solstice the sun would be above the horizon for about 16 hours ;   at the Winter Solstice for about 8 hours ;   at the Equinoxes for 12 hours.

The lengths of the " apparent " courses of the sun will thus be proportional to the time that the sun is above the horizon.

Similarly, the " apparent " course of the sun may be ascertained for any other given latitude (such as the equator, tropics, polar circles, poles).

Dawn and Twilight. Light from the sun can reach us even when the sun is below the horizon, provided that the angle of depression of the sun is not more than 18°. *Direct* light, of course, ceases as soon as the sun disappears below the horizon. But *indirect* light may reach us : (a) by *refraction*—that is, by the bending of the rays as they pass from one " medium " to another which has different optical properties (layers of air at different temperatures may possess such properties) ; (b) by *diffused reflection* from " banks " of clouds, etc. ; (c) by the *scattering* of light by countless millions of minute particles of dust, etc., which are floating about in the atmosphere, particularly in its lower layers.

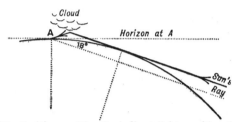

The limiting position for indirect light reaching A

The sun's light (" white " light) is made up of a number of " primary colours " (the " colours of the rainbow "), *blended* together. Each primary colour has a definite wave-length, that of *red* being the longest, and that of *violet* being the shortest. The amount each colour is " bent " by refraction depends on the wave-length, the light of longest wave-length being least refracted. During the processes of refraction, reflection and scattering, the colours of shortest wave-length are quickly " lost ", but those of longest wave-length are capable of greater penetration, and hence predominate in the composition of indirect light.

At the first sign of the dawn, therefore, it is the deep red which appears (that is, the least refracted and least scattered colour). As the angle of depression of the sun below the horizon decreases, colours with gradually decreasing wave-lengths enter into the composition of the indirect light. Thus, the sky just above the eastern horizon changes to orange, then gold, and then to a clear bright yellow, at which stage the sun may be expected to " appear ".

During twilight this order of colours is reversed. Just after sunset the sky above the western horizon is a clear bright yellow. Gradually the colour changes to a rich gold, then to orange, and finally to warm reds which deepen as night falls ; the most refracted colours disappear before the longer wave-length colours which are less refracted.

The actual colour tones and the duration of the dawn and twilight vary considerably from day to day, but, in general, the duration of twilight is longer than that of the dawn. (The conditions necessary for the refraction, reflection, and scattering of light are usually more favourable in the evening than in the morning.) Nor are the duration of the dawn and twilight by any means equal all over the earth. In the tropics, where the sun approaches the horizon at an angle which is never very far from the vertical, the duration of both the dawn and twilight is short. By comparison with the British dawn and twilight, the transition from day to night within the tropics is a remarkably short period. High mountains produce very much the same sort of effect. In high latitudes the sun approaches the horizon very obliquely, and will therefore take a correspondingly longer time to reach an angle of depression of 18°, with the result that both the dawn and twilight are well-marked periods. This is shown in the diagram, where

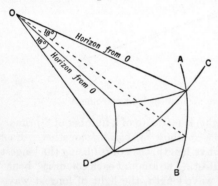

two very different apparent paths of the sun cross the twilight zone. The line *AB* shows the shortest possible crossing of the twilight zone, when the sun, as viewed from *O*, approaches the horizon vertically; *CD* shows the apparent path when the sun, as seen from *O*, approaches the horizon obliquely. The sun will clearly take longer to cross this zone by the path *CD* than by the path *AB*.

The Equation of Time. The earth revolves around the sun in a huge ellipse which, however, does not differ greatly from a circle. Assume for a moment that the earth's orbit is actually a circle, and that the sun is situated at its centre. The radius of this circle would then be about 93 million miles, which is the earth's mean distance from the sun. Now, the velocity of a planet about its parent body depends on the gravitational pull between them, and this, in turn, depends on the distance between their centres. (The actual relation is not quite so simple as this.) If, therefore, the earth's orbit were really a circle, the earth would revolve round the sun with uniform velocity. This means that the solar day (the interval between two successive noon elevations of the sun) would be uniform throughout the year.

But the earth's orbit is not quite a circle; it is an ellipse, and the sun is situated, not at its centre, but at one of the two foci. (Just as a circle can be described about a centre, so an ellipse can be described, by applying the appropriate laws, about two points known as its foci.) The distance of the earth from the sun therefore varies according to the position of the earth in its orbit. At its shortest this distance is about 91½ million miles (December 21) ; at its longest it is about 94½ million miles (June 21).

When the earth is closer to the sun it moves faster along its orbit ; when it is farther away it moves more slowly. Rotation is not affected. Thus the solar day varies.

A method has been devised to obviate such inconveniences as a *varying length* of day would inevitably cause. Time based on observations of the noon sun is known as **apparent time**, and it is the time that the sundial records. If, now, we average the solar days throughout the year, we can obtain a value for a uniform day ; this is the **mean solar day.** This is the time which is generally in use—the time on which **Greenwich Mean Time** is based, for example. The divergence between mean solar time and apparent time is known as the **Equation of Time** and has a maximum value of about 16 minutes.

The position of the sun with reference to the earth's orbit is illustrated (in exaggerated form) in the diagram where F_1 represents the sun and F_2 the other focus of the elliptical orbit.

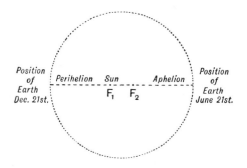

Measurement of Latitude. In these days, when travel by sea and air is so general, the determination of position (or navigation) is an increasingly important science. Latitude is normally determined by one or other of the following methods :

(i) *Observation of the sun* as it crosses the meridian (that is, at noon). The noon elevation of the sun is measured by means of the sextant, and the latitude can then be determined by referring to the " Nautical Almanac ".

(ii) *Observation of the stars.* The angle of elevation of a known star on the meridian is observed, and the latitude can again be found by referring to the " Nautical Almanac ".

(iii) *Observation of the Pole Star.* This requires an observation of the star's true altitude, together with an observation of local apparent time. As before, the " Nautical Almanac " is consulted.

Measurement of Longitude. An observation of local apparent time can readily be made (for example, by observation of the noon sun). Local apparent time must then be converted to local mean solar time by means of the Equation of Time, and then a comparison can be made with Greenwich Mean Time.

Formerly the only method of determining Greenwich Mean Time was to carry an accurate chronometer. Nowadays accurate time signals are radiated at regular intervals by certain wireless stations.

CHAPTER II

THE " SOLID " EARTH

BEFORE turning to the more prominent features of the build and constitution of the earth itself, it will be instructive to examine certain of the established facts which relate to the solar system and some of the theories which have been advanced, from time to time, to explain the origin of the earth.

The Solar System. The earth is only one of a number of planets which revolve round the sun.

	Diameter	Mean Distance from sun	Number of satellites
Sun	886,400 miles	—	—
Mercury	3,030	36 million miles	0
Venus	7,700	67	0
Earth	7,918	93	1 (The Moon)
Mars	4,230	142	2
Jupiter	86,500	483	9
Saturn	73,000	886	9
Uranus	31,900	1,782	4
Neptune	34,800	2,792	1

In addition there are, between Mars and Jupiter, many hundreds, if not thousands, of planetoids (frequently, though less correctly, called asteroids), the largest of which is Ceres, about 500 miles in diameter. These are, in fact, minor planets. Quite recently (1930) yet another member of the solar system was discovered outside the orbit of Neptune. This " new " planet, Pluto, is evidently very small—perhaps even smaller than our moon—and rather resembles a planetoid.

This particular arrangement of the solar system has attracted considerable attention in recent years because, it is claimed, it may well throw light on the mode of evolution of the system, and hence on the origin of the earth (see p. 25).

The Value of Theories. After a careful study of the earth had once been started certain facts gradually came to light. Men of science then tried to weave these facts into a pattern ; in other words, they evolved theories to account for what they observed. Right or wrong, such theories are most valuable in furthering knowledge.

From a general theory, it can frequently be deduced that " properties " other than the facts already observed should become evident. The theories often suggest exactly what should be looked for. If, then, these " theoretical properties " do, in time, become " observed facts ", support is added to the theory. If theoretical properties do not at once become evident, it is not necessarily because the theory is at fault ; our methods of observation might not be sufficiently delicate. If, however, facts observed afterwards show that the theoretical properties do not exist, or are only partially correct, the existing theory must be either modified or replaced by an entirely new one which will satisfy all the known facts. As more and more facts become known, theory after theory might become necessary, each one approaching nearer and nearer to the truth as portrayed by up-to-date knowledge.

This is very much the position we are in to-day concerning many of the problems connected with the origin and subsequent development of the earth.

THEORIES CONCERNING THE ORIGIN OF THE EARTH

Kant's Theory. In the middle of the eighteenth century, Kant, the great Prussian philosopher, advanced his theory of the universe. He assumed that there was first a vast cloud of supernaturally created matter. He further assumed that the millions and millions of particles, falling in towards a common centre under their mutual gravitational attraction, would collide and so generate heat and rotation in the mass. In this way a vast hot nebula would come into being, rotating so rapidly that rings of matter would be thrown off from its equator by centrifugal force. These discarded rings would " condense " into planets, leaving the residual mass in the centre as the sun. In a similar way, each planet would throw off rings to form satellites. Thus, he supposed, the solar system was " born ". Although this theory is fundamentally unsound (in that the rotation of the nebula could not have been produced by the collision of particles within the original cloud) it is, nevertheless, of great interest in that it was the forerunner of the famous " Nebular Hypothesis " which was generally accepted up to comparatively recent times.

The Nebular Theory. This theory, as generally understood, was first advanced by Laplace, the eminent French mathematician and astronomer, towards the close of the eighteenth century. Unlike Kant, Laplace did not attempt to show how the rotation came into being ; he assumed supernatural agencies. Thus he started with a nebula, already hot and rotating. This gaseous mass, he now assumed, would cool and, as a result, contract. Contraction would increase the speed of rotation which would, in turn, increase the centrifugal force at the equator. In time, when this equatorial centrifugal force exactly balanced the gravitational attraction, an equatorial ring would be able to stand away from the contracting mass. This ring would later " condense " to form a planet, and so the process would go on until the solar system as we know it to-day came into being.

Both Kant's theory and the Nebular theory, which assume that the origin of the earth and other planets was in a nebula, therefore assume that the earth passed from a gaseous to a molten state, during which phase a solid crust formed.

Our modern knowledge shows that the nebular hypothesis, in its simple form, is not a wholly satisfactory theory, but that it is not without its uses.

Tidal Theories. At the beginning of the twentieth century the Planetesimal Hypothesis was advanced. This theory supposes that the solar system came into being when another large star passed so close to the sun that the resulting gravitational attraction caused the sun to break up. (The sun is only one of many stars in the universe.) The theory further supposes that, following the disruption of the sun, small particles of solar matter were thrown very great distances and drawn forward in the direction of the passing star. In time, under gravitational attraction, nuclei were formed and these, in turn, became " planetesimals "—very small planets—which, in their turn, became planets.

This theory does not, therefore, assume that the earth was ever wholly in a molten state. It does admit that heat would undoubtedly be generated and that pockets of molten material would probably appear in the earth ; and it does assume that all the materials of the earth came from the planetesimals (and hence from the sun), added bit by bit so that, in effect, the earth " grew ". (This theory is one of the " Tidal Theories ". The subject of " Tides on the Earth " will be dealt with later (see p. 117). For the present it is sufficient to note that a fluid body can suffer great distortion as a result of gravitational attraction. Such distortion may be referred to as " tidal distortion ".)

More recently still, other tidal theories, with various modifications, have been put forward. Thus, it has been pointed out that if a star, several times larger than the sun, were to pass the sun within a certain limiting distance, the tidal distortion produced might be so great that the sun would break up. Moreover, in the disruption, comparatively substantial masses of the sun might be thrown out into space with very little scattering. Gravitational attraction would bring about concentrations of such solar matter ; and so the planets would be " born ", all of the same age and all revolving round the sun.

New Theories. Weizsäcker's Theory is tantamount to a restatement of the nebular hypothesis, modified so as to overcome some of the difficulties encountered by earlier theories of this kind. The fundamental hypothesis is that a nebulous envelope was rotating round an already existing sun, and that initially the envelope was of the same chemical composition as the sun. It is then argued that the present planets, which are of different chemical composition, represent only a small fraction of the original mass of the envelope.

Alfvén's Theory postulates that the planetary system came into being following the passage of the sun through an interstellar cloud, when the collision of neutral atoms, falling towards the sun under gravitational attraction, produced heat and ionization. The ions, moving under the influence of the sun's electromagnetic field, which was sufficiently powerful to counteract gravity, accumulated near the sun's equatorial plane, where they again became neutral and hence acquired gravitational orbits.

In time, more facts about the universe may become known, and the origin of the earth may then become less of a mystery.

INTERIOR OF THE EARTH

The Core. Whatever the actual constitution of the earth, we now know that, in many respects, it is almost as rigid as if it were made of steel throughout. Further, whereas the average density of the surface rocks is rather less than three times that of water, the density of the earth as a whole is about five and a half times that of water. (The earth has actually been " weighed " by applying the principle of gravitational attraction.)

This established fact leads to the belief that the density of a central core of the earth must be high—seven or eight times that of water. Here we encounter a major difficulty, for the temperatures and pressures prevailing in this central core must greatly exceed any that can be created on the surface. (As we pass down through the earth's outer rock layer we know that the temperature increases at an average rate of about 1° C. for every 100 ft. of descent.) Since we cannot carry out experiments under comparable conditions of temperature and pressure, we cannot say, with any certainty, in precisely what state the materials at the centre of the earth exist. It may well be that they exist in a state very different from any we know on the surface. However, as a result of the many and careful observations that have been made of the earth's " behaviour ", and in particular from an examination of records of earthquakes, it is possible to draw certain conclusions.

It is now widely believed that the high density of the central core is not due to pressure, but that the materials there are naturally heavy (that is, they would still be heavy if they were on the surface). It has therefore been suggested that the core is largely metallic, probably consisting mainly of nickel-iron. This would seem to agree fairly well with what has already been said about the earth's rigidity.

The Crust. Surrounding this core is a zone of rock material, the upper part of which we know, by direct observation, is crystalline. The lower part is beyond the reach of direct observation at present, and the same uncertainty as exists in the case of the core must persist here. However, it is probably not too rash to suggest that the separation of the crystalline " crust " from the metallic " core " bears some resemblance to the formation of the stony slag in the smelting furnace. If we accept this, we might carry the suggestion a stage further ; although the earth now behaves as a solid, it has probably passed through a molten or liquid phase.

It is frequently claimed that, because molten lava flows from the earth during volcanic activity, the interior of the earth must be in a liquid state. This is by no means necessarily so. We have already admitted that uncertainty must exist because we do not know the effects of the very high temperatures and pressures prevailing below the crust. But, in the case of a volcano, we can most certainly assume that when the pressure is released locally (as it is when the crust is fractured) the temperatures are such that the materials underlying the crust, in the neighbourhood of the fracture, can become molten, even if they were not so already. It is probable, therefore, that the sudden release of pressure over a comparatively small area brings into being a pocket of molten lava, which flows out on to the earth's surface.

Seismological Evidence. Before attempting to complete the picture of the earth as it is to-day, brief reference must be made to one of the most important methods of observation of the constitution of the earth, namely, seismology, or the study of earthquakes. When an earthquake occurs (that is, when there is a fracture and local movement of some part of the earth's surface), " waves " travel out from the centre of disturbance in a variety of ways and are recorded on instruments known as seismographs, which detect even slight vibrations of the earth's surface. By a careful study of such records, made at a great number of places for any one earthquake centre, it has been possible to calculate the speeds of the various " waves " through the different " zones " or " layers " of the earth, and hence to determine the different densities of the zones or layers. Largely as a result of this method, we are able to deduce certain definite properties of the earth. Silicates, which include the minerals felspar and mica, predominate in the crystalline portions of the earth's crust, and we can now say that there are at least two zones or layers in the crystalline " crust " : an upper layer of lighter silicates (mainly granitic) and a lower layer of somewhat heavier silicates (mainly basaltic).

So far, however, observers are not agreed on a uniform classification of these different layers. While noticing that some prefer to speak of an upper layer as the sial and of a lower layer as the sima, it would be as well, perhaps, to be content with the simpler terms " crust " and " substratum ". (" Crust " used in this sense is not identical with sial, but includes also the upper part of the sima.) For most purposes it is sufficient to regard the earth as having a more or less solid crust, some 40–50 miles in thickness.

We shall return later to this subject of the earth's structure in layers or shells (see p. 31).

THE OCEANS AND THE CONTINENTS

Most people are familiar with some of the legends of " lost continents "; many are equally familiar with the historical facts of changing coast-lines.

These two aspects of a changing earth surface are very different. The first involves a major earth-movement (a tectonic movement) ; the second involves only a local change in the relative levels of land and sea—and frequently only a very small change—which might be due to a variety of causes.

The " ground-plan " of the present-day earth shows that about 29 per cent. of the total surface is land, while the remaining 71 per cent. is water. Study of the general lay-out of the continents and oceans on a globe will show that the north polar area is an almost land-locked expanse of water—an " ocean-basin ". Surrounding this "Arctic Ocean " is an almost continuous land-girdle, from which the great land masses seem to " hang " southwards. Three such groupings of land can be recognised, and in each group we notice that, in a general way, the land-masses taper towards the south. This is broadly true of North and South America, of Europe and Africa, and of Asia and Australia. Now turn to the south polar area. Here we find a land-mass, completely surrounded by a " water-girdle ", from which the great oceans extend northwards, separating the continents. Just as the continents taper to the south, so do the oceans taper to the north.

Now let us look at these continents and oceans in another way. As a result of the vast amount of exploration and surveying that has been done over the earth's surface, both the heights of the continents and the depths of the oceans are now known with very fair accuracy. The accompanying diagram (p. 29) illustrates these features. Along the Y-axis are plotted heights above sea-level and depths below sea-level. Along the X-axis is plotted the total area of the earth's surface at each particular height and depth. Thus, between sea-level and 600 ft. above sea-level there are about 15 million square miles of land. We therefore plot along the X-axis a length, representing 15 million square miles, to correspond to a change of height along the Y-axis from sea-level to 600 ft. above sea-level.

Two features are immediately apparent from this diagram. First, nearly one half of the total land area is at a height of 600–3,000 ft. above sea-level. Another quarter is less than 600 ft. above sea-level. Secondly, well over a half of the total ocean floor is at a depth of

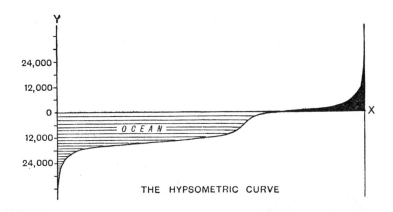

THE HYPSOMETRIC CURVE

12,000–18,000 ft. below sea-level. Generalised in this way, the " solid crust " of the earth appears to conform to two main levels ; there is an " average " ocean floor and an " average " continental surface. A third feature, also clearly shown in the diagram, is that these two levels are joined by a relatively steep slope—the continental slope. Fourthly, the very high parts of the land and the very deep parts of the ocean form, in the aggregate, a relatively insignificant proportion of the earth's total area.

We shall have occasion to refer to these important aspects of the earth's build again (see pp. 31 and 32).

Now examine the cross-sections (below) through the actual ocean floors. They are, of course, greatly exaggerated, but they give a clear idea of the form of the ocean floor, nevertheless.

The first thing to note is that generally the oceans are not deepest in the middle. This is contrary to what might be expected, and to early conceptions of the " ocean basin ". Until accurate and extensive sounding had been carried out, it was widely believed that the ocean

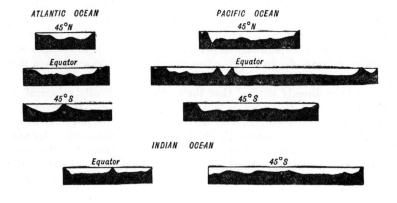

floors somewhat resembled a relatively shallow saucer. Actually they are more like soup-plates, deepening rapidly from a comparatively narrow rim.

These prominent features of the continents and oceans can be represented in a generalised cross-section, taken through a typical continent and ocean basin (see diagram).

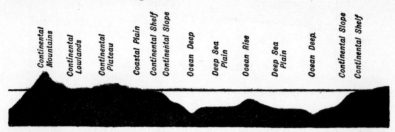

Although there is a suggestion of permanence about such an arrangement of land and water (very different from the former conceptions of ocean basins as shallow depressions, and continents as slight upward warpings), it must not be thought that the oceans and continents have necessarily always maintained their form and position exactly as we know it to-day.

ORIGIN OF THE CONTINENTS AND OCEANS

Tetrahedral Theory. This theory, which was evolved in the second half of the nineteenth century, was inspired by the peculiar arrangement of the continents and oceans. It is a well-known fact that whereas the sphere has the least possible surface area for a given volume, the tetrahedron (a pyramid on a triangular base), of all the regular figures, has the greatest. This aspect of the sphere and tetrahedron makes the theory look very attractive at first sight, for if we assume that a spherical earth cooled and contracted, the " solid " crust, unable to contract at the same rate as the " molten " core, would tend to conform to a figure of much smaller volume in proportion to its surface area. (Further, experiment shows that a sphere tends to collapse into a tetrahedron ; for example, when the air is withdrawn from a thin spherical shell.)

We have already noticed that the earth is practically spherical, so the tetrahedral tendency is not very pronounced. However, the similarity is interesting. The north polar area (slightly flattened) would come in the centre of the triangular base ; the south polar area (slightly bulging) would form the apex of the pyramid ; the great ocean basins (Atlantic, Pacific and Indian) would form the three flat faces ; the great continental " belts " would form the three ridges running from base to apex. Lines drawn on the globe well illustrate this tetrahedral arrangement. Attractive as this theory looks, it is not now generally accepted.

Wegener's Theory of Continental Drift. This theory, advanced in the early years of the present century, takes us back to the layer build of the earth. It had long been noticed that different parts of the earth's surface, now widely separated, are very similar, sometimes in their build, sometimes in some peculiar form of animal life or vegetation. Thus, the Brazilian Highlands, the African Plateau, the Indian Deccan and Western Australia present a marked similarity of build ; living marsupials (animals with pouches for carrying their immature young) are found only in Australia and Chile, though fossil remains have been found in other parts of South America ; certain types of vegetation, notably the Glossopteris flora associated with the coal-bearing beds of the southern continents and India, are found only in these same areas.

Again, from a study of rock formations, fossil remains of flora and fauna (natural vegetation and animal life), etc., it is now known that many parts of the earth have not always had the same climate as they experience to-day. This would involve either a variation in the climatic zones (and hence a fundamental change in the solar system), or a drifting of land-masses from one climatic zone to another. (In part, the observed facts could be explained by appreciable changes in the elevation or depression of the land-masses.)

Some support for the theory of " drift " was found in the shapes of eastern South America and western Africa ; one could easily imagine that these two areas had once made a good fit. Even this fit, however, when examined on the globe, is not so good as it appears at first. A better case could most certainly be made for the islands lying in the north-east of the American continent (Greenland, Baffin Land, etc.).

According to Wegener, then, the great land-masses originally formed one major unit, named by him " Pangaea ". From this proto-continent two continental masses eventually evolved : a northern block, comprising what is now North America, Europe, and Asia, and a southern block, comprising what is now South America, Africa, Peninsular India, Australasia and Antarctica. Separating these two blocks was the " Tethys Sea ". Later, by a similar process of " drifting ", the continents assumed their present shapes and position.

Wegener's theory, in its original form, is no longer acceptable, but the general conception of continental drift is by no means dead. In fact, when dealing with many of the problems connected with the build of the earth, it is convenient to think of the continents as " rafts of sial floating on a layer of rather denser sima ".

Theory of Subsidence and Uplift. This theory, formerly more widely held than now when applied to major continental areas, is another attempt to explain the many points of similarity already noticed over widely differing parts of the southern hemisphere. In this case it is assumed that one great continent (to which the name " Gondwanaland " has been given) extended from Brazil, through Africa and India, to Western Australia. The build of such a continent, forming from the molten material of the earth, would have been sensibly uniform over its entire area ; flora and fauna would have developed along comparable lines over its entire area. Then, it is assumed, this continent was fractured and large areas foundered beneath the sea. From that time, with the land-bridges broken, flora and fauna would develop independently, but would continue to show their common ancestry. To accept this theory, however, is to concede that a large part of the present Indian Ocean was once part of a continental mass.

Yet, in some respects, the idea of subsidence and uplift is of the greatest importance in the study of certain features of the earth's build. We shall have occasion to refer to it again at a later stage (p. 43).

Theory of Isostasy. Consideration of a simple problem in flotation will assist in understanding this principle.

Suppose that we have two solid cylinders of equal weight, W, and equal cross-sectional area, A. Let the density of one be D, and of the other d ; and their heights H and h respectively. Their volumes will then be AH and Ah respectively, while their weights will be AHD and Ahd respectively.

$$Thus\ AHD = Ahd = W.$$

Suppose these cylinders could be floated (with their axes vertical) in a liquid of density D_1. Now apply Archimedes' Principle.

Since the weights of the two cylinders are equal and since their areas of cross-section are equal, they will displace the same volume of liquid, and hence have the same depth immersed. Let this depth be x. Then the weight of liquid displaced is AxD_1.

$$Thus\ AHD = Ahd = AxD_1,$$
$$and\ HD =\ hd\ = xD_1.$$
$$Thus\qquad H = \frac{xD_1}{D}\ and\ h = \frac{xD_1}{d}.$$

Therefore, if D is greater than d, h will be greater than H.

Thus the two cylinders will be immersed to the same depth, but the cylinder made of the less dense material will stand farther out of the liquid.

In this simple analogy we see the principle which underlies the conception of isostasy. The less dense parts of the earth's crust " float " higher out of the supporting " fluid " than do the denser parts. In general, observation supports this idea. The continental masses are composed, in the main, of the lighter sial, while underlying the ocean floors is, in all probability, the relatively denser sima.

Returning to the analogous problem of the floating cylinders for a moment, it was noticed that the cylinders were immersed to the same depth. Expressed in another way, this means that the cylinders appeared to " stand " on the same plane—the plane containing their bottom ends. In the case of the earth we have to imagine, then, a level (called the level of compensation) somewhere below the surface of the earth, on which the overlying masses can be regarded as " standing ". This is what is implied in the meaning of the word isostasy (from the Greek *iso-* and *statós*, meaning " equal-standing "). The masses can be considered as " standing " on the level of compensation and balancing one another.

We are now in a position to appreciate that many of the problems connected with the origin, development, and build of the earth are exceedingly complex and not easily explained. The explanations are always somewhat of the nature of trial and error. So long as a theory is capable of explaining all the known facts it must be considered satisfactory, but when other facts are revealed which cannot be adequately explained, another theory, or a modified form of the existing theory, at once becomes necessary. It is the complexity of these problems which makes them, at the same time, baffling and interesting.

CHAPTER III

THE EARTH'S CRUST

SO far we have referred only to crystalline rocks. These are the rocks which " solidified " from the earth's " molten " materials. Observation shows, however, that crystalline rocks now appear on the earth's surface only over relatively small areas. Some of these areas have already been mentioned : parts of the Brazilian Highlands, of the African Plateau, of the Indian Deccan, and of Western Australia. Other areas include parts of north-east Canada, of north-east Siberia, and of the country round the northern part of the Baltic Sea.

But even the hardest rocks can be worn away by natural agencies and their disintegrated materials re-made into " new " rocks. Many of these " new " rocks are " laid-down " in water and, as a result, occur largely in horizontal layers. (These horizontal layers, as we shall see, may later suffer various distortions.) Rocks which are formed in this way are called " sedimentary " rocks, and, because of their arrangement in layers, also " stratified " rocks (from the Latin *stratum*, meaning " something spread out, or a bed ").

By far the greater part of the earth's land surface is to-day covered with such sedimentary rocks, in some cases extending to a depth of several miles. But if all the sedimentary rocks were spread evenly over the continents they would, in all probability, not exceed a depth of half a mile, or, say, about one per cent. of the total thickness of the crust. We were, therefore, justified in ignoring the presence of such rocks until now ; in the constitution of the earth's crust they are relatively insignificant. When dealing with the earth's surface, however, we can no longer ignore them, for they predominate.

CLASSIFICATION OF ROCKS

To the geologist, rocks include not only the hard, massive slabs or boulders of popular usage, but also the sands, clays, muds, etc., so commonly found in some parts of the earth's crust. We therefore have to deal with a great variety. Now, although the study of " rocks ", as such, is mainly the concern of the geologist, the geographer cannot ignore it because so much that concerns him depends on rock formations. For example, soils depend largely on the nature of the underlying rocks, and soils, in their turn, help to determine the natural vegetation, the type of agriculture, etc. Some industries depend largely on rocks ; the localisation of such industries will depend partly, at least, on the distribution of those rocks.

It is usual to classify rocks, partly according to their age and manner of formation, and partly according to their appearance.

1. Igneous Rocks (from the Latin *ignis*, meaning "fire"). These rocks have all solidified from molten material. As a result they are usually either crystalline in structure or glassy in appearance. They can be further sub-divided into :

(a) Plutonic Rocks (in classical mythology Pluto was the god of the "infernal regions"). These rocks were formed at some considerable depth in the earth's crust where they cooled slowly. The crystalline structure is hence usually very marked and the crystals usually large, as, for example, in the case of granite.

(b) Volcanic Rocks (Vulcanus was the Roman god of "fire"). These rocks were formed when molten material (lava) poured out on to the earth's surface and cooled relatively quickly. Sometimes this lava spread out in great sheets (rather like pan-cakes) as, for example, in parts of the Snake River Basin of North America and over parts of the North-West Deccan of India (the "Deccan Trap"). At other times it flowed only a relatively short distance and, interbedded with other rock debris ("ashes", etc.), helped to build up the numerous volcanoes (active, dormant and extinct) appearing in various parts of the world. Due to the greater rate of cooling the crystals are usually small, and there are frequently large quantities of glassy material present. Basalt is a good, and widespread, example of a finely crystalline volcanic rock. A good example of the glassy type is tachylite or basalt glass.

2. Sedimentary Rocks (literally "rocks formed from sediment"). At a later stage we shall discuss how rocks are broken up by natural agencies and how the disintegrated materials are carried away by rivers and deposited on the floors of the shallow seas surrounding the land. During these processes the disintegrated and transported materials are, to a large extent, sifted. Thus materials of the same kind and size tend to be deposited in the same area. Hence the composition of the "sediments" deposited in shallow seas depends partly on the nature of the rocks over which the rivers flow and partly on the sifting processes. These sediments "bed down" in roughly horizontal layers and, due partly to the pressure of overlying sediment (that is, later deposition) and partly to permeation by other substances which act as a kind of "cement", gradually form compact "rock strata".

The most common rocks of this class are gritstones (of coarse texture), sandstones (of rather finer texture), shales (smooth to the touch, but crumbly) and clays (very smooth to the touch). In addition, there are the sands and gravels, which have bedded but not consolidated. It is clear that these rocks vary enormously in their composition, hardness, appearance and usefulness. It will also be clear that their age of formation also varies enormously, the lower strata being older than the upper (unless the strata have suffered great distortion after deposition). It will further be clear that these processes are still operating.

Another class of sedimentary rock is formed by the remains of marine organisms (both animal and plant) which accumulate on the sea floor. Since the durable parts of these organisms are confined to the shell, skeleton, etc., the rocks so formed consist mainly of calcium carbonate which the organisms have extracted, during growth, from the sea water. Impurities (that is, substances other than calcium carbonate) give rise to the variety of colours seen in these rocks. Most common of the rocks in this class are limestone, chalk and coral. (Over the deep ocean floor, marine organisms, volcanic dust, etc., are the cause of the oozes deposited there. These form much more slowly than the sedimentary rocks of shallow seas. We shall return to this subject later ; see p. 105.)

Yet another class of sedimentary rock—in many respects the most important of all the rocks—occurs on the sites of former " swamp forest " (possibly akin to the present mangrove-swamp). These large areas of dense vegetation were, some 200-300 millions of years ago, alternately just above and below the level of the sea. Thus the remains of the vegetation, growing when the areas were above sea-level, are inter-bedded with other sedimentary deposits. Pressure of overlying sediments has transformed the forest remains into compact masses in which the principal substance is carbon. In this way the world's vast stores of coal have come into being.

It is well known that there are many different types of coal. Broadly, however, we may group all these different types into one or other of four classes. First, there is lignite, an inferior brown coal which is often not considered a true coal. Its carbon content is low— about 45 per cent. Secondly, there is the wide range of " household coals " (which are also very important in industry). These are known as bituminous coal ; the carbon content is about 70 per cent. Thirdly, there is anthracite, the dustless and smokeless coal, with a carbon content exceeding 90 per cent. Fourthly, there are the hard steam coals, intermediate between bituminous and anthracite.

Opinions are not wholly agreed on the causes which have differentiated these various coals. Some believe that differences in the original vegetation are partly responsible ; others that pressure, and perhaps changes in temperature, have produced these different coals from the same vegetation. The evidence derived from the coalfields does not appear to be wholly conclusive. True, in some coalfields (for example,

South Wales) where there is evidence of greater pressure, there is found coal with a higher carbon content.

In the same series we may, perhaps, include **peat**, a very early stage in the transformation, and graphite or black-lead, a very advanced stage, with a carbon content of 95 per cent. It is very doubtful, however, if the peat which develops so widely on moorlands, etc., in the British Isles would ever become true coal.

3. Metamorphic Rocks (from the Greek *meta-morphe*, meaning " change of form "). These rocks, as the name implies, have been changed from their original state. This has usually been brought about by changes in temperature or pressure, or by a combination of both. Thus, in volcanic activity, rocks will be subjected to intense temperatures by the outpouring lava, with the result that there will be contact metamorphism. Sedimentary rocks, buried deeply under more recent deposits, may be subjected to such great pressures during " earth-movements " that they take on an entirely new appearance, frequently crystalline. In such ways sandstones are changed to quartzites, limestones to marble, clays and shales to slates. The schists and gneisses (of, for example, the Highlands of Scotland), formerly held by some to be " original " rocks, are now generally admitted to be metamorphic (possibly changed from granite).

4. Wind-formed Rocks. These rocks can usually be classified as sedimentary in that they show stratification, but they are distinguished from the normal sedimentary rocks by properties due to the fact that wind, and not running water, has been the transporting agent, and that the disintegrated materials have been bedded down on land instead of under water. (Such rocks may have been submerged under water afterwards, but water appears to have played no part in their actual formation). Rocks of this kind will clearly accumulate where there is a drift of wind-borne material in a prevailing direction and where there is little or no running water to complete the transportation to the sea. It is the sort of deposition one would expect to find in desert areas.

Most notable of these wind-formed rocks is **loess**. It is found over thousands of square miles in North China, in a belt across Europe from the Black Sea to the North Sea running along the southern edge of the European Plain, and over parts of the Central Lowlands of North America. In its original state it is yellow, but the soil derived from it is frequently black, due to the presence of humus (decayed vegetable matter). (Note the Black Earth Region of Europe.) Loess is easily worn away by running water, as is seen in the case of the Hwang-ho of North China, also called the Yellow River because of the load of yellow loess held in suspension.

Two important features of desert areas are sand-storms (wind-borne sand) and inland drainage basins (basins into which the intermittent water drains and from which it escapes only by evaporation and perco-lation into the ground). In such " basins " salts accumulate (for example, the famous " Nitrates " region in the Atacama Desert of North Chile). Because of the nature of the rock and the presence of salt beds, the New Red Sandstone of the English Midlands is often considered to be of desert origin.

LAND FORMS

The influence of the physical characteristics of the various rocks on " land-forms " will be discussed in detail later. For the present, it will be sufficient to study a good geological map of the British Isles and notice what rocks predominate in the different major areas of relief.

A possible arrangement of various igneous rock-formations and their relation to sedimentary rocks is indicated in the accompanying dia-gram. It must be remembered that rocks which have formed at some considerable depth in the earth's crust may, in time, appear at the surface.

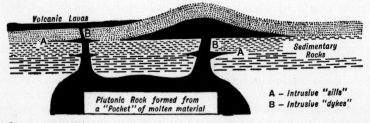

Rocks formed when lava pours out on to the surface are sometimes referred to as effusive rocks (for example, the basic lava-sheets) ; when the lava is thrown out violently the resulting rocks are called eruptive rocks. When rocks are formed from molten material which has been forced in between other " older " rocks they are referred to as intrusive rocks. If such intrusive rocks occur in a roughly vertical position (that is, in fissures in the older rocks) they are called dykes ; if in a roughly horizontal position (that is, between the different strata of older rocks) they are called sills. When sedimentary strata are forced apart by the intrusive materials we may get laccoliths or laccolites (dome-shaped masses) or phacolites (lens-shaped masses). Large, roughly dome-shaped masses of plutonic rock (frequently granite) which plunge steeply to great depths are called bathyliths. The " pocket " (see diagram) might well become a bathylith when the overlying rocks have all been worn away.

From the nature of their formation it is clear that igneous rocks of the kind shown in the diagram must be " younger " than the rocks which underlie them ; they might also be " younger " than the rocks immediately above them.

FORMATION OF MAJOR FEATURES OF THE EARTH

There is good evidence for believing that the earth's relief features are by no means permanent ; they are, in effect, the result of **earth-movements.** The mechanism of earth-movements is extraordinarily complicated but, for the present purpose, it is sufficient to consider only two main types of movement. These are produced by : (a) *radial forces* (that is, forces which act either towards, or away from, the centre of the earth) and (b) *tangential forces* (that is, forces which act in a plane parallel to the surface of the earth at any particular point).

Radial forces will tend either to lift or to depress parts of the earth's crust bodily. They therefore tend to form large land areas and are sometimes called epeirogenetic forces. Such forces have brought into being the large areas of the Central Lowlands of North America, the Russian Plain (" Russian Platform "), the African Plateau, the Indian Deccan, and many similar areas. In all these cases vast areas have been " lifted " with very little disturbance.

Tangential forces, on the other hand, will tend either to compress or to extend those parts of the crust where they are acting. In compression, parts of the crust will tend to buckle up, forming mountains ; in extension, fractures will tend to develop and parts of the outer crust will subside. These are therefore mountain-building forces and are sometimes called **orogenetic forces.** To them are due the great mountain ranges of the Himalayas, Rockies, Andes, Alps, etc. In all these cases the original rock formations have been appreciably distorted.

MOUNTAINS

We can recognise four classes of mountains : (a) fold (or folded) mountains, (b) block mountains, (c) volcanic mountains, (d) residual mountains (or mountains carved during the process of denudation).

Fold Mountains. These are due to forces of compression in the earth's crust and we may visualise their formation in two main ways : either by two substantial blocks in the crust moving towards one another, or by one substantial block moving towards a stable block. In either case the materials between the blocks will be crushed into folds, somewhat after the fashion of the folds produced in a pile of blankets when pressure is exerted from either or both sides. This analogy is by no means perfect, for the forces in the crust are very

D

complex, but it serves to illustrate the general effect. Rocks, as we know them on the earth's surface, would clearly crack and crush if subjected to intense folding forces, but at some depth in the crust, pressure would probably render them sufficiently plastic to bend without cracking. Then, when the overlying rocks had been worn away, the " folded rocks " would appear at the surface and the " folds " would be clearly seen. Such folds are particularly noticeable in stratified rocks. In a quarry, for example, minor folds can often be detected.

The diagram illustrates the formation of fold mountains when two substantial blocks are supposed to move towards one another. In such a case, if we assume that the pressure exerted from one side is approximately equal to that exerted from the other, we should expect a symmetrical arrangement. This is rarely found.

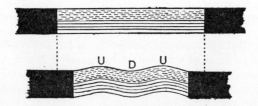

The formation of fold mountains when one substantial block is supposed to move towards a stable block is also illustrated. If, in the diagram, we assume that the greater pressure is exerted from left to right we shall, in general, get folds as shown.

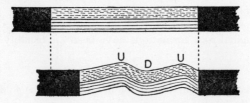

In both diagrams it will be noticed that there is an effective shortening of the crust. The original " spherical " surface has been thrown into " waves ". The crests of these " waves " are called upfolds or anticlines, marked U ; the troughs are called downfolds or synclines, marked D.

Because of the complexity of the forces of compression brought into play, Fold Mountain Systems are generally very complicated, and various types of folding are evident. Some of these are shown in the following diagrams.

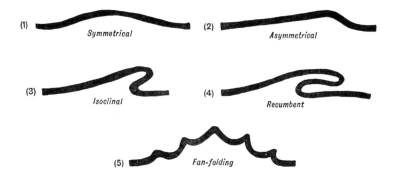

(1) Symmetrical   (2) Asymmetrical

(3) Isoclinal   (4) Recumbent

(5) Fan-folding

Sometimes, too, in the process of folding, fractures occur in the crust, and large masses of the crust may " slide " forward over other parts of the crust. Such sliding movements are called thrusts and they take place along thrust planes. The over-riding part of the crust is frequently called a nappe (from the French *nappe*, meaning " table-cloth ").

In complicated Fold Mountain Systems such as the Alps, all these different types of folding are to be found, although they are seldom so simple as indicated in the diagrams above. Moreover, denudation (the wearing away of the upper rocks, perhaps to the extent of thousands of feet) frequently makes recognition of the folds extremely difficult.

In the long geological history of the earth there have been at least three major mountain-building phases. The first of these is often called the Caledonian (because it is evident in Scotland). Then, it appears, a great mountain range extended from Scandinavia, through the Highlands of Scotland and through Northern Ireland. The highlands seen in those countries to-day are but remnants of the original range. The second great mountain-building episode is sometimes called the Altaid, although in Europe it is usually referred to as the Hercynian or Armorican. Remnants of Hercynian ranges are to be seen in widely separated areas : the Appalachians in North America, the Pennines in England, South Ireland, South Wales, South-west England, North-west France, the " Massif Central " of France, the Rhine Highlands, Bohemia, the Cape Ranges of South Africa, the Great Dividing Range of Australia, the Altai of North-east Asia, etc. The third and " youngest " of the major mountain-building episodes is usually called the Alpine. Belonging to this class are the Alps and other mountain chains of Southern Europe, the Rocky and Andean systems, the Himalayas and other mountain chains of Southern Asia.

Because they are the "youngest" (and hence less worn down) the Alpine systems show their folding very clearly. For this reason they are sometimes called Young (or New) Fold Mountains. The Hercynian systems, greatly worn down and often "shattered" by later earth-movements, do not show their folding so obviously. They are some-times called Old Fold Mountains. The Caledonian systems show their folding even less, and evidence of folding can usually only be inferred, and that only after the most careful study.

To the geographer, perhaps the most important features of the newly folded systems are their heights and ruggedness, for on these features so many others depend. Great mountain barriers, three, four, or even five miles above sea-level, are formidable obstacles to movement ; moreover, they have an important effect on climate and vegetation. The older folded systems (because they have been worn down and smoothed) are not often serious barriers, either to move-ment or climate, but they are not without their influence.

A generalised cross-section of the Pennine Arch through the High Peak is given in the accompanying diagram. The coal measures, once probably continuous across the arch, now appear only on the flanks.

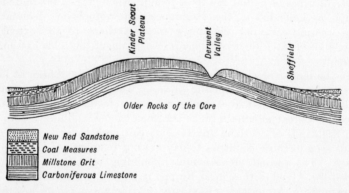

Block Mountains. Quite frequently, during earth-movements, fract-ures (or faults) develop in the crust. Then great masses of the crust either subside below the general level, or rear above it. In this way steep-sided "blocks" come into being.

Diagram a illustrates what might happen during earth-movements when forces are pulling apart. The crust will clearly be in tension and any adjustment will tend to produce effective lengthening of the crust. Diagram b illustrates the case when forces of compression operate, and

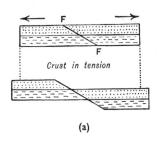

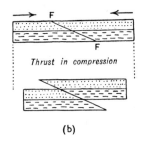

(a)   (b)

when the rocks fail to "fold" or have reached the limit of folding.
Thus the adjustment tends to produce effective shortening of the
crust ; compression produces a thrust.

Extending this conception somewhat, two of the more important
relief forms due to faulting can be usefully examined. In the formation
of Block Mountains or Horsts it is assumed that the crust is in tension
and that major faults develop. (These faults appear at the earth's
surface as roughly parallel lines.) Then it is supposed that the block
enclosed by the faults stands relatively at rest, and that the surrounding
parts of the crust, pulled outwards, subside, their faulted edges sliding
down the wedge-like sides of the upstanding block.

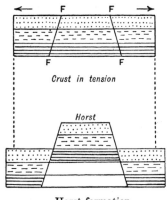

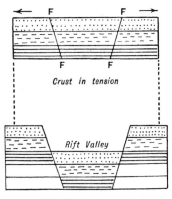

Horst formation   Rift Valley formation

In the formation of Rift Valleys (which are really the counterpart of
horsts) it is supposed that a part of the earth's crust has been let down
between two earth-blocks which are moving apart. In general, rift
valleys are relatively long and narrow ; the famous Rift Valley of the
Rhine is some 200 miles long, but only 20 miles wide.

The structure of block mountains and rift valleys is not often so
simple as that indicated in the diagrams. More generally, instead of
two major faults, we find two sets of parallel faults which give rise to a

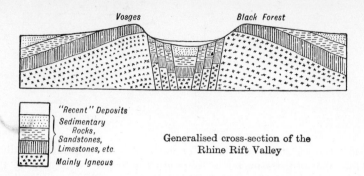

Vosges   Black Forest

"Recent" Deposits
Sedimentary
Rocks,
Sandstones,
Limestones, etc.
Mainly Igneous

Generalised cross-section of the
Rhine Rift Valley

feature known as step-faulting. The Rift Valley of the Rhine illustrates
this type of structure.

So far it has been assumed that the subsiding parts of the crust are
let down in a generally horizontal position. This does not always
happen. Quite frequently subsidence is accompanied by pronounced

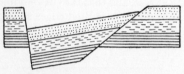

tilting. The diagram illustrates
this in the case of a **fault valley.**

Land-forms (block mountains,
rift valleys, fault valleys, etc.)
which owe their origin primarily,
if not exclusively, to faulting of
the types just described, are

An asymmetrical fault valley

sometimes referred to as examples of block-faulting. Now, although
faulting in various degrees is very widespread over the earth's crust,
true block-faulting is not nearly so common. Often, too, denudation
has so modified the existing land-forms that it is difficult to say just
how important a part faulting has played in the structure.

One of the best of known examples of block-faulting occurs in the
Great Basin of North America, in the States of Nevada and Utah.
Here, although denudation has modified the original forms, true
block mountains, typical rift valleys, and asymmetrical fault valleys
are all clearly recognisable.

Of the better known rift valleys we have already referred to that of
the Rhine. Even more remarkable are the great rift valleys of East
Africa which extend from Lake Nyasa in the south to Syria in the north.
The major "lines" of these rift valleys can easily be traced on an
ordinary physical map, for the elongated depressions are clearly
shown : the central valley of Syria and Palestine (containing the Dead
Sea), the Gulf of Suez and the Gulf of Akaba, the Red Sea, the Gulf of
Aden, Lakes Rudolf, Nyasa, Tanganyika, Edward and Albert. In
South Australia, Spencer's Gulf and Lake Torrens occupy a similar rift
valley. The Central Valley (better called " Lowlands ") of Scotland is

certainly bounded north and south by fault lines (the Helensburgh-Stonehaven and Girvan-Dunbar " Lines "), but other agencies have also helped in the development of this rift valley so it is not such a good example as the Rhine Rift Valley.

The Caledonian and Hercynian remnants of the continent of Europe, though often referred to as " blocks ", and though often showing signs of some degree of faulting, do not, in the main, owe their present form to block-faulting, and in that sense they are not strictly blocks. It is preferable to call them massifs, a name by which they are generally known (for example, Massif Central of France).

Volcanic Mountains. Reference has already been made to the ejection on to the earth's surface of volcanic materials from holes or fissures in the crust. These volcanic materials, " thrown " or " poured " out on to the crust, differ considerably from one part of the earth to another, and so give rise to very different land-forms.

Basic lavas, which are poor in silica and rich in iron and magnesium, are naturally very fluid, and flow for a very long way before solidifying. One of the most outstanding of the basic volcanoes is Mauna Loa, in the Hawaiian Islands. Its base is on the sea floor, and from this base, which is more than 100 miles in diameter, it reaches a height of 30,000 ft. It is thus a flat cone, the sloping face of which makes an angle of about 5° with the horizontal. Of a similar type are the basic lava sheets of the Deccan Trap Region in the north-west of the Indian Deccan, of the Snake River Basin in North America, and of Antrim in Northern Ireland. The Antrim type (where is found the famous basalt Giant's Causeway) is repeated in some of the islands to the west of Scotland, notably Mull and Skye, and this suggests that there might once have been a vast lava sheet in this region which has since been shattered.

Acid lavas, which are rich in silica and poor in iron and magnesium, are very viscous and flow only for a short distance. These therefore tend to build " piles " or " mounds ". One of the most remarkable eruptions of this type was that of Mt. Pelée in Martinique in 1902. The lava, too viscous to flow at all, simply piled up like a huge pillar, about 700 ft. above the summit of the existing cone.

Most volcanoes fall rather between the two extreme types just described. Of this intermediate type we may notice the well-known Mediterranean volcanoes, Vesuvius, Etna and Stromboli, the famous Japanese volcano, Fuji Yama, the Andean volcanoes, Cotopaxi and Chimborazo, etc. They all show well-developed cones. The formation of a typical intermediate type volcano is illustrated in the diagram (p. 46). Before the eruption there are usually earth tremors. Then follows a violent outburst of steam, gas, etc., during which phase, rock debris is hurled from the vent. This rock debris (sometimes called " ashes ")

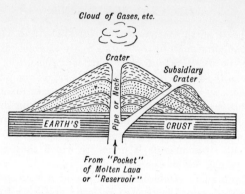

Cloud of Gases, etc.

Crater

Subsidiary
Crater

Pipe or Neck

EARTH'S CRUST

From "Pocket"
of Molten Lava
or "Reservoir"

naturally falls round the vent, at no very great distance from it. Then lava pours from the vent and flows over the ash layer. A period of quiescence usually follows during which the lava solidifies. Later another eruption throws more ashes out on to the solidified lava, and these ashes are, in turn, buried under another layer of lava. In this way a volcanic cone, consisting of alternate ashes and lava, is built up layer upon layer.

Volcanoes which erupt at fairly frequent intervals are styled *active*; when no eruptions have occurred over a long period, but when the possibility is always present, they are said to be *dormant*; when no eruptions have occurred within historic time, and when such occurrences are highly improbable, they are considered *extinct*.

Sometimes extreme explosive violence accompanies volcanic eruptions. Thus, in 1883, a particularly violent explosion took place during the eruption of Krakatoa, a small island in the Straits of Sunda (East Indies). A part of the island literally disappeared, rock debris was hurled great distances, and the volcanic dust, thrown into the upper atmosphere, is considered largely responsible for the particularly brilliant sunsets seen in various parts of the world between 1883 and 1885.

Closely related to volcanic activity, apparently, are earthquakes, which are tremors or convulsions of the earth's crust. Both occur in regions of crustal instability (that is, in regions of "recent" uplift or depression). Most prominent of such regions is that bordering the Pacific Ocean (popularly called the "Fiery Ring of the Pacific"). Both volcanoes and earthquakes are common features of North Island, New Zealand, of the East Indies and Japan, of Kamchatka and the Aleutian Islands, and of the Andes. In North America the volcanoes are nearly all extinct, but devastating earthquakes do occur from time to time as, for example, that of San Francisco in 1906. Other prominent regions are those of the Mediterranean, the West Indies, and the African Rift Valley. Associated with the folds of southern Asia are a number of extinct volcanoes, and a few active ones in the Bay of Bengal. The violent earthquake at Quetta of 1935 was just one of many reminders that such dangers are ever present in this area.

Terrible as the consequences of eruptions and earthquakes frequently are to human life and property, it is easy to over-emphasise their importance in earth-building. Volcanic activity has certainly added a few land-forms to the earth's surface, but, in the aggregate, they form a relatively insignificant portion of the total surface. Earthquakes, while influencing life over considerable areas, have produced no great land-forms ; in certain localised areas they have, perhaps, altered relative levels to the extent of a few feet.

Residual Mountains. When an area is " lifted " above sea-level, various agents begin their work of wearing it down again. This process, which goes by the name of denudation, will be dealt with in detail later, but for the present it may be noted that rocks do not all wear away at the same rate. Thus an " original " highland area might well be " carved " into an area of mountain and valley. Such **residual mountains** (that is, mountains left standing after surrounding areas have been worn away) are frequently called **Mountains of Denudation.**

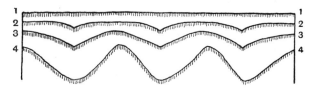

The form of such mountains will clearly depend partly on the original highland formation, and partly on the work done by the agents of denudation. In areas such as the Scottish Highlands, the English Lake District, and Wales, many examples of residual mountains are to be found. The successive stages by which a generally level highland area might be reduced to an area of residual mountains and deep valleys are illustrated in the diagram.

PLAINS

Plains are areas of low and generally level land. When very near sea-level they are usually flat, but when raised slightly are frequently " rolling " or " undulating " (wavy), due to the presence of broad river valleys.

It is, perhaps, simplest to classify plains according to their formation.

Plains of Deposition. Plains of this class consist of sediments which have been " bedded down " in water and then raised slightly without deformation. In this way a large area of low and generally flat land comes into being (for example, the plains of the Mississippi Basin in North America, the great Russian Plain, the Pampas region of Argentina, the Murray-Darling Basin of Australia, etc.). Such areas have a generally flat appearance for possibly hundreds of miles. As they are relatively near sea-level (frequently not more than 600 ft.) denudation is very restricted and, at most, these true plains attain a rolling character.

Coastal Plains is the term given to plains of deposition and gentle uplift when they border the sea. Outstanding among plains of this class is that of the south-eastern United States of America, from Chesapeake Bay to Florida. We may refer to this area as a " low raised coast ".

Another type of plain which may well be put in this general class is that formed on the site of a former lake which has been filled by deposits brought by inflowing rivers. As will be seen later, fast-flowing rivers " carve away " the land over which they flow to make their valleys. The materials so worn away are carried by the river, and constitute its " load ". If the speed of the river slackens, some of this load is deposited on the river bed, and when the river enters the still water of a lake, practically all the remaining load is deposited on the lake bed. In time, the original lake will become a plain crossed by one or more river channels. The fertile Red River Basin, to the south of Winnipeg in central Canada, has been formed in this way, on the site of " Lake Agassiz ".

Of a similar type are the deltaic fans (small plains) which form round the mouths of rivers where they enter relatively still water ; for example, where rivers flow into fiords or other tideless seas, or where swift tributary streams join a slow-moving river.

Another type of plain due to deposition is the flood plain. These are found along those courses of a river where there is little or no gradient and where the river, in consequence, is flowing very slowly. The river's " load " is gradually spread over the bed which, therefore, slowly rises. When the river comes down in flood, both its volume and speed are increased. Quite frequently in such cases the flood water spreads over considerable areas well away from the normal channel. The swirling flood waters carry a substantial " load " which is spread over the land alongside the river. In this way very flat plains—sometimes extensive—may come into being. Rivers like the Hwang-ho, in North China, and the Mississippi, in North America, have very extensive flood plains, but most rivers possess them in varying degrees.

Plains of Denudation. " Plains " of this class are seldom " true " plains and are usually better described as peneplains (or peneplanes) (from the Latin pene, meaning " almost "). As their descriptive title suggests, they are formed by the wearing down of other land forms.

Now, however uniform the surface of a rock formation may be, agents of denudation seldom wear it away evenly over its entire surface; more often the new surface has a hummocky appearance. But in spite of the uneven surface there is usually a marked uniformity in the heights of the hummocks (that is, there is a general " summit level "). After peneplanation an area might be subjected to another uplift. Denudation would proceed anew and would continue until a second peneplanation had been achieved. Such a land-form is known as an "ancient peneplain ". Among the most extensive peneplains are the Finnish Peneplain (the area round the Gulf of Bothnia), North-East Siberia, and the Hudson Bay Lowlands. To the geologist, all three areas form parts of well-known shields.

Plateaux. In general, a plateau is an area of highland which possesses some measure of uniformity in its surface relief. Its popular description—a tableland—is in some respects rather misleading, for it suggests a perfectly level surface which is everywhere at the same height above sea-level. It further suggests that the plateau must stand above surrounding areas. None of these features is an absolute requirement.

Since plateaux are highland areas they are naturally subjected to progressive denudation. Rivers may " trench " deeply into their surfaces (for example, the Spanish Meseta and the Indian Deccan) with the result that those surfaces are anything but even. But, as in the case of peneplains, there is usually a general " summit level " ; the ridges are all much of the same height. These are called dissected plateaux.

Some plateaux are definitely tilted (the Indian Deccan has its western edge considerably higher than its eastern, the Brazilian Plateau is highest along its south-eastern edge, the Central Plateau (Massif Central) of France is also highest along its south-eastern edge, the African Plateau is likewise highest along its eastern and south-eastern edges, etc.).

Certain plateaux are surrounded by higher land (for example, the plateaux enclosed by the ranges of the Rocky, Andean, and Himalayan systems, etc.). These are called intermont plateaux (from the Latin inter, meaning " between ", and mons, meaning " mountain ").

So far we have inferred that the use of the word " plateau " should be restricted to areas which are distinctly highland. This is not necessarily so. Certain relatively low upland areas might well be termed plateaux (for example Salisbury Plain and parts of the English Chalk and Limestone " Ridges ").

The Plateau of Antrim in Northern Ireland is a particularly interesting example of a plateau built of basic lava ; Lough Neagh occupies the depression formed when the lava poured out on to the surface and so left part of the crust unsupported.

CHAPTER IV

LAND SCULPTURE

THE various processes which are involved in the " sculpturing " of the earth's land masses are frequently grouped together under the heading sub-aerial denudation, or simply denudation (from the Latin *denudare*, meaning " to lay bare ").

Included in denudation we may, in the first instance, recognise three distinct processes : (1) the actual breaking away of particles or fragments from the original rock masses ; (2) the transportation, possibly by stages, of these disintegrated materials to their ultimate destination, the sea floor ; and (3) the " carving " or " modelling " of valleys and other relief features.

The first of these processes is concerned with the breaking up of exposed rock masses by the action of the weather and is generally known as weathering ; the second concerns " vehicles " capable of carrying the broken or decomposed rocks—running water, moving ice, and wind ; the third concerns " tools " capable of " chiselling " into the rock formations, and is generally known as erosion (from the Latin *erodere*, meaning " to gnaw away "). Erosion is carried out mainly through the agency of water, ice and wind.

WEATHERING

Weathering may best be considered as being of two distinct types. If the rock disintegrates without chemical change we may regard the process as one of " mechanical weathering " ; if disintegration is accompanied by, or the result of, chemical change, we may think of it as " chemical weathering ".

Mechanical Weathering. (i) In climates where there is considerable difference between day and night temperatures (notably in the " hot deserts "), rocks alternately expand and contract to an appreciable extent. The composition of rocks, and especially of the coarsely grained and crystalline rocks, is very different from that of the metal poker which can be subjected to alternate heat and cold without apparent damage. The various " ingredients " which go to make up a rock expand and contract differently. Further, the surface layers will be subjected to greater heat by day (exposed to the sun) and to greater cold by night (exposed to cold air) than the interior of the rock. If rocks were good conductors of heat (as good as a metal poker) there would be a much more uniform distribution of heat through the rock mass than actually occurs. The result of all this is that there is unequal expansion and contraction in different parts of the same rock. This differential expansion sets up enormous stresses in the rock which ultimately cause it to break up. Such disintegration is normally of two types : the rock may break into blocks due to the internal strains (block disintegration), or it may gradually crumble into its constituent mineral grains (granular disintegration). The rock debris accumulates at the base of the rock mass to form screes.

(ii) If water permeates a rock mass and then freezes, the great expansive force will be sufficient to set up enormous stresses in the mass (1 unit volume of water becomes 1·09 units on changing to ice). This is particularly noticeable where there are crevices. Each time water collects in the crevice and freezes, the crevice will be made slightly larger. In time block disintegration will result. Every time a block is dislodged it leaves a new face exposed to the attack of the weather. As for the block itself, it will come to rest near the base of the rock mass, where it will suffer further disintegration as time goes on. The "Edges" in the Millstone Grit country of the High Peak region of the Pennines have screes of this sort strewn along their bases.

(iii) There is a certain mechanical aspect to the action of rain and wind on some rock formations. Rain, merely by beating against a surface, may dislodge small particles. The work of rain, however, is largely chemical and erosive. Similarly, the wind, by blowing particles of sand, etc., against a rock surface, can dislodge small particles. In general, however, the work of the wind is better classified as erosive.

Chemical Weathering. (i) Rain, falling through the atmosphere, dissolves an appreciable quantity of carbon dioxide and so becomes a dilute solution of carbonic acid, which has very marked effects upon some rocks. Thus, in the case of limestones, calcium carbonate, the main constituent, is dissolved out, leaving the insoluble components loosened, and thereby open to the attack of other agents. This form of chemical disintegration is clearly seen in typical chalk and limestone country. It is also to be seen in many buildings and monuments, for limestone is a common building material ; after a comparatively short time, the lettering on such monuments is no longer legible, and the entire surface usually acquires a pitted and crumbly form.

Wherever carbonates are present this process goes on in greater or lesser degree, whether the rocks are " hard " or " soft ", whether they are crystalline or sedimentary ; true sands and clays, however, which contain no carbonates, are unaffected by such action.

In the case of granite, decomposition of felspar, one of the constituents, leads to the formation of kaolin (hydrated aluminium silicate) ; this is a fine, white china-clay, which absorbs moisture readily, and is used in the manufacture of porcelain and pottery.

(ii) Some rocks disintegrate by simple solution; for example, gypsum and rock-salt. If fully exposed to weathering in a moist climate, their disintegration would be comparatively rapid.

(iii) Rain water, passing through the atmosphere, and surface water, in contact with the atmosphere, usually contain " free " oxygen in solution. Such free oxygen is therefore available for oxidation, which is particularly marked in rocks containing iron compounds. The reds, browns and yellows of some of the surface rocks (and of boulders in the streams) in, say, the Sheffield area, indicate pronounced oxidation.

(iv) Moist air (quite apart from rain) can also bring about rock-decay. The oxygen and carbon dioxide, both very abundant in the atmosphere, form, with the various substances in the rocks, oxides, hydrates and carbonates, which are generally more open to attack by the weather than the original rocks.

(v) Plants, partly because their roots drive down into crevices and prize them wider, and partly because their foliage keeps surface moisture in contact with the rock surface for considerably longer periods than would otherwise be the case, also assist rock-decay. Further, a certain amount of acid is present in the water film surrounding roots, and this will act on some rock constituents.

TRANSPORTATION AND EROSION

Transportation is closely bound up with erosion; these two aspects of denudation will be better understood if considered together.

(A) THE WORK OF RUNNING WATER

Over the greater part of the earth's surface, rivers are the most important of the erosive agents. Even in desert areas the effects of inter-mittent torrents following sporadic downpours are very pronounced.

Rivers. A river obtains its water, directly or indirectly, from rain-fall and other forms of precipitation (snow, etc.). This precipitation may either drain off the surface on which it falls straight into the river, or soak into the ground until, at a lower level, it reaches the surface again in a spring which " feeds " the river. The surface run-off will clearly be dependent on the day-to-day rainfall. After heavy storms or prolonged steady rainfall, there will be a considerable supply of water from this source; there may be even more than the river can cope with, resulting in serious floods lower downstream. The supply from springs will depend, not on the day-to-day rainfall, but rather on the average rainfall over a period, for the entry of such water into the river is delayed. Whether rain tends to run off, or soak into, the surface depends, of course, on the nature of the surface rocks. In the case of such rocks as Millstone Grit and many of the crystalline rocks, it tends to run off ; in the case of certain of the limestones and chalks, it tends to soak in. Other factors which affect the supply of water draining to a river include the vegetation cover (for plants both use water and check its downhill drainage), and evaporation.

Since the rainfall is usually heaviest in highland or hilly areas, rivers generally rise in relatively high country. From their source they then follow a generally downhill course, and usually in a well-defined channel, until they empty their water into the sea, or perhaps into a lake. This well-defined channel is largely the result of work done by the river. Originally, no doubt, the escaping water followed such hollows or depressions as Nature had provided, but once the course had become defined, the shaping of it was due to the river itself.

The Course of a River. A typical river course must now be examined, observing the various characteristics in the different stretches or reaches and studying the work done by the river at various stages.

The Upper Course of the river, in its hills or mountains, is frequently referred to as its Mountain Course, Hill Course, or Torrent Course. Here the volume of water is small, but the stream is very swift, for the gradients are steep. In the river bed, rock fragments of all sizes are strewn. The racing water swirls round the larger boulders, " pushes " the rather smaller ones downstream by " fitful jerks ", and churns the sand and silt from the rocky bed. Here and there will be cascades, waterfalls and rapids ; elsewhere there may be quiet stretches where the stream opens out into a string of shallow ponds, and where the water may be delightfully " fresh ".

After a period of prolonged drought the water may dwindle to a mere trickle, or it may dry up altogether, especially if the stream depends on surface run-off. Then the course will be marked by the rock-strewn bed, with, perhaps, a pool here and there. But in flood all is different. Even the large boulders may be " eased " downstream. There is evidently much energy available for work. The shape of the valley here shows exactly what that work is. The river is cutting down into the rocks—and the work is done by the boulders and rock-fragments it pushes along, and by the smaller pieces it carries. These rock fragments are the " cutting-tools "; the energy to drive this " erosive-machine " is provided by the torrent. Because the stream here is concerned chiefly with the downward cutting, the torrent valley is deep relative to its width, and hence steep-sided or even gorgelike. The actual form of the valley will depend on the local rocks. If these resist weathering, a gorge will result; if they yield to weathering, a relatively deep V will usually result. But the mere fact that such rocks form the " higher " parts of the region normally implies that they are of the more resistant type, and in general, therefore, torrent track valleys are relatively deep and narrow.

The Middle Course of the river is where it leaves the hills or mountains and comes out into the foothill country. This stretch of the river is usually called the Valley Course or Foothill Course. Here the volume of water is considerably greater, for the effective catchment area (the area draining to the river) has been increased, partly, perhaps, by the confluence of several tributaries. But although the volume has increased, the rate of flow has decreased noticeably because the gradients are less. In most parts of this section, however, there is still appreciable movement of water, and, in the main, the river is still "cutting down", but at a reduced rate. This allows weathering more time to work. The result of this is that the valley has been "cut back" into the form of a wide V. Moreover, the reduced downward cutting enables the river to carry out some measure of lateral cutting (that is, widening of its actual bed) to accommodate the increased supply of water. This, too, is achieved by the load of rock fragments, partly carried, partly pushed or rolled. In certain parts of the Valley Course, however, where there are relatively level stretches, downward cutting may have ceased, at least temporarily.

Now, the load a river is capable of carrying depends very largely on the rate of flow. In level stretches the rate of flow will be generally slow, and much of the load, particularly the larger fragments, will be deposited on the bed. (If, at any time, the rate should increase, some of these deposited fragments will be picked up again and transported farther downstream.) Deposition over a long period will clearly mean an appreciable building up of the bed. If the river comes down in flood, therefore, with a greatly increased volume, and with a greatly increased rate of flow, the banks might not be able to contain all the flood water. This water, with a considerable load consisting largely of silt, might then spread over the low-lying land alongside the banks. The silt would then be deposited, and it would naturally tend to accumulate in the hollows. In due course the flood water would recede, but the layer of silt would remain. In time local flood-plains would be built up, consisting of rich alluvial deposits.

The Lower Course of the river extends from the point where it leaves the foothills to its mouth and is, in general, across a plain. This stretch is usually called the Plain Course. Here the river is wide and slow-flowing; the volume of water has probably been greatly increased by the confluence of still more tributaries, and the gradients are gentle, sometimes scarcely noticeable. The slow-flowing water deposits all but the finest particles of its load and so builds up its bed. In the main, downward cutting has ceased, and deposition replaces erosion as the work of the river. (The level of the sea or lake into which the river flows will clearly limit the extent of downward cutting. Should this level change, the work of the river will be ad-

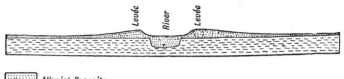

Alluvial Deposits
Surface Rocks before deposition

justed to the new conditions.) As a direct result of this persistent and widespread deposition, extensive flood-plains are formed, exactly in the same way as the local flood-plains of the Valley Course. However, since they are often a predominant feature of the Plain Course, their build must be studied more closely.

During floods, a considerable load of alluvial deposits is spread over those low-lying areas reached by the flooding sheet of water. During the actual " invasion " the flood water may be moving quite rapidly, taking its load with it. Then there may be a period of days, or even weeks, when the sheet of water is relatively still. That is when the load is deposited. During the " retreat ", the flood water usually moves slowly so that the deposits are not greatly disturbed. Such disturbance as does occur tends to move deposits from the rather higher parts into the hollows, and so to level the " plain ". Further, because the land adjoining the banks is covered by a greater body of water than more distant parts, and because it is reached more often by flood water, there is usually a marked tendency to greater deposition along the banks than elsewhere. Moreover, much of this deposit will consist of the rather heavier rock debris which the flood water has been unable to " carry " farther. In time, therefore, we may find that although the river is building up its bed, flood water is also building up its banks. In such cases it sometimes happens that the river is actually above the level of the surrounding plain (see diagram).

Along the lower course of the Mississippi these natural embankments are known as levées. They are also a common feature along the lower courses of the Hwang-ho and Yangtse Kiang in China. Because they are made of alluvial deposits, these levées are not particularly strong, and they are easily breached by a river in flood, frequently with disastrous effects on life and property. As will be seen from the diagram, the flood water, when it has once escaped from its channel, will not easily be able to return to that channel when the flood subsides. Artificial strengthening of the levées has long been practised in various parts of the world ; but even that is only partially successful, for the river goes on building up its bed. To safeguard such areas from the disasters of flooding, either deposition must be stopped (by increasing the rate of flow) or the deposits must be removed from the bed (by dredging). To increase the rate of flow is not always possible ; to remove the deposits would, in certain cases, be a tremendous undertaking. In the case of the Mississippi it has been estimated that, during the year, the river carries to the sea more than 500 million tons of material, two-thirds of which is carried in suspension, while most of the remainder is in solution. The proportion drawn along the river bed is small (about one-twelfth), but even this amounts to some 40 million tons. In cases of this sort it is clear that Nature has presented man with a very difficult problem.

Erosion in the Plain Course. Although the work of a river in its Plain Course is largely " constructive ", it is, nevertheless, capable of considerable erosion. (The term corrasion is frequently used to denote river erosion ; " vertical corrasion " means " downward cutting ", " lateral corrasion " means " widening ".) Such erosion, however, is primarily concerned with cutting into the banks. This may involve a general widening of the bed to accommodate the increased volume during floods, but more often it involves the shifting of the entire bed. This is seen in the case of meanders, another characteristic feature of the Plain Course.

Over the plain we may assume that, in the first instance, the land was practically flat. There would, in all probability, be no obvious course for the river ; it would therefore wind about (or " meander ") on its way to the sea. But even if its course had been straight originally, various agents could have diverted it. A resistant rock formation might have checked lateral corrasion in a particular direction, causing the erosive work of the river to be concentrated on the opposite bank. This, in time, would give rise to a pronounced bend. Even " accidents " might play their part. A fallen tree might well prevent, at least for some time, further erosion at some particular point of a bank, again diverting the main effect of the river to the opposite bank.

Except when a river is in full flood, there is scarcely any movement of the water under the banks on straight reaches. Out in the middle of the river the current might be quite appreciable. We should therefore expect a certain amount of deposition under the banks, but considerably less, if any, in the middle. Conditions are rather different, however, on a " meandering stretch ". Under the bank on the inside of the bend there is still practically no movement. Out in the middle the current is much as it was before. But under the bank on the outside of the bend there is now considerable movement. It is as if the water there is being " thrown " against the bank. There will thus be erosion of the outside bank, but under the inside bank there will be deposition. In this way, by cutting away the outside of the bend and by building up the inside, a meander, once started, tends to grow. In the process the river may " shift its bed " completely.

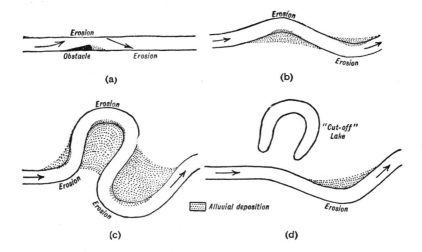

Erosion

Obstacle   Erosion

(a)

Erosion

Erosion

(b)

Erosion

Erosion

Erosion

(c)

"Cut-off" Lake

Alluvial deposition

Erosion

(d)

After a time, when the " loops " have become very pronounced, the river, coming down in flood, may shorten its course to the sea (and hence increase its gradient and rate of flow) by cutting across the " necks " of one or more of these loops. Even after the flood waters have re- ceded, the river may well maintain itself in its new and straightened channel. The abandoned loop will then be a cut-off lake (also called an ox-bow or a mortlake). In time the cut-off lake will become gradually filled in by flood alluvial deposits and will then appear merely as a shallow depression, characterised, however, by the presence of dampness and marsh plants. The stages in the development of river meanders and the formation of cut-off lakes are indicated in the diagram above.

In addition to the lateral shifting of the river bed, there is frequently a tendency towards a generally down-stream shifting, as shown in the diagram.

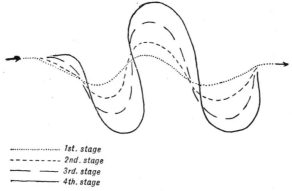

.... 1st. stage
---------- 2nd. stage
—— —— 3rd. stage
———— 4th. stage

Downstream shift of meanders

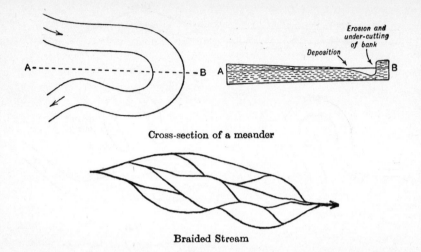

Cross-section of a meander

Braided Stream

A cross-section through a typical meander shows that in general there is a marked difference between the bank on the outside of the bend (steep and under-cut) and that on the inside (gently shelving).

Sometimes, over its flood-plain (or alluvial flat), several alternative courses, which are usually " linked " together, are used by a river. Such a feature is known as a braided stream. In such cases the land between the streams is generally very flat and liable to flooding.

Utilisation of Rivers and their Courses. Before leaving the subject of rivers and their valleys, some of the more important uses to which they have been put in their different sections will be discussed.

In its Upper Course a river will clearly be of no use for navigation. Water-power, however, is normally abundant and is a valuable source of energy, which is often developed in hydro-electric stations. Highly important also are the reserves of water available for domestic purposes. The rainfall is usually relatively heavy, and if natural lakes are not available the deep and narrow valleys are easy to dam ; and the reservoir so made will be well above the area it is required to serve (for the main centres of population are down on the plains) with the result that little or no pumping is necessary. Further, as the catchment area is well away from settlement and industry, the water will be relatively uncontaminated.

Occasionally these upper courses determine the routes of railways and roads, for they may lead to passes or to the best points for tunnels. The land alongside the river is not normally good farmland, but it does often provide good grazing for sheep.

In its Middle Course the river is still of little use for navigation, except, perhaps, in short reaches. Now that the valley is much wider and includes local flood-plains, there is more room for both settlement and agriculture. Villages are a common sight, strung out along the river, and market towns frequently grow up round important confluences. Whether the land is devoted to arable farming or to pasturing cattle will depend on a number of factors—climate, soils, etc.—but, compared with the Upper Course, it is a relatively prosperous area. The broad, open valleys generally provide good routes and so frequently become rail and road highways.

In its Lower Course, the broad, deep river, flowing across a level plain, is admirably suited to navigation. In the case of the really important rivers, large ports therefore tend to grow up somewhere along the lower stretch, the exact location depending on a number of factors. If the climate demands it, irrigation is usually a fairly simple matter, for on the flat land, canals will serve to carry the water great distances, and if dams are built upstream the supply of water can be regulated. The rich alluvial land is usually valuable for agriculture, but here again the type will depend on climate, etc. The only obstacles to communications are generally the wide rivers themselves. Provided therefore, that bridges, etc., are available, there is little difficulty. As a result of all these factors, and many others which may be locally important, the plains are, in the main, areas of relatively dense population, engaged partly in agriculture, partly in industry, partly in commerce, etc.

Diagram (a) shows a section along the course of a typical *mature* river. Such a section is sometimes called a thalweg (from the German, meaning "valley way"), or a long-profile (in contrast to a "cross-section"). Diagram (b) illustrates cross-sections of the course.

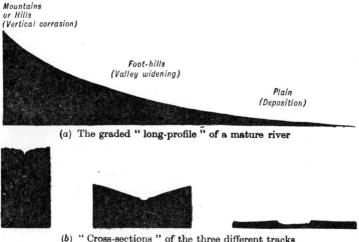

Mountains
or Hills
(Vertical corrasion)

Foot-hills
(Valley widening)

Plain
(Deposition)

(a) The graded " long-profile " of a mature river

(b) " Cross-sections " of the three different tracks

Erosion in its Upper Course, and deposition in its Lower Course, may both help to lengthen a river. Consider the erosion first. At its source, where the river is cutting down, it is also cutting back into the hill. Some interesting consequences of this feature of river erosion are to be seen. Suppose that we have two separate river systems, starting on a fairly level plateau surface, and flowing in opposite directions. Now suppose that the headstreams of one of the systems cut back at a faster rate than those of the other. (This is quite commonplace, and might be due to unequal distribution of rainfall, or to inequality in the resistance of rock formations, etc.) The headstreams of the more " aggressive " system might well cut back across the headstreams of the " weaker " system, " capturing " them and diverting water from the weaker system into the stronger.

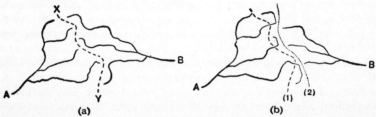

(a)   (b)

In diagram a the two original systems are shown. The broken line, XY, is the water-shed or water-divide, that is, a line drawn to separate two different drainage-areas. (On the actual ground a typical water-shed might be the crest-line of a ridge, for example.) In diagram b the headstreams of the stronger system, A, have cut-back and " captured " the headstreams of the weaker system, B. Notice how the water-shed has been pushed back—from (1) to (2)—and how the points of capture are marked by right-angle bends. These are frequently referred to as elbows of capture. After capture, river-cut gaps may be left in the new divide, but they are now dry, and known as wind-gaps.

The land about the headstreams need not be flat. Streams " working back " from opposite sides of a hill range can achieve the same results. Thus, in the case of the Pennines we find a certain amount of river capture where we have opposite pairs ; for example, Ribble-Aire. The " western " Ribble, with rather heavier rainfall, has been able to encroach somewhat on the drainage basin of the " eastern " Aire, effecting capture here and there. Very noticeable, sometimes, are the captures brought about by streams " working back " along some particular rock formation. The Yorkshire rivers Swale, Ure, Nidd, Wharfe and Aire, have all been diverted into such a stream, the Ouse ; while the same thing is seen in the case of the Sheffield rivers Don, Little Don, Ewden, Loxley, Rivelin, Porter and Sheaf.

Rivers, the general direction of which conforms to the " original " surface slope, are often referred to as consequent streams. Rivers which develop later, as tributaries cutting-back along some less resistant rock formation, are known as subsequent streams. By their own work they bring into being a new surface slope which is more or less at right angles to the original slope. Rivers which, as a result of erosion, are able to develop in a direction opposed to the original surface slope, are known as obsequent streams.

A river such as the Medway (Kent) illustrates all three types. The original drainage slope was from the centre of the Weald, and the consequent reaches of the Medway are therefore those with a generally south-north slope. But subsequent reaches have developed in a generally east-west direction, in the Vale of Kent. The southern slopes of the North Downs now drain to the Vale of Kent, and this drainage is obsequent.

Delta Formation. At its mouth a river is extended by the formation of a delta, frequently a fan-shaped area crossed by several distributaries (that is, where the river has divided into separate channels before emptying its waters into the sea).

Two major conditions are essential for the formation of river deltas : (a) the river must carry an appreciable load, and (b) the river silts must be allowed to accumulate on the gently shelving sea-floors of the shallow waters off the mouth of the river. The first of these two conditions is best realised where there is rapid erosion over a considerable stretch of the course ; that is, where the river and its main tributaries have extensive mountain tracks, and where there is an absence of lakes to " filter " the water. The second condition is best realised where deposition reaches its maximum just off the mouth of the river, and where there is no tidal scour to remove the deposits.

Thus, for delta formation, the river should have a " Plain Course " sufficiently long to ensure that there is no appreciable current off its mouth. The presence of such a current, extending the " line of the river ", would clearly delay deposition, perhaps until beyond the really shallow waters. Further, there must be little or no tide ; that is, the river should flow either into a land-locked sea or into a sea where local conditions reduce tidal action to a minimum. In the practically tideless Mediterranean Sea we find such well-formed deltas as those of the Rhone, Po, and Nile. At the head of the Persian Gulf we find the common delta of the Tigris and Euphrates. In open seas we find the delta of the Rhine, where a high tide, advancing from one direction, is more or less " neutralised " by a low tide, advancing from another. These delta-lands are frequently among the most fertile areas in the world.

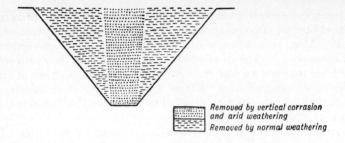

Removed by vertical corrasion
and arid weathering
Removed by normal weathering

River Erosion in Arid Regions. So far we have discussed the work
of a river when vertical corrasion is accompanied by normal weathering.
In arid regions, however, the weathering of rocks is very different from
that described above, for water is virtually absent. A well-watered
river, fed by the rains or snows falling over a distant area, might cross
a desert region on its way to the sea (for example, the River Colorado
crosses the Arizona Desert ; the Orange River crosses the southern
edge of the Kalahari Desert). Vertical corrasion of the river bed would
proceed according to the rate of flow, load carried, nature of rocks, etc.,
but there would be very little valley widening. The resulting valley
would thus be a gorge, deep, narrow, and with precipitous sides. The
world-famous Grand Canyon of the Colorado is an outstanding example
of such river-cut gorges. In moist climates canyons (from the Spanish
cañon) would soon weather back to V-shaped valleys. The development of a canyon relative to a normal valley, is illustrated in the
diagram.

(B) THE WORK OF MOVING ICE

To-day ice-sheets (extensive masses of ice) exist only in polar regions,
but valley glaciers are to be found in all the really high mountain areas.
In polar regions the precipitation is mainly in the form of snow and,
because of the generally low temperatures prevailing throughout
most of the year, this snow accumulates, layer upon layer. If there
were no means of dispersing these ice sheets the accumulation would
clearly go on indefinitely. As it is, some of the surface snow " evapor-
ates ", for there are sunny periods and the air is often dry. Further,
where the ice sheets come down to the sea, they " calve " ice-bergs.
There is thus a kind of balance between the snow precipitated and the
snow and ice dispersed.

In high mountain areas we find a similar balance. Above a certain
height, the snow-line, which varies with latitude and a number of
other factors, snow and ice cover the area all the year round. This
snow-line ranges from sea-level in polar regions to about 18,000 ft. at
the equator ; in the Alps it has an average height of about 9,000 ft.

In such mountain areas the precipitation is again largely in the form of snow. The dispersal of the accumulating snow and ice is accomplished partly by "evaporation" and partly by valley glaciers which move down the valleys and then melt, to form and feed rivers.

Within these relatively small polar and mountain areas, ice is still playing its part in modelling the earth's surface. At other times in the earth's long history, ice has covered much more extensive areas. During these periods (Ice Ages or Glacial Epochs) the role of ice as an erosive agent was accordingly more important than it is now. (Why there should have been these Ice Ages is a controversial question and wholly outside the scope of this book.)

A close study of the surface rocks and land forms, once buried under ice sheets but now uncovered again, has taught us much about the work of ice during its "advance" and "retreat". It is known, for example, that at the stage of maximum glaciation, nearly the whole of the British Isles (except the area south of a line from the Severn Estuary to the Thames Estuary) was under a series of ice sheets. On the Continent of Europe, ice extended from Scandinavia across the northern part of the European Plain. In North America a vast ice sheet stretched from the north across the area now occupied by the Great Lakes to reach its southern limit near the confluence of the Ohio and Mississippi. Further, many of the mountain areas then had ice-caps much more extensive than those of to-day. With the "retreat" of the ice sheets, the work of normal sub-aerial denudation was resumed, but many of the "recently" glaciated areas have not been altered greatly by other agents since glaciation. In such areas we find many features which are characteristically glacial in origin.

By virtue of its structure, ice, although a solid, can "flow". True, the rate of movement of valley glaciers is generally slow, varying from a few inches to several tens of feet a day. Nevertheless, moving ice is a powerful erosive agent. Whether it is more so, or less so, than running water is again a very controversial point which will not be debated here. We shall content ourselves with a study of some characteristically glacial features.

Ice, like running water, can wear rocks away and transport the rock fragments. These rock fragments, held firmly in its mass, are, in effect, the cutting tools of an erosive-machine which derives its driving force from the enormous weight of ice sliding slowly, but almost irresistibly, down a valley. Over lowland areas the piled-up ice masses push "tongues" out well beyond the main mass, and such tongues are capable of movement. Thus, both in the mountains and over the lowlands, glaciation can completely re-model surface relief features, partly by erosion, partly by transportation and re-deposition.

(i) **Glaciated Valleys.** A cross-section of a typical glaciated valley is shown in diagram (i). Several of its more prominent features are at once evident. (*a*) There is a deep, flat-floored trough ; (*b*) steep walls rise from the sides of this trough ; (*c*) above these walls are broad ledges or "shoulders" ; (*d*) above the shoulders normal mountain slopes lead to the heights ; (*e*) tributary streams, draining the mountain slopes, plunge from the shoulder into the trough ; (*f*) such a pronounced break of slope will clearly be a source of water-power.

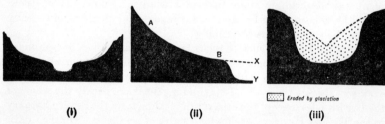

Eroded by glaciation

(i)   (ii)   (iii)

These tributary valleys, which appear to "hang" above the main valley trough, are called **hanging valleys**. It is as if the trough had been over-deepened by ice action during its temporary occupation by the valley glacier. The gradients of the tributary streams, down the mountain slopes and across the shoulder, seem to suggest a former confluence at a considerably higher level (diagram ii). In general this is quite likely, for the glacier would normally occupy a river valley which would then be modified by it. With the return of milder conditions the glacier would "abandon" the valley in its uphill "retreat", leaving the river to resume its work. Most of the so-called "glacial valleys" therefore owe their present form partly to the work of rivers and partly to the work of glaciers, although the influence of the glacier frequently predominates. In the diagram the tributary valley (*A—B*) "hangs" above the main valley (*Y*). *XY* indicates the extent of "over-deepening" which might be attributed to glaciation ; *X* the level of the confluence in the former river valley ; *Y* the level of the confluence in the present glaciated valley.

It is interesting to compare the forms of glacial and river valleys. The river valley is usually referred to as V-shaped ; the glacial valley is often styled U-shaped (diagram iii). The "U", it will be seen, refers to the trough, the part most influenced by the glacier and hence most typically glacial. Above the shoulder, normal sub-aerial denudation usually predominates, for this part was not generally continuously under ice. Sometimes, however, more than one shoulder is to be seen up the valley slopes. This feature seems to indicate that greatly varying amounts of ice occupied the valley at different times, giving rise to an alternation of glacial erosion with normal sub-aerial denudation.

(ii) **Glaciated Mountains.** Just as glaciated valleys possess certain characteristics so, too, do glaciated mountain ranges. In general, we may say that mountain areas which have been subjected only to normal sub-aerial denudation, especially in a reasonably moist climate, show smooth, rounded features. On the mountain slopes this is particularly the case, for rock debris accumulates there, smoothing out the underlying irregularities. In glaciated mountains, on the other hand, many sharp-edged features are to be seen, for one of the effects of ice erosion is to " pluck " away substantial masses of loosened rock. Even the slopes have often been scraped bare of rock debris, except for recently accumulated screes. In general, there is a bold and varied relief—the kind of scenery that appeals to tourists—although many of the individual rock surfaces may well have been smoothed and polished as a result of the ice action.

One noticeable feature of the higher areas of glaciated country is the occurrence of sharp-edged ridges which stand out above the general level. Sometimes the crest-line of these ridges, frequently called arêtes, runs roughly horizontal, at other times it may be inclined. Sometimes, too, several such ridges may converge on rugged peaks which have a generally pyramidal form. Between the converging ridges armchair-shaped depressions are often to be found. These have a generally flat floor, have higher land rising sharply from probably three sides, and fall away rapidly on the fourth side. The flat floor is either marshy or largely occupied by a lake. Small streams usually drain the steep slopes leading down to the hollow, and a considerable stream usually drains the depression. These remarkable depressions are often called **cirques** (from the French), but they are also known as **cwms** (in Wales) and **corries** (in Scotland). Diagrams *a* and *b* show the typical long-profile and cross-section of a cirque. It will be seen that the typical cirque somewhat resembles an " amphitheatre " at the head of a mountain valley.

If several cirques are situated about a pyramidal peak, erosion around the sides and back of the cirques may eventually lead to the destruction of the peak. In a similar way, if two cirques are situated back to back on opposite sides of a ridge, they may eventually be the

(a)   (b)

Long-profile (*a*) and Cross-section (*b*) of a cirque

cause of a break developing in the ridge. Such breaks in ridges are often called cols. More usually, however, cols link two normal valleys which have " eaten back " from opposite sides of a ridge.

(iii) **Moraines.** Features resulting from the various materials re-deposited by glaciers and ice sheets are generally called moraines.

(a) The rock debris which falls on to the sides of valley glaciers from relief features protruding above the ice is often deposited as a low ridge of loose material along the valley side. Such deposits are known as lateral moraines.

(b) When two tributary glaciers join on entering the main valley, their lateral moraines may unite to form a medial moraine.

(c) When a glacier has gone so far down a valley that it begins to melt, the rock debris which it has been carrying will be deposited across the valley to form a terminal moraine. Such a moraine may be sufficient to dam the valley and cause a lake to form. These three types of moraines are illustrated in the diagram.

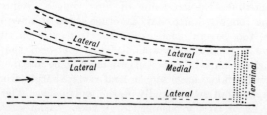

(d) When a glacier or ice sheet melts (due, possibly, to a return of generally milder conditions) the "load" it carries will be deposited over the area covered by the ice, as a ground moraine. This load will have been derived, partly from materials worn away from the surface over which the ice has passed, and partly from materials which have fallen on to the ice from protruding rock masses. Much of it will have been reduced to very fine particles due to the continual grinding process. The larger rock fragments will have been greatly smoothed and rounded. This glacially deposited material is frequently referred to as boulder clay.

Boulder clay does not often occur prominently in mountain areas, for after deposition it is subjected to normal sub-aerial denudation and worn away fairly readily. Over lowlands, however, boulder clay and other glacial debris (glacial drift, as it is often called) frequently plays a very prominent part in shaping relief features.

(iv) **Glaciated Lowlands.** The sheets of glacial drift are sometimes so thick that, if removed, extensive areas would be below sea-level. This is particularly the case with the coastal areas extending from Bridlington Bay to the neighbourhood of Lowestoft, and from Morecambe Bay to the Mersey. In addition, even greater areas have such a thick glacial covering that the underlying rock formations are obscured. So important are these glacial deposits in determining the relief and surface conditions of such areas that " Drift Editions " of geological maps have been specially prepared for them ; the underlying rock formations are shown on the " Solid Editions " of geological maps.

Glacial Drift is of two main types : (a) boulder clay deposited by the ice sheet itself when it melted, and (b) gravels and sands deposited by water along the margins of the ice sheet. Consider the case of an ice sheet advancing across a lowland area. Along its front edge there would often be sufficient " free " water to wash out sand and gravel from the edge of the ice sheet and deposit it as bedded sands and gravels in front of the advancing sheet. These sands and gravels would gradually be covered by the ice as it moved on. Meanwhile, the sand and gravel zone would also move on, always keeping in front of the advancing ice. Suppose the ice sheet now retreats. Its load of boulder clay will be deposited on top of the sands and gravels, and " free " water will wash out more sands and gravels on top of the boulder clay. When the ice sheet has finally disappeared the deposits will be in the form of a sandwich. In the case considered, boulder clay is sandwiched between two layers of sands and gravels. Ice sheets, however, seldom appear to have made one simple advance and one simple retreat. More often, it appears, they oscillated, with the result that the arrangement of boulder clay and " outwash " sands and gravels is usually much more elaborate than is suggested above.

After a glacial dump has been left by an ice sheet, normal sub-aerial denudation acts upon it. The mass as a whole is not generally very resistant, due largely to the soft and impermeable nature of the boulder clay. An outwash zone is therefore formed. The larger gravels are re-deposited by water along the outer edges of the dump ; the smaller sands are carried considerably farther ; the fine clays are probably carried away altogether.

Glacial Drift country is very varied, partly because there may, or may not, be sands and gravels, and partly because the boulder clay itself can be derived from such a variety of sources. The glacial deposits take on something of the character of the local rock formations, and something of all the other rock formations over which the ice passed before depositing its load. Thus, to reach East Anglia, the ice crossed the chalk belt, with the result that much of the East Anglian drift is a chalky boulder clay—easy to work and very fertile. This type of boulder clay country is, in effect, a low plateau.

Drumlins. Sometimes the glacial deposits present a hummocky surface in which a complicated arrangement of low, elongated hills can be discerned. These low hills, which may vary in height from mere mounds to considerable hills of, perhaps, 300 ft., are called drumlins. They are nearly always elongated in the direction of the ice movement, and are composed wholly of boulder clay (that is, bedded sands and gravels are absent).

Eskers and Kames. These are long, winding, steep-sided ridges composed mainly of gravels and sands. There are considerable differences of opinion as to their precise origin, but they are a characteristic feature of glaciated lowland country.

Glacial deposits, as we have seen, frequently occur in a hummocky form. Because of this and the impermeable nature of boulder clay, lakes and ponds are frequently to be found in the hollows.

A minor consequence of glaciation—but a very interesting one, nevertheless—is the occurrence of **erratics**. These are " foreign " rock boulders left stranded by the ice sheets in an area where rocks of that type do not form part of the local formation. Thus, when erratics from the Southern Uplands of Scotland are found in the Eden Valley, one infers that an ice sheet pushed out a tongue from these Scottish Uplands across the Solway Plain and up the Eden Valley. The presence of drumlins in the Eden Valley, elongated in the direction of the valley, helps to support this view of the direction of movement of this particular ice sheet. Further evidence of the direction of movement of the ice can sometimes be gained by **striations** (parallel scratches) on the rock surfaces over which the ice has passed, for these striations will clearly be in the direction of movement.

(C) THE WORK OF WIND

In moist climates the work of wind is not often conspicuous, for it is overshadowed, or even obliterated, by the work of water. In arid areas, however, wind is the chief agent of erosion. It must be remembered, though, that even arid areas receive sporadic, and sometimes torrential, rainfall. Such " downpours " may be quite local, and they may be at intervals of several years, but they may well occasion the temporary predominance, if only over relatively insignificant areas, of the work of running water.

Because the work of wind is largely confined to desert areas, our knowledge of such erosion is less complete than that of the types already discussed, for there are still many gaps in detailed study of the world's great deserts. Yet these arid areas occupy nearly a third of the earth's present continental surface.

In the hot deserts, erosion will depend on several well-defined " controls ". One of these, heat by day and cold by night, has already been discussed under the heading of " Mechanical Weathering " and it has been seen how rocks are broken up into blocks and ultimately into sand. Another important control is the lack of a substantial vegetation cover. Rock surfaces are therefore exposed directly to eroding forces. A third control is the rapid evaporation. Thus the sporadic rains, even when torrential, are localised in their erosive effects. The water pours into deep gullies, rushes along for a relatively short distance, and finally ends as a thick paste. The streams, unless fed from sources outside the desert, are purely intermittent and scarcely ever reach the open sea. Usually they either dry up in the desert itself or flow into a salt lake. Such areas are called inland drainage basins. Under these conditions the work of the wind predominates.

The chief ingredient of ordinary sand is quartz, a mineral which is harder than most of the other rock-forming minerals. Carried along by the wind, quartz has much the same effect as a sand-blast. It can polish and etch rock surfaces, and can actually carve rock masses into fantastic shapes. Thus, it is not uncommon in desert areas to find mushroom-shaped rocks. There appears to be both an upper and a lower limit to really effective wind erosion. Near the ground there is too much friction, with the result that the sand-blast loses a great deal of its cutting power. Above a certain height the wind cannot lift the larger pieces of quartz. So we find rock masses supported on relatively slender stems—like mushrooms. In time, of course, the stem would be cut completely through and the rock mass would fall. Then the sand-blast would begin to re-shape it all over again.

Sand Dunes. More important is the transportation and re-deposition of disintegrated rock materials. The formation of "loess" has already been mentioned as a case in point. In the desert itself, sand dunes are of common occurrence. In some ways comparable are the coastal dunes of, say, many parts of Western Europe. In one very important respect, quite apart from several others, these coastal dunes differ from desert dunes; they are usually "tied down", frequently by grasses, both naturally rooted and artificially planted. In the "Landes" district of south-west France conifers have been successfully established on them. In the desert the dunes "wander" with the wind. Over many of the great deserts, particularly the Trade Wind Deserts, the winds are fairly steady in direction throughout the year, with the result that the dunes take up definite forms and tend to move in definite directions. The diagrams illustrate the shape of a typical dune

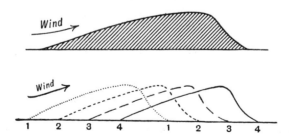

(note carefully the relative slopes, one gentle and slightly convex, the other steep and slightly concave), the general manner in which dunes move (or migrate) with the wind, and a crescentic dune or **barkhan**. Effects similar to these can sometimes be seen when the wind " drifts " powdery snow.

(D) THE WORK OF UNDERGROUND WATER

The precipitation falling on an area is dispersed in some or all of four ways : (i) it may run off the surface to form streams ; (ii) it may soak into the ground ; (iii) it may be used up by the vegetation cover, or (iv) it may evaporate and return to the atmosphere as water-vapour. We are now concerned with that part which soaks into the ground.

Whether or not water will soak into the ground clearly depends on the nature of the particular rock formation, and here two distinct types of rock must be recognised. Those which allow water to pass through them freely are said to be **permeable** or **pervious** ; those which do not allow water to pass through them freely are styled **impermeable or impervious**. (The terms " porous " and " non-porous " should not be used in this general descriptive sense.)

Much of the water which soaks into the ground enters and follows joints (planes, possibly produced by shrinkage, which tend to divide the rock formation into separate blocks), faults, crevices, bedding-planes, etc. Such features tend to develop into considerable channels, and serve to make the formation as a whole permeable. A compact crystalline rock, certainly not porous, might well be permeable, if only to a limited extent. The case of limestone is particularly interesting in this respect. Many of the limestones are hard, compact, and extensively used in building ; they are not porous. Yet " jointing " is one of the predominant characteristics of limestone formations ; they are very permeable. True, some formations might be both porous and permeable. A bed of loose (unconsolidated) sand generally allows water to drain through it. In such a case the pore spaces become filled with water and the whole mass becomes saturated ; it might be termed " porous ". Further, because of the loose texture of such a formation, the water would drain right through (the surface tension would not be sufficient to hold the water within the mass) ; it is also " permeable ". The same might be said of a bed of gravel. Some of the softer chalks also display the same characteristics, but owing to the

finer texture, more of the water is held within the mass. Chalk, however, usually shows jointing as well, and is therefore permeable. Clays,
on the other hand, though often porous, are generally very impermeable. The constituent particles which comprise clay are so fine that the
pore spaces are exceptionally small. Water may penetrate clay but
will be held within the mass, making the formation as a whole impermeable. When saturated with water, clay is plastic, easy to mould and
easily worn away. Even when thoroughly wet, however, it will not
allow water to pass through it. These characteristics have an important
bearing on the resulting land forms, for they modify erosion. The distinction between " porosity " and " permeability " is a very real one
and must be thoroughly appreciated.

Under the ground, at depths which vary with circumstances, ground
water is usually to be found. This level may be called the saturation
level, but it is frequently called the water table. To think of it as a
table, however, is very misleading, for it is seldom flat for more than
relatively short distances. The level of underground water depends
on a number of factors, of which the most important are : (i) the
amount and distribution of rainfall ; (ii) the nature of the rock formations ; and (iii) the surface relief of the land areas. It would
be surprising, therefore, if the saturation level were, in general,
a " table ".

Ground water plays its part in land sculpture in two very important
ways. By " feeding " rivers from springs it helps to maintain the flow
of those rivers and so assists normal river erosion. By working on the
rocks below the surface it is directly responsible for certain features in
the surface relief.

Springs. A spring is the name given to ground water which flows
out on to the surface. In the accompanying diagram the shaded
part represents an impermeable rock layer, the upper surface of
which is slightly tilted from right to left. Resting on this layer is
a permeable mass which has been worn down so that the slope in
the general direction of the bedding plane, the dip slope, is gentle,
while the slope facing in the opposite direction is steep, the scarp
slope. (This is quite a common arrangement, for example, in

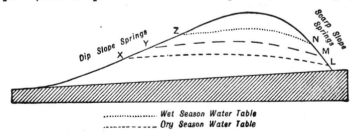

.... *Wet Season Water Table*
-------------- *Dry Season Water Table*

F

the scarplands of South-East England.) Rain falling on the permeable mass will soak into the ground, but it will not be able to penetrate the impermeable layer. The lower layers of the permeable rock will therefore tend to become saturated as more and more water finds its way down into the mass. The " water-table " will thus take up some such position as *YM*, which conforms somewhat to the surface relief. After prolonged rainfall the water-table will tend to rise nearer to the surface, say to the position *ZN*. After prolonged drought, however, the water-table will tend to fall, to the position *XL*.

When the water-table is in the position *YM*, the " table " is not flat, but generally convex towards the surface. This, in effect, means that water is piled up in the middle of the permeable mass. There is thus a head of water. This head of water (or hydrostatic pressure) will tend to force water out of the mass at points below the saturation level. Springs may therefore be expected at points lower down the slope than *Y* and *M*. Those lower than *Y* will be the " dip slope springs "; those lower than *M* the " scarp slope springs ". If, now, heavy and prolonged rain should occur, there might be a tendency for " wet season springs " to appear higher up the slopes (in the diagram, below *Z* and *N*). After prolonged drought, on the other hand, there will be a tendency for springs higher up the slope to cease. (In the diagram the dry season spring-lines will be below *X* and *L*.) After an exceptionally severe drought the scarp slope springs may cease altogether, due to the fact that the ground water may sink so low that it no longer has any head in that direction. So long as there is any ground water left in the mass there must be a head for the dip slope springs, and they are therefore usually the more reliable.

Because of the importance of water to man, **spring-lines** were early chosen as suitable for settlement, for example, in Chalk country.

It may happen that the permeable layer is largely covered by impermeable rocks, and comes to the surface only in one place. This outcrop of the permeable rock may be referred to as the **catchment area**. Rain falling on the impermeable surface will largely run off into streams, but

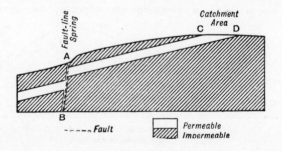

rain falling on the permeable outcrop (*CD* in the diagram) will tend to soak into the rock. So long as this ground water is trapped between the two impermeable layers it cannot escape. In the diagram, how-ever, there is indicated a major fault (*AB*) and a " downthrow " of the strata. Provided, therefore, that there is sufficient head, this ground water may be driven out through the fault, giving rise to fault-line springs.

Oases. An oasis is an isolated, fertile region within a desert ; its existence is due to the presence of water. Generally this means that, over some particular area, ground water becomes available, but the meaning might be extended to include those areas, otherwise desert, which are watered by a river and so made fertile. Thus Egypt might be called an oasis ; it is surrounded by desert but is watered by the Nile, which draws its vast supplies from areas outside the desert. Without the Nile, Egypt would, indeed, be a desert. What is usually understood by the term " oasis ", however, is a limited area which depends on ground water for its fertility. Thus an oasis might be a

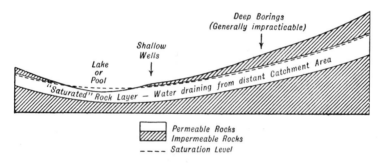

small settlement dependent on a few springs or wells, or it might be an area comparable with an English county and watered by a lake and numerous outlying wells. The diagram shows how the surface relief might very well bring a lake into being. If the water-table is far below the surface, only deep borings can reach the ground water ; if it comes near the surface, shallow wells will suffice ; if it comes to the surface, marsh or bog normally results ; if it comes " above " the surface a lake will form.

Artesian Wells and Basins. Somewhat akin to the type of oasis described above is the Artesian Basin (from the name " Artois " of an old province in north-east France, where this method of boring was first adopted in Europe). In the artesian basin, however, the ground water does not naturally reach the surface ; it requires the boring of wells and, perhaps, pumping. The general conditions which give rise to the formation of artesian basins will be understood from the

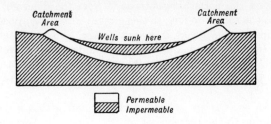

diagram, which shows a permeable layer sandwiched between two impermeable layers, the whole arrangement being bent into a downfold or syncline so that the permeable layer does, in fact, reach the surface on the edges of the " basin ". The permeable outcrops provide the catchment areas. Rain falling on these catchment areas sinks into the permeable rock layer, where it is trapped between under-lying and overlying impermeable strata. To reach this ground water it is necessary to sink wells through the upper impermeable layer. If there is a sufficient head, the ground water will gush up through the boring ; if there is insufficient head, pumping will be necessary.

An artesian basin similar to the type described above underlies the London area. The London area is, in fact, a basin. To the north-west lie the Chilterns (chalk) ; to the south lie the North Downs (chalk) ; these hills are the outcrops of a chalk syncline (downfold). Within the basin there is a layer of London Clay ; underlying the chalk is another layer of clay (but, of course, older than London Clay). The Chilterns and North Downs form the catchment areas. Until London became such a vast " settlement " this artesian basin was its main source of water for domestic purposes. It is no longer adequate and the Thames and its tributaries now provide the greater proportion.

A double catchment area is not essential for the effective formation of an artesian basin, as is shown in the case of most of the artesian basins in Australia, where they are very widespread and extensively utilised. The generally synclinal arrangement is, however, very important. The largest and most important of the Australian basins underlies a great part of the Central Lowlands, extending from the Gulf of Carpentaria Lowlands southwards into the Murray-Darling Basin. Its only effective catchment area lies to the east, where the permeable rock crops out along the Great Dividing Range. To the west the conditions become progressively arid. Further, in the west there is no major permeable outcrop even if there were rain ; the sedimentary strata abut on to the old hard crystalline rocks of the Western Plateau.

Australia serves to illustrate the great value of artesian water. Taken as a whole, Australia is the " driest " of the continents. Further,

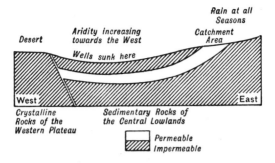

Central Lowlands Artesian Basin of Australia

large areas which normally receive a fairly adequate rainfall for at least certain types of farming, experience periodic and severe droughts. It so happens that artesian water is available over many such areas. Here, however, one very important characteristic of artesian water (and of all ground water in greater or lesser degree) comes to the fore. Due to its passage through the rocks, possibly for very considerable distances, the water dissolves mineral salts. This makes it unsuitable for irrigation purposes, for evaporation of the water from the soil would soon lead to a harmful deposit of these salts in the soil. Nevertheless, it is most valuable for feeding to stock. Special " stock roads " lead to the artesian wells, and in times of drought, cattle and sheep may be taken hundreds of miles and thus saved. Even so the exceptionally severe droughts experienced from time to time still cost Australia many valuable stock. But so important is the artesian water, that wells have been sunk in some places to depths of several thousand feet, and no large " station " is complete without its own well.

Geysers. Geysers are usually associated with areas of present or recent volcanic activity ; for example, North Island, New Zealand, and the Yellowstone Park, North America. The ejection of the hot water is intermittent, and sometimes at remarkably uniform intervals.

It appears that ground water (and perhaps seepage from the oceans) becomes superheated as a result of its proximity to masses of hot rock and the intense pressures prevailing. Then, as in the case of a volcano, there is a " flash point " when a violent eruption occurs. Quiescence follows, and later another eruption. Not all geysers, however, are violent ; some have settled down into a steady rhythm.

Mineral Springs. Springs which contain, in solution, an unusually high proportion of mineral salts, or some distinctive mineral salt, are known as **mineral springs.** Some of these have well-known medicinal properties and so lead to the growth of watering-places or spas. (Spa, a famous watering-place in Belgium, noted for its " Pouhon Spring ", has given its name to all places of this type.) In England we have such well-known spas as Bath, Buxton, Harrogate, etc. One of the most celebrated of all the spas, perhaps, is Lourdes, in the south of France, at the foot of the Pyrenees. Hundreds of thousands make the " pilgrimage " there every year, to the spring which is credited with miraculous powers.

Landslides (or Landslips). Ground water, partly by increasing the weight of the rocks which it saturates, and partly by lubricating fault-planes, bedding-planes, etc., is often a cause of landslides (or landslips), especially during periods of alternate freezing and thawing. In general,

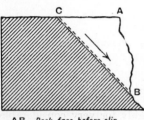

AB – *Rock face before slip*
CB – *Rock face after slip*

the effect of a landslide is to reduce the slope of an exposed surface, for the rock masses which slide are normally wedge-shaped. They are particularly common along parts of the glacial drift coast of eastern England where the sea has under-cut the rock formation and produced either cliffs or steep faces. Such uncon-solidated formations are not very re-sistant to active erosion, and do not, therefore, readily lend themselves to steep-faced relief. Landslides also occur, from time to time, in quarries, mines, cuttings and embankments, and they are sometimes of considerable local importance. Taking the earth as a whole, however, they are relatively insignificant in the shaping of relief features.

Dry Valleys. Dry valleys, a characteristic feature of chalk and limestone country, though not actually modelled by ground water, are nevertheless closely associated with it. They are dry because the water table lies below even the bottoms of the valleys.

As has already been seen, both chalk and limestone are permeable rocks, and many of the softer chalks are also porous. Rainfall therefore tends to soak into the rock, and to sink until it reaches the satura-tion level. On the lower slopes this saturation level, or water-table, may come to the surface. Then streams will be able to flow over the surface. If, on the other hand, the saturation level is well below the surface, there will, in general, be an absence of streams and of other surface water. Yet many of the dry valleys are river-formed. Though dry—and perhaps for a very long time—they show features which are defin-itely associated with river valleys, such as terraces, river-gravels, etc. It can therefore be said with certainty that such valleys were carved by running water.

Two explanations in particular may account for this great change from river-valley to dry-valley ; in some cases the change may be due, in part, to both. One possible cause is that the valleys were actually carved about the time of the last great ice age and just after. Then there may have been periods when there was considerable surface water to drain away, but when the sub-soil and rocks just below the surface were frozen. The freezing of a saturated rock would clearly render it impermeable. These conditions are frequently encountered in sub-polar areas to-day. For the greater part of the year, surface temperatures may be well below freezing ; for a short time, surface temperatures may rise above freezing ; a little below the surface, rocks will remain frozen all through the year. There is a short period, therefore, v hen surface water will remain on the surface no matter what the normal nature of the underlying rocks may be, and when it will perform the work of river erosion.

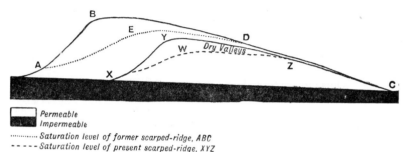

Permeable
Impermeable
.... Saturation level of former scarped-ridge, ABC
- - - - - Saturation level of present scarped-ridge, XYZ

The second possible cause is that there has been an appreciable lowering of the saturation level. Such a lowering could be brought about by a marked diminution in the rainfall, for after periods of prolonged drought the saturation level falls. But a lowering could also be achieved by the wearing away of the land-form, and this is the more likely cause. The diagram illustrates the lowering of the saturation level in a scarped-ridge by the wearing back of the scarp. Assume that the " original " land-form is represented by the cross-section ABC. Assume further that the scarp-face (AB) is being attacked by erosive agents. (This is quite usual. A river, flowing along the foot of the scarp, will assist the comparatively rapid erosion of the scarp-face.) In the original position the saturation level would approximate to AED. Therefore, below the point D, streams could flow on the surface of the slope DC. Now suppose that the scarped-ridge has been worn away to XYC and that the saturation level has thereby been lowered to XWZ. In the new position, streams will be able to flow on the surface only below Z. Any valleys which had been eroded between D and Z will now be " dry ". If these river-eroded valleys had been cut deeply into the surface, and if the scarp-face had been cut back sufficiently far (that is, D higher up the slope than Y) a distinct " break " might have occurred in the ridge. Such breaks in the crest-line are called cols. They have frequently become important

controls in lines of communication, for valleys lead up to them and
they form the lowest crossing-places.

Occasionally, due to abnormal, or seasonal, raising of the water-
table, streams may temporarily occupy " dry valleys " ; such streams
are called bournes.

Further characteristics of Limestone Country. Limestone country
(and this, in many respects, includes Chalk, for both are essentially
calcium carbonate) shows certain definite characteristics which depend,
to a very large extent, on the particular properties of this class of
rock. Both tend to form upland country. This is not because the
rock is hard (some chalks are quite soft), but because of the absence
of surface drainage, due to its permeability. One of the most powerful
of the erosive agents—running water—is therefore very restricted in
its effect. The work of underground water, on the other hand, is of
the greatest significance, due to the well-developed system of jointing
and the solubility of calcium carbonate in water containing carbon dioxide. Thus rain-water (which contains carbon dioxide), by a process of
solution, enlarges joints and makes underground channels which penetrate deeply into the rock. The formation of dry, rocky plateaux, dissected by joint-fissures, is therefore a characteristic feature of most limestone regions ; for example, the North Pennines, around the head-
waters of the Ribble, where the bare surfaces are known as clints.

Underground rivers. If the water-table is at (or above) the surface,
a river can flow over limestone country ; if the water-table sinks
below the surface, the river will disappear into the ground down to the
level of the table. Thus, when crossing the chalk of the North Downs,
the River Mole (note the name) disappears, only to reappear lower
downstream. The Tarn, in the Causses Region of southern France
does the same thing on an even greater scale. The holes through which
such rivers disappear are known as swallow holes.

Subsidence. Associated with underground drainage we sometimes
find subsidence which is noticeable on the surface. The roof of an
underground channel may in time collapse, forming a long and narrow
gorge. One of the best-known examples of this kind is, possibly, the
Cheddar Gorge, in Somerset. At other times subsidence may lead
only to hollows and depressions appearing at the surface. These are
known as dolines.

Caves and Caverns. Where the underground channels have been
greatly enlarged, due to pronounced solution in some particular place,
we find caves and caverns. The most famous of them have become
popular tourist centres as, for example, Gough's Caves at Cheddar,
the Blue John and Speedwell Caverns in the South Pennines. Inside
the caves, stalactites and stalagmites are often to be found, the former
hanging from the roof rather like icicles, the latter built up from the

floor rather like pillars. They are composed of calcium carbonate, and are caused by ground water containing carbonates and other minerals in solution dripping from the roof and so forming deposits both above and below. Stalactites and stalagmites " grow " at very variable rates, but always slowly ; in some cases the rate has been estimated at less than an inch in a thousand years.

The characteristic features of limestone country are extraordinarily well developed in the area which lies to the east of the northern Adriatic, and here they have been most carefully studied. This region was formerly known as the Austrian " Karst ", but later became the Italian " Carso ". It is customary, therefore, to speak of limestone areas which display well-developed underground drainage, dry valleys, caves, dolines, etc., as karst regions. The South Pennines and the limestone zone around the south-western borders of the Massif Central of France (the " Causses ") are similar, if not identical, to the Karst proper.

THE CYCLE OF DENUDATION

In the light of what has been said of earth movements and land erosion, it is now possible to trace the evolution of some of the earth's major landforms (see accompanying diagram).

(*A*) Sedimentary strata are resting on crystalline rocks as deposited, the whole being below sea-level. Here, then, deposition of fresh sediments will be taking place.

(*B*) Uplift has occurred, and the strata have been pushed up into folds. (In certain cases this may not happen, of course. The strata may be raised gently to form plains or plateaux.)

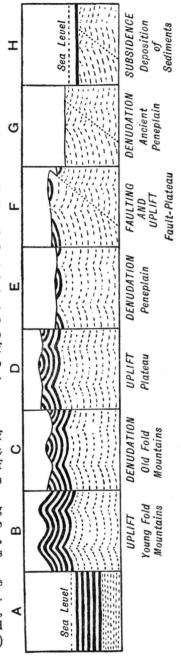

H — SUBSIDENCE — Deposition of Sediments

G — DENUDATION — Ancient Peneplain

F — FAULTING AND UPLIFT — Fault-Plateau

E — DENUDATION — Peneplain

D — UPLIFT — Plateau

C — DENUDATION — Old Fold Mountains

B — UPLIFT — Young Fold Mountains

A — Sea Level

Such " recently " uplifted mountains are known as **young fold moun-tains** ; for example, Alps, Rockies, Andes, etc.

(*C*) Denudation has made considerable progress. The upfolds, stretched and weakened, have been worn away far more than the downfolds which, compressed and strengthened, now form the highest parts. These are **old fold mountains**; for example, Appalachians.

(*D*) The whole area has been uplifted afresh, to form a plateau. Erosion will therefore proceed with renewed vigour ; in some cases rivers may cut fresh courses, in others they may become more deeply *incised*, or ~~entrenched~~, in their " original " channels.

(*E*) The area has, at long last, been worn down to a **peneplain** ; denudation is now greatly restricted in its influence.

(*F*) Faulting has occurred and a part of the mass has been uplifted yet again to form an old, **fault-bounded plateau**. (In the diagram a thrust-fault is suggested.)

(*G*) Denudation has reduced the area to an **ancient peneplain**, and normally, if no further earth-movements intervened, this process would continue until the entire area was practically at sea-level. In certain cases the peneplain might tend to rise slowly, uplift approximately balancing the very reduced denudation. The shield lands of North-East Canada, North-East Asia, and the Gulf of Bothnia are possibly of this type.

(*H*) The " cycle " has been completed, for the area has sunk below the sea once more, and the deposition of sediments is beginning all over again, on the denuded remnants of the former contorted rock formations.

It is by no means certain that this same area would ever again go through identical, or even similar, processes of " evolution ", for the mechanism of earth-movements is exceedingly complicated.

CHAPTER V

THE OUTLINE OF THE LAND

MARINE SCULPTURE

THE study of land sculpture must now be extended to the margins of the land.

Marine Erosion. First consider the case of an area of land which has just been submerged, thereby producing a coastline of submergence. In general the lower parts will be drowned, and the sea will wash against the relatively steep slopes of prominent hills. Now wave action is a powerful erosive agent. The large quantities of water, battering against a rock face, can themselves have an important erosive effect, particularly when the water is forced into crevices or cavities. Then the crevices tend to become enlarged, partly by the pressure of the water which has been driven in like a wedge, and partly by the compression of air trapped in the cavity.

More important, however, is the work done by the " load " of such pounding waves. Strong waves, breaking on a rock surface, can throw substantial pieces of rock debris with considerable violence; larger pieces are rolled along by the waves. Such action, moreover, is rather like that of a cross-cut saw, for the load is not only brought in on the wave but it is also carried out again on the backwash. As a result of this constant pounding and rolling, the rock debris is soon smoothed into pebbles, but they are still capable of erosive action, nevertheless. These apparently endless quantities of rock debris are the cutting tools of an erosive machine which derives its power from the release of enormous energy during wave action.

It will be at once evident that there must be an upper limit to this type of erosion, namely, the limit reached by the highest waves. But there is a lower limit also. Below a certain depth the waves are effectively damped out and the sediments there are scarcely ever disturbed. We are therefore concerned with the zone between these two limits. Above the upper limit, normal sub-aerial denudation will become effective and this, combined with the marine erosion in the wave zone, may become an important factor in determining the form of coastal features. Normal erosion must therefore not be ignored when dealing with marine erosion.

Abrasion Platform and Beaches. The formation of a coast-line in a recently submerged area is illustrated in the diagram (p. 82). The various stages are in alphabetical order.

(a) The sea is washing against a former hillside at X. Wave action will therefore tend to wear away a notch between the high- and low-water

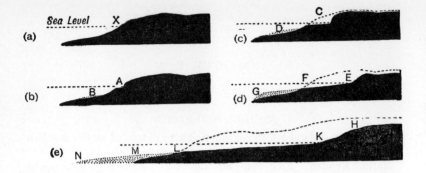

marks. This is shown at A in (b). The rock debris worn away will be washed down the hill slope and will come to rest below the level of wave action, where it will accumulate (B).

(c) The process is carried a stage further. A marked wave-cut bench backed by steep cliffs (C) has now come into being, and an appreciable accumulation of sedimentary deposits (D) has resulted. Meanwhile normal erosion has lowered the general level of the land slightly. (The original surface is shown by the broken line.) At C, however, marine erosion is still dominant; that is, wave action is cutting into the base of the cliffs so fast that the cliff form remains, although the whole coastline is receding inland.

(d) The wave-cut bench has broadened into an abrasion platform (E–F), while the sedimentary deposits have been built up to produce a seaward extension of this platform (F–G). At the same time, normal erosion has become relatively more important, with the result that the cliff tops have been worn back more than their bases, producing steep slopes rather than sheer faces.

(e) The fully developed stage. (This is often called the mature stage and is comparable to the "graded profile" of a mature river.) There is now a very extensive abrasion platform (K–L) and very considerable sedimentary deposits on its seaward side (L–M–N). Further, there is an absence of pronounced cliffs; instead we find a fairly steep slope (H–K) leading down to the sea, due to the fact that normal erosion has at last taken control.

As the coastline recedes inland the abrasion platform offers increasing resistance to wave action and so hinders the wave attack; at the same time the increasing height of the cliff-face presents normal erosion with a greater surface on which to work and this, in turn, provides a bigger "load" for the waves to move. Thus handicapped, marine erosion is checked, but normal erosion goes on apace, wearing the top of the cliff ever back. The original land surface, shown by the broken line in (e), has therefore been greatly altered by the combined action of marine erosion and normal erosion.

In such a process, several factors must be considered, for the resulting coastline will depend on their collective action. First, the nature of the rock will clearly be an important factor, because some rocks wear away more quickly than others. Secondly, we must consider the erosive agents, both marine and normal ; thirdly, the " load " which the waves have to carry ; and fourthly, the transportation of this load. If the erosive agents, acting on a less resistant rock, provide a greater load at the bottom of the cliffs than the wave scour can adequately cope with, there will be an accumulation of rock debris on the shore, giving rise to pronounced beaches, or beach terraces, and masses of scree at the cliff-foot. Wave action will gradually sift and sort these materials, forming possibly several beach terraces in the process.

Bay Formation. Frequently several different levels of terraces can be seen, corresponding to the high- and low-water marks and perhaps to storm marks, that is, when wind-driven waves have reached abnormally high levels. If, on the other hand, there is insufficient load for the wave scour, the rock debris will be removed from the cliff-foot and very little material will be left on the wave-cut benches and abrasion platform. Further, the cliff base will not long have the protection of fallen debris against wave attack and vigorous erosion is to be expected. These aspects of erosion and transportation are very important along some coasts, frequently in the case of bays.

The diagram shows how erosion may produce a bay. The two resistant belts of rock stand out as headlands or points, and the less resistant rock between them has been eroded away to a much greater extent to form a bay. Such a bay will continue to extend inland so long as the wave scour is capable of removing all the rock debris which accumulates at the head of the bay. Should the accumulation of rock debris prove too great for the wave scour to clear, however, deposition will take place at the head of the bay. Until the headlands are then worn back, thereby giving the wave scour increased vigour, the bay will

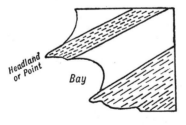

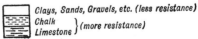

Clays, Sands, Gravels, etc. *(less resistance)*

Chalk
Limestone } *(more resistance)*

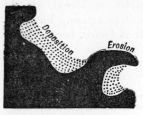

"Bay-head" Beaches
(Deposition)

not penetrate any farther inland. Features of this kind clearly depend for their continuance on the delicate balance maintained among the several forces involved. Any disturbance of that balance will result in the feature being transformed. In this way a bay may become silted-up, or renewed wave attack may begin at its head.

A good example of alternate bays and headlands is to be seen along the eastern side of the Purbeck coast of Dorset—Durlston Head, Durlston Bay, Peveril Point, Swanage Bay, The Foreland, Studland Bay.

The general arrangement of " bay-head " beaches, when deposition is taking place, is illustrated in the diagram above.

Off-shore bar. Now consider the case of an area of land which has recently been raised gently above sea-level, thereby giving rise to a coastline of emergence. In general the sea will wash against a surface which shelves slightly, perhaps almost imperceptibly. Because of the shallowness of the off-shore water, the larger and more destructive waves will lose much of their energy before reaching the actual shore. Even so, the erosive effects of the waves which do manage to reach the land margin may be sufficient to produce a line of low cliffs. (We may define the " shore " as the zone between the high- and low-water marks. The landward side of the shore, that is, the land margin just beyond the reach of the sea, is the coastline proper.)

More important, however, in this instance, is the formation of a submarine bank off the shore, that is, in the water which is too shallow to allow of the passage of the more powerful waves. Such a bank, built by the action of the smaller waves, eventually reaches the surface as an off-shore bar. Between the bar and the land will be a lagoon which will later probably develop into a salt-marsh. Here and there the bar will be breached to admit the passage of tidal water. Meanwhile, wave scour is proceeding on the sea floor where the more destructive waves " break ", that is, some distance to seaward of the bar. In time the abrasion platform so formed will reach the bar and the more powerful waves will then be able to begin their attack on the bar. As the waves extend their erosion towards the land the bar will be pushed back across the salt-marshes.

Finally, with the deepening of the off-shore water during this process, the most powerful waves will be able to begin their attack on the land margin proper. The tendency then will be for wave action to extend the abrasion platform inland to distances which vary according to local circumstances ; if there is lack of uniformity in the rock formations and marked differences in the degree of sub-aerial denudation from one point to another, the coastline may be expected to become progressively irregular.

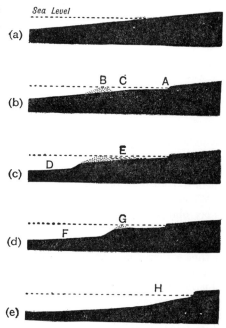

The various stages are illustrated in the accompanying series of diagrams.

In (a) a gently shelving land surface has just been raised above sea-level. Stage (b) shows the formation of low cliffs (A) and the offshore bar (B) with its accompanying lagoon (C). In (c) erosion of the sea floor on the seaward side of the bar has produced an abrasion platform (D); the lagoon is developing into salt-marsh (E). In (d) the abrasion platform has been greatly extended (F) at the expense of the bar (G), which is being "pushed" towards the land across the former salt-marsh. Stage (e) shows the abrasion platform and wave-cut bench extending right up to the land margin (H); the bar has been completely removed by erosion, and the cliffs are now fully exposed to wave attack.

FACTORS MODIFYING MARINE SCULPTURE

So far we have examined the normal evolution of coastlines when areas have been either submerged or gently raised, and we have seen how bays, headlands, and beaches come into being. Some of the more important factors which modify this normal development must now be considered, for local conditions may well produce coastal forms very different from those already discussed.

(a) **Wind Waves.** It is a well-known feature of ordinary sea-waves that they tend to make straight for the shore no matter what the outline of the shore may be. In other words, the wave-front tends to conform to the outline of the shore. This is known as **wave refraction**; the wave-front is bent. As the wave enters shallow water its forward speed is checked by what amounts to "friction" on the bottom. Further, the shallower the water the greater the brake applied. In this way the wave-front becomes bent and swings round almost parallel to the shore. Such waves will therefore tend to carry their load

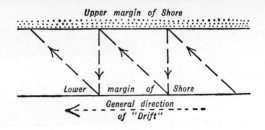

straight up the shore and, on retreating, straight down again. Whether, on balance, they erode or deposit depends on factors which have already been discussed. There will be little tendency, however, for them to transport any materials along the shore.

When waves are wind-driven they may, and often do, approach the shore obliquely. Wind-waves will therefore tend to carry their load obliquely up the shore. But the retreating wave will generally follow the direction of steepest slope ; that is, straight down the shore. There is thus a zigzag movement of the load along the shore. Wind waves can, in this way, produce a longshore drift of rock materials. This is illustrated in the diagram above. It is quite common to find pebbles on the shore which must have come from another part of the coast many miles away. They may have come by this means. Such drifted material may take a very important part in the formation of sub-marine banks and off-shore bars, and of spits and beaches.

(b) **Currents.** Tidal currents are a very common feature of off-shore water, but their rate of flow is seldom more than 2–3 knots. In very exceptional cases this rate may be exceeded as, for example, when tidal water flows through a narrow strait to form a race. In general, however, the comparatively small velocity of tidal currents does not make them capable of transporting large quantities of shingle. They are, nevertheless, capable of transporting the finely disintegrated materials and, by so doing, they may play a very important part in the development of local coastal features. Thus sediments may be removed from one part of the coast and deposited on another with far-reaching consequences as, for example, in parts of eastern England.

The combination of wind-wave drift and current drift may well account for many of the coastal features which involve the transport and re-deposition of rock materials. On these points, however, our knowledge is far from complete. Some of the questions raised, therefore, are of a highly controversial nature.

(c) **Storms.** Storms, because of their violence, can, in a very short time, produce marked effects in coastal areas, but, because of their irregularity, such effects are not usually cumulative. Thus, one particularly violent storm may throw up a bank of shingle well beyond the

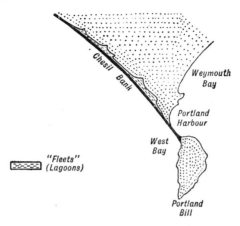

The Chesil Bank, Dorset

normal high-water mark. At a later date an even more violent storm
may throw up a ridge on top of the earlier bank.

An outstanding example of this kind is the Chesil Bank of the Dorset
coast (usually known locally as the Chesil Beach). It joins the " Isle "
of Portland to the mainland and sweeps away to the west in a broad
curve for nearly twenty miles. Behind the bank, shallow lagoons,
known as fleets, have been formed.

(d) The Nature of the Coastal Rocks. The nature of the coastal rock
formations will clearly influence the form of coastal features. So
varied are the rocks, and so varied the resulting forms, however, that
we cannot do more than touch on certain aspects of the subject here.
It has already been seen how alternate belts of hard and soft rocks
give rise to an alternate bay and headland coast when those belts run
out to sea. In general, those rocks which resist erosion (both normal
and marine) lend themselves to cliff formation ; those which do not
resist erosion so well frequently weather back in gently sloping lines.
Sometimes, however, marine erosion may so outpace normal erosion
that even the so-called soft rocks are cut into cliff faces. Such cliffs
are not usually very stable, and landslides are to be expected, as, for
example, in the Glacial Drift coastal areas of eastern England. In
coastal evolution so many factors are involved, and many of them are
possibly of a freak nature, that it is undesirable to push these generalis-
ations too far.

Interesting examples of many different coastal types abound round
the shores of Great Britain. The Dorset coast provides another good
illustration. Eastwards from the " Isle " of Portland sweeps the broad
Weymouth Bay, generally a low coast. Then comes a series of small
bays in a generally rocky coast with cliffed headlands and boulder-

G

88

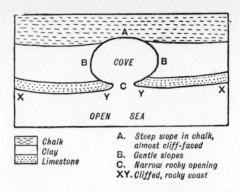

Chalk Clay Limestone	**A.**	Steep slope in chalk, almost cliff-faced
	B.	Gentle slopes
	C.	Narrow rocky opening
	XY.	Cliffed, rocky coast

strewn shores. Farther to the east the coast, still cliffed, takes on a smoother outline, although both coast and shore are essentially rocky. In this stretch of coast occurs Lulworth Cove. Here the sea has breached a thin " curtain " of hard limestone along the coast and has attacked the softer rocks behind with marked success. The rapid penetration inland has now been checked by massive deposits of chalk. It is to be expected, therefore, that further erosion will take place mainly along the less resistant belt, and that the " cove " will become progressively elongated in a direction generally parallel to the coast line. Here, however, a balance must be struck sooner or later for, with increased penetration, marine erosion will tend to decrease relative to normal erosion, while at the same time the ability of the sea to transport the accumulating load will decrease. The general arrangement of this type of coast is illustrated in the diagram above.

COASTAL FEATURES DUE TO DEPOSITION

In this class, reference has already been made to beaches which may result either because the load is too great for the wave scour to remove or because materials have been thrown up during storms. Of a rather different type are the spits, banks and bars which are a common feature of some coastal areas.

Spits are " fingers ", consisting largely of sand, which often occur where there is a pronounced bend in the coastline (diagram i). There is historical evidence that some, at least, of these spits " grow " (or " contract "), though usually slowly. In certain cases an average annual growth of a few feet, and occasionally of several yards, has been estimated. The seaward end of a spit is often curved towards the land, and sometimes off-shoots, called lateral spits, strike off from the main spit (diagram ii). If a spit grows right across a bay, or if two spits grow from opposite sides and join, a bay-bar may be formed (diagram iii). Such bars may be completely covered at high-water, but they are always a hindrance to shipping. Farther off-shore, submarine

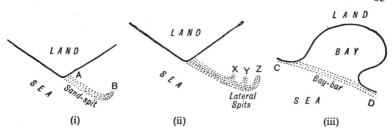

banks sometimes occur, and at low-water they are frequently recognisable even if they fail to reach the surface. These, too, are a danger to shipping (that is, for large vessels) and the navigable channels through them must then be buoyed. In some areas sandbanks tend to shift their position; continual sounding is then clearly necessary if shipping uses these waters.

Spits or bars which extend across bays and estuaries give some measure of protection against wave action and tidal scour. In the relatively slack water behind such a spit or bar, considerable silting may take place with the result that " new land " eventually comes into being. Romney Marsh on the Kent coast owes its origin to some such process; in the Norfolk Broads the same sort of process is still very active.

Spits, bars and banks are a common feature of the coasts of East Anglia, the Severn Estuary and Cardigan Bay, to name but a few areas.

Sand-dunes. Deposition resulting partly, perhaps, from storms and partly from wind-blown sand may give rise to the dune coasts which are such a marked feature of the " Landes " region of south-west France, of the Netherlands, and elsewhere. Unless these dunes are " tied down " by vegetation they may well be a menace to good agricultural land lying behind them on account of the drift of sand. The Landes region has been successfully planted with conifers which, in addition to checking the inland drift of sand, provide valuable products.

CLASSIFICATION OF COASTLINES

A small-scale physical map of the world will be sufficient to indicate some of the approaches to this subject. A first sub-division might be made on the basis of the length of coastline in relation to the area bounded. We could then distinguish between " short " coasts and " long " coasts. Or again, the heights of the bordering lands might be made the first consideration, and a distinction drawn between " highland " coasts and " lowland " coasts. A third method of classification might be to consider whether the coastline runs parallel to the " grain " of the land structure or cuts across it, and so to distinguish between "longitudinal" (or *concordant*) coastlines and "transverse" (or *discordant*) coastlines. Yet another method might be to consider the age of present coastlines, recognising that some have been "recently" raised and others depressed, while others have maintained their broad outline for considerably longer periods. We could then distinguish between "raised coasts", "drowned coasts" and "stable coasts". (Used in this sense "raised" means that the land has risen relative to the sea; "drowned" that the sea has risen relative to the land. Such changes in relative level could be achieved either by a movement of the land or by a change in the level—possibly as a result of a change in volume—of the sea, or by a combination of both processes.) Taking all these various factors into consideration, a great variety of coastal types would clearly be afforded and an elaborate classification would be necessary to embrace them.

However, certain coastal types have distinctive characteristics, which can be used as the basis of a simple classification.

(a) **The Fiord Coast.** On the coasts of Norway, western Scotland, British Columbia, southern Chile and south-western New Zealand, there are many long and narrow inlets, called fiords (or fjords). The distinctive characteristics of such coasts have long occasioned much controversy and there is still far from universal agreement on some of the points at issue. In their general form fiords are typically glaciated troughs, with all the usual features of glacial sculpture present, namely, steep, parallel walls rising straight from the water, hanging valleys, over-deepened rock-basins along their floors, and truncated spurs along their sides (that is, spurs which have had their ends worn away by ice erosion during the passage of glaciers).

There is often a remarkable rectangular plan to a fiord and its numerous branches; tributary branches are usually almost perpendicular to the main inlet, and the many bends in the fiord itself are often practically right-angles. This pronounced feature has led some observers to believe that fault-lines have dominated the existing form of the typical fiord; ice, in their view, has merely modified the fissure valleys. To certain other observers ice has played the dominant part, widening and deepening the original river valleys.

Another distinctive feature is the floor of the fiord. This often consists of deep rock-basins which are sometimes even deeper than the sea-floor outside the fiord. These rock-basins are separated from the outer sea-floor by submerged sills, bars of rock across the lower end of the glacial valley, frequently covered by glacial material—the terminal moraines of the valley glaciers. To explain how these deep rock-basins have come into being some observers suggest that the land has been depressed (or the sea-level raised), so forming a drowned coast. Others do not admit this, but insist that ice-erosion is almost entirely respon-

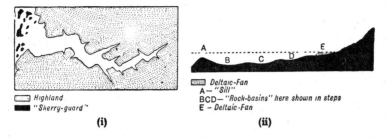

Highland
"Skerry-guard"

(i)

Deltaic-Fan
A — "Sill"
BCD — "Rock-basins" here shown in steps
E — Deltaic-Fan

(ii)

sible. (Actually ice-erosion, unlike water-erosion, can proceed at quite appreciable depths below sea-level.)

In, or just away from, the mouth of a fiord small islands are frequently found. Off a coast such as that of Norway these islands form a kind of outer screen to the coast, known as a **skerry-guard**. In the relatively protected waters of the fiords and inside the skerry-guard the Norsemen early acquired skill in the arts of navigation and set out to reach Britain, Iceland, Greenland, and probably the eastern seaboard of North America.

Fiords make fine, deep, sheltered harbours, but there is little room for settlement round them, because of the steep, walled sides ; and communications inland are usually difficult, because of the mountainous country behind them. It is rarely, therefore, that they provide good sites for large ports. Communications in such country are generally carried out by water ; settlement is restricted to narrow ledges wherever they may chance to occur, or to the more extensive areas in the hanging valleys above the fiord ; agriculture is confined to the deltaic-fans which are occasionally to be found where streams enter the fiord or, again, to the hanging valleys.

Diagrams (i) and (ii) show the general plan of a typical fiord (note the rectangular pattern of the fiord and its branches) and a generalised long-profile of its floor.

(b) **The Ria Coast.** In south-west Ireland (Dingle Bay, Kenmare River, Bantry Bay), south-west England (Plymouth Sound), north-west France (Brest), and north-west Spain (Vigo) we find just a few of the many examples of a ria coast—a " drowned " transverse coast.

In some respects rias appear to resemble fiords. They frequently penetrate far inland, winding as they do so, and they are usually backed by relatively high land. But they differ in one important respect : they have not been glaciated. In essence they are drowned river valleys. Instead of " walls " rising from the water's edge, the land slopes more gently in the typical river V-form. Further, in the areas mentioned above, the highlands are not strictly comparable with those of Norway, north-west Scotland, etc. (the fiord regions). Communications inland are not, therefore, so difficult from rias as from fiords. But they are frequently too difficult to allow of the development of first-class ports along their excellent water-fronts ; they are better suited to naval bases than to commercial ports.

Like fiords, rias often branch in a complicated way, but after the pattern of a river system, not after the " rectangular " pattern of the fiord. In another important respect rias differ from fiords : there is no skerry-guard and no sill; and soundings show that the water shallows steadily inland.

The diagrams below show a typical branching ria (the highland has been shaded to indicate the wide valley form) and the long-profile of its floor. Note how the long-profile resembles the graded long-profile of a mature river valley, and how it differs from that of a typical fiord.

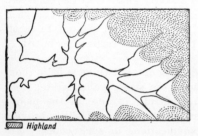

Sea Level

Highland

(c) The "Dalmatian" Coast. On the eastern seaboard of the Adriatic Sea (along the coast of Dalmatia) there is another, and different, type of coastline. Because it is so well developed here the name " Dalmatian " has been applied generally to other coastlines of the same type. Along the coast of Dalmatia the " grain " of the country is parallel to the coastline; it is, in fact, a longitudinal coast. Like the typical ria coastline, that of Dalmatia has been drowned, but the difference in structure produces very different effects. There are chains of long and narrow islands lying off, and parallel to, the coast ; they are the tops of former mountain ranges. Between these islands and the mainland are long and narrow stretches of water ; these occupy the sites of former valleys (drowned longitudinal valleys). The coastline, which is usually backed by a coast range, is sensibly unbroken for considerable distances. Then there may be a breach where the sea has penetrated right through the coast range to drown the lower parts of the next succeeding longitudinal valley. These various and distinctive features are illustrated in the diagram (p. 93).

Such coastlines are usually very mountainous (even the islands are hilly) and communications inland are generally difficult. Here, again, there may be many excellent, sheltered harbours, but few good ports.

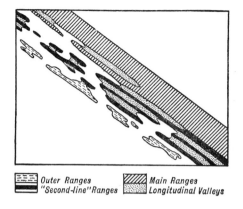

Outer Ranges
"Second-line" Ranges
Main Ranges
Longitudinal Valleys

Dalmatian Coast

Although the western coasts of the Americas illustrate this same general longitudinal grain, the distinctive Dalmatian type of coastline is not everywhere in evidence throughout their great length. Further, in the extreme north and south, glaciation has produced the characteristic fiord type, modifying what would otherwise be a Dalmatian coast. Notice, however, the Lower California Peninsula and the Gulf of California; they conform to the Dalmatian pattern, and on a very large scale.

(*d*) **The "Haff-Nehrung" Coast.** This type of coast is seen at its best, perhaps, in East Prussia. A long spit, growing across a bay and covered by low sand dunes (German, *Nehrung*), may cut off a shallow lagoon (German, *Haff*) and so give a smooth outline to the coast. Such lagoons tend to become filled in, in time, partly by silt brought down by the rivers which drain into them, and partly by wind-blown sand. The general form of a " haff-nehrung " coastline as found in East Prussia is illustrated in the diagram below.

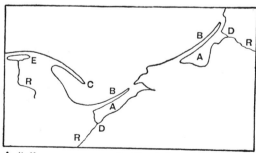

A. *Haff*
B. *Nehrung*
C. *Partly-formed Nehrung*
D. *River Deltas*
E. *Shallow Lake (formerly a Haff)*
R. *River*

(e) **The Estuary Coast.** Estuaries, such as those of the Thames and Severn, are really the drowned lower courses of rivers, and in some respects they may therefore be termed lowland rias. When a large area is drowned, rivers which previously formed part of one drainage system may be able to reach the new coastline independently, each draining to its own estuary. When Britain was joined to the Continent (as, indeed, it once was) the Thames, as the dominant stream, would have collected the drainage of Essex and north Kent, as well as that of other areas lying farther afield. Now the rivers of Essex and north Kent drain to their own estuaries.

CHAPTER VI

LAKES AND ISLANDS

LAKES AND LAKE BASINS

LAKES are bodies of water, large or small, which have accumulated in hollows (or " basins ") in the earth's surface. By their very nature they are essentially temporary features; for if rivers drain into them deposition will gradually raise the floors of their basins, and if rivers flow from them erosion of the outlet channel will gradually lower their water surfaces. In certain cases, too, deposition resulting from wind-blown sand may help to curtail their existence.

Rivers invariably carry in solution a certain amount of mineral salts. When lakes have no river outlet, these salts tend to accumulate in the lake basin, for evaporation carries off only the pure water. Such lakes are known as inland drainage basins; for example, Caspian Sea, Dead Sea, etc. In time their waters become very salty. When, how-ever, lakes are drained by rivers, the salts do not tend to accumulate, and their waters remain fresh; for example, Windermere, Lake Geneva, etc.

Lakes may be formed in a variety of ways, some of which will now be discussed.

FORMATION OF LAKE BASINS

(1) **Earth-movements.** Many of the very deep lakes were probably formed by earth-movements. When a " block " is lowered between faults, a natural basin is provided into which water can drain. Or, again, faulting may lead to the formation of fault-valleys, on the floors of which water may well accumulate. The origin of lakes as deep as Lake Baikal in southern Siberia (it is 4,500 ft. deep in one part, but its surface is only 1,500 ft. above sea-level) would be difficult to explain otherwise. The Dead Sea, Lake Rudolf, Lake Nyasa, Lake Tanganyika, Lake Edward, Lake Albert, etc., have formed on the floor of the great African Rift Valley. They are all deep; the Dead Sea has a maximum depth of nearly 1,300 ft. Loch Ness occupies part of the floor of the fault-valley of Glenmore; its depth exceeds 700 ft. in several places.

The Great Lakes of North America owe their present form to a combination of several factors, but earth-movements have played a part. With the exception of Lake Erie (maximum depth 180 ft.) they are all deep; Lake Superior has a mean depth of 900 ft. although its surface is only 600 ft. above sea-level.

Lake Titicaca and Great Salt Lake occupy depressions in the " inter-mont " plateaux of the Andes and Rockies respectively, and are there-fore associated with earth-movements.   Lake Titicaca lies more than 12,000 ft. above sea-level and has a maximum depth of 700 ft. ;   Great Salt Lake lies more than 4,000 ft. above sea-level and has a very variable area and depth due largely to the climatic control.

Even the Mediterranean Sea probably owes much to the same general kind of earth-movement, for some, at least, of its several basins are due to foundering.

Sometimes a warping of the earth's crust, resulting from earth-movements, and especially during folding, may convert a river valley into a lake basin by raising its lower end.   Lake Geneva (Rhone) and Lake Constance (Rhine) were probably formed in this way.

(2) **Deposition.** Most of the relatively shallow lakes are probably formed by the deposition of a barrier across a river valley, and this may occur in several ways.

(a) A tributary stream may build a deltaic fan across the compara-tively level floor of the main valley.   In this way Lake Brienz has been separated from Lake Thun (Switzerland).   Now Lake Brienz stands some 20 ft. above Lake Thun, " ponded back " by the deltaic fan of a tributary stream.   In the English Lake District we find an example of the same kind where Lake Bassenthwaite has been cut off from Derwentwater.

(b) Morainic debris deposited by valley glaciers is a common cause of lake formation.   Sometimes the lateral moraine of one valley may dam a tributary valley, but more often it is the terminal moraine which is responsible.   Many of the lakes in the English Lake District (for example, Windermere) and the Scottish Highlands (for example, Loch Lomond) are of this type.

(c) Lava streams may dam river valleys and so form lakes.   One of the most notable of this type is Lake Taupo, in the volcanic region of North Island, New Zealand

(d) A dam may also be formed by a landslide.   Where a river has been cutting down vigorously for a considerable time, and possibly undercutting the rock formations, there is a tendency to landslips. Masses of rock debris may then fall across the valley, making a dam which is usually not very compact and hence not very substantial. Quite large lakes may be dammed back for a time, but they are usually short-lived.   Such dams may collapse suddenly, causing disastrous floods downstream ; for example, that on the Upper Ganges which collapsed after about two years, towards the end of the nineteenth century.   Many of the small mountain tarns, however, which form behind land-slip dams, appear to be much more permanent.

(e) Man-made dams are sometimes used to convert river valleys into reservoirs to meet the needs of large cities. In the Millstone Grit country of the Pennines such " artificial lakes " are quite common ; the several tributary valleys of the River Don largely supply Sheffield with its domestic water ; the Etherow helps to supply Manchester. In the Derwent Valley (Derbyshire) the Lady Bower Dam, when completed, will hold back a very considerable " lake ".

(f) In its flood-plain a river may so raise the land near its banks that tributaries are unable to maintain their courses. The flood deposits of the main river then, in effect, dam back the tributaries, which therefore spread out over parts of the flood-plain in shallow lakes. As the level of this tributary water rises, it will tend to " wander " parallel to the main stream until it is either lost by evaporation or able to join the main stream where, for some reason or other, the flood-plain has not been raised to the same extent.

Even when the tributaries do succeed in joining the main stream, there is still a tendency for some of these shallow lakes to persist, with the result that in warm, dry climates, an abnormally high proportion of the total flow is lost by evaporation. All these features are well illustrated in the case of the River Murray and its tributaries (Australia).

(g) A river may shorten its course, and so increase its gradient, by leaving one or more of its meanders. Flood deposition at the two ends of the abandoned meander converts it into a lake. These cut-off lakes are a feature of the Lower Mississippi and of the Murray and its tributaries. Usually they are known as ox-bows or mortlakes, but in Australia they are known as billabongs. Many of them degenerate, as a result of later deposition, into marshy depressions which are filled with water only during times of flood.

(h) Deposition of silt in a river estuary (for example, behind a spit), or the extension of a delta into the sea may give rise to the formation of shallow lakes. As the silting-up process continues, these lakes (or broads) are gradually reduced in size. Ultimately, if no other forces operated to counteract the effect, they would disappear altogether. Examples of this kind are to be found in the Norfolk Broads and in the deltas of the Mississippi (North America) and Po (Italy).

(i) When storm beaches are thrown up across the mouth of a bay or river, land drainage may accumulate behind the beach to form a lake or, if the barrier is incomplete, a sea-water lagoon. The fleets behind the Chesil Bank, on the Dorset coast, are of this type ; so also is Dubh Loch, which has been cut off from Loch Shira (Inveraray), and the Looe in Cornwall.

(j) A glacier itself may dam back a tributary and so form a lake. Outstanding among the European glacier lakes is the Marjelen Sea, dammed back by the Aletsch Glacier (Upper Rhone).

(*k*) When a glacier or ice sheet melts, the ground moraine is deposited very unevenly to form a hummocky surface. Water may collect in the hollows and so form pools or lakes as, for example, over parts of the North German Plain.

(*l*) Trees falling across a stream may serve to start a dam and so form a lake ; the activities of the beaver may have similar results. Like land-slip dammed lakes, these lakes are of a very temporary nature.

(3) **Erosion.** Rivers, by a scouring action upon their beds, often emphasised by the varying resistance of the rock formations, may scoop out shallow basins. When the water diminishes, a string of shallow lakes may result. This is quite frequently the case when water comes over a fall ; the greater scouring there may form a marked basin at the foot of the fall.

Glaciers and ice sheets, by removing weathered rock and by their general erosive action, may leave many shallow hollows in a surface. Glaciated regions show many examples of this type, both in the mountains, where we find glacial tarns and cirque lakes, and on the lowlands, where we find shallow rock basins.

Wind eddies over an undulating plain may move sand and form shallow lake pans. Some of the salt lakes (only periodically filled) in the Central Lowlands of Australia are probably of this type.

(4) **Volcanic Activity.** In addition to the possibility of lava streams damming river valleys (referred to above), volcanic activity may lead to the formation of lake basins in two distinct ways.

(*a*) The outpouring of lava often leaves the surface of the earth in the region of the volcano or fissure unsupported, so that the crust caves in and forms basins which are comparatively wide and shallow. A good example of this type is Lough Neagh in Northern Ireland ; the effusive lava appears on the surface in the basalt Antrim Plateau.

(*b*) Sometimes water accumulates in the craters of extinct volcanoes to form crater lakes. Lake Avernus, near Naples, is an example.

(5) **Minor and Local Subsidence.** In limestone areas the removal, in solution, of calcium carbonate by underground water often leads to the development of surface depressions. Because of the permeable nature of limestone these depressions are frequently dry, but after prolonged rainfall they may contain water. Should the limestone form lowland country, as over much of central Ireland, depressions may form the basins of perennial lakes.

In mining areas the removal of underground rock sometimes gives rise to a similar effect. Surface depressions result, and these become shallow lake basins. This is particularly noticeable in the salt-mining areas (for example, the Weaver Valley in Cheshire), especially when the salt is removed by pumping water into the beds and pumping brine out, for no supports are then left to the " roof ".

VALUE OF LAKES TO MAN

Water Storage. A large lake in a river valley is an important factor in regulating the flow of the river. By storing water during periods of heavy and prolonged rainfall, it helps to minimise the effects of flooding downstream ; by releasing water during a dry season it helps to maintain a steady flow. This is particularly important for irrigation and, where suitable lakes do not exist, artificial reservoirs have, in many notable cases, been constructed ; for example, Aswan (Nile), Sennar (Blue Nile), Boulder (Colorado), Lloyd Barrage at Sukkur (Indus), Burrinjuck (Murrumbidgee), etc.

A regular supply of water is invaluable also for the development of hydro-electric power. A large lake above the falls providing the power helps to ensure this ; for example, Lough Derg above the Falls of Killaloe in connection with the Shannon Scheme.

Lakes, both natural and artificial, are important sources for the supply of water to large cities ; for example, Thirlmere (Manchester), Vyrnwy (Liverpool).

Transport. Large lakes may provide cheap transport for heavy and bulky goods over considerable distances. Of particular interest in this respect are the Great Lakes of North America. In a normal year the tonnage passing through the Sault Ste. Marie Canal (between Lakes Superior and Huron) exceeds the combined tonnage passing through the Suez and Panama Canals. Most of this vast tonnage consists of heavy and bulky goods such as grain, timber, iron ore, coal, etc.

Further, the Great Lakes have played a most important part in the development and organisation of American industry, by bringing together widely separated raw materials and sources of power.

Effect on Climate. Very large lakes have an appreciable effect in moderating the climate of the lakeside country. The " Lake Peninsula " in North America, between Lakes Huron, Erie and Ontario, has much milder winters than would otherwise be the case, with the result that important fruit belts occur in this region.

Alluvial Beds of Former Lakes. The beds of former lakes, because of the thick deposits of rich alluvial soil, usually provide valuable agricultural land. The fertile Red River Valley, to the south of Winnipeg (site of the former " Lake Agassiz ") has already been referred to in this respect. In Great Britain the fertile Vale of Pickering, now drained by the Yorkshire Derwent, was formerly an old lake bed. The original outlet of the Derwent, near Filey, was blocked by glacial deposits, with the result that a lake formed. Ultimately these lake waters escaped by cutting a new channel near New Malton and draining inland to the Ouse. In the meantime, however, rich alluvial deposits had been spread over the lake bed.

ISLANDS

For most purposes, islands may be conveniently classified under two broad headings : (a) continental islands, and (b) oceanic islands.

Continental Islands. These suggest a former connection, or some definite association, with the neighbouring continent. Generally it may safely be said that such islands were, at some time in the distant past, actually joined to the continent, from which they were afterwards separated by the subsidence of a " land bridge ", or by a raising of the sea-level which drowned the lower connecting links. They therefore frequently possess structural features which show marked continuity with those of the continent from which they have been separated. The rock formations are often similar, if not identical. They frequently lie near the neighbouring continent, usually on the continental shelf. Very often, too, the vegetation and animal types (flora and fauna) are similar to those of the mainland, though sometimes rather poorer in variety, due to more restricted development after " insulation ".

Continental islands usually conform to one or other of three different types :

(1) Rock stacks, or pillars of hard rocks which have resisted wave erosion better than surrounding rock formations and have therefore become detached. Numerous examples are to be seen round the coasts of Britain, from the " Old Man of Hoy " (off the Orkneys) to the " Needles " (off the Isle of Wight).

(2) Archipelagoes, or island groups comprising hundreds, or even thousands, of islands of different sizes.

(3) Festoons, or island-loops, which suggest a former outline of the continent. Continental islands of this type are a feature of the Pacific coasts of Asia.

Islands, which may also be classified as " continental ", sometimes possess characteristics which are contrary to those stated generally above. Thus the island festoons of eastern Asia and the East Indies are separated from the mainland by very deep seas, suggesting foundering of certain parts of the earth's crust on a pronounced scale. Yet the evidence of structure, flora and fauna points to a former connection. Similarly, Madagascar is separated from Africa by the deep Mozambique Channel. Here, again, the evidence of structure points to a former connection. In the case of Madagascar, however, the separation probably took place so long ago that the island has had time to develop certain types of flora and fauna which are peculiar to itself, although the general African type is still in evidence, even if lacking much of the variety found on the continent.

The case of New Zealand, Fiji, and certain other of the Pacific Islands is even more marked than that of Madagascar, because the

separating distances are so much greater. Such remote islands are not
merely " insulated " ; to a large extent they are virtually " isolated ".
Their flora and fauna may have developed from the same early types
as have those of the continent, but they have developed very differently,
giving rise to characteristic and peculiar present-day forms. It may
well be claimed, however, that such islands are not strictly " continental " in the usually accepted sense of the term.

Oceanic Islands. Oceanic islands, which rise sharply from the ocean
depths, do not necessarily bear any relation to the nearest continent ;
should there be any, such relation would be purely accidental. Further,
oceanic islands often lie at very considerable distances from the nearest
land-mass ; their flora and fauna must necessarily have evolved, therefore, from types which have been able to cross the intervening sea.
There will not usually be the variety or richness found on the mainland,
while some types may have remained extraordinarily primitive.

In general, oceanic islands may be classed under one or other of two
headings ; sometimes they owe their present form to a combination
of both processes.

(1) Volcanic Islands, as the name suggests, owe their origin to
volcanic activity. They may have their bases on the floor of the
ocean " deeps ", or on the top of an ocean " rise ". Quite frequently
they reach very considerable heights and, in a number of cases, their
volcanoes are still active.

Above the Central Atlantic Rise there is Ascension Island (with
Green Mountain rising to 2,870 ft.) and Tristan da Cunha. St. Helena
rises from the " deep sea plain " of the South Atlantic. In the Indian
Ocean there is Réunion (with Piton des Neiges rising above 10,000 ft.)
and Mauritius (which has no really high mountains). In the Pacific
Ocean there are the Hawaiian Islands (with Mauna Loa exceeding
13,000 ft.) and the Galapagos Islands, which are remarkable for their
peculiarities of flora and fauna.

(2) Coral Islands. The Maldive Islands of the Indian Ocean, and
the Ellice, Gilbert, and Marshall Islands of the Pacific Ocean are in
this class. Moreover, extensive coral reefs are found in the Hawaiian
Islands and around Mauritius, both of which are primarily of volcanic
origin. The Bermudas, too, consist largely of coral, and it is here that
we find the present-day northern limit of the reef-building coral polyps.
Unless other factors have taken a part in their formation, coral islands
are invariably low.

Coral and the Coral Polyps. Coral is a limestone deposit formed
from the " skeletons " or framework of various minute and simple
marine organisms. It is found in various colours (the " black " and
" red " were early prized for ornamental purposes) and " grows " into
a variety of shapes.

The reef-building polyps can only flourish under certain conditions :

(i) The temperature of the water must not fall below 68°F. This means that they are practically confined to tropical waters, and even there, they will grow only if there are no cold currents. For this reason (as will be seen later) coral is usually found off eastern coasts ; seldom off the west.

(ii) The water must not be more than about 150–180 ft. deep ; a depth not exceeding 90 feet is ideal.

(iii) The water must be normally saline (salty), that is, it must be free ocean water and well away from the mouths of rivers.

(iv) The water must be free from silt and sediment. Again the mouths of rivers are unsuitable.

(v) There must be an adequate supply of food. Again free ocean water is essential.

Coral reefs and islands are composed principally of rock which bears but little superficial resemblance to what is generally understood by "coral". The foundation is usually a compact white limestone to which are added coral fragments, washed there by wave action from another part of the reef, skeletons of other organisms, shells, sand, etc. On such a mass the living polyps build. In the case of certain reefs in the West Indies it has been estimated that, starting from a base 40 ft. below sea-level, the surface of the sea would be reached in about a thousand years.

Classification of Coral Islands and Reefs. Coral formations can best be sub-divided into three classes, one of which often develops from another.

(i) **Fringing Reefs.** These are found extending outwards from the shore of an island or the mainland. There is no channel between the reef and the shore (diagram *a*).

(ii) **Barrier Reefs.** These are found at some distance from the shore, from which they are separated by a definite channel (diagram *b*). Such a reef may be largely submerged, a line of breakers in the sea indicating its position. Where it emerges above sea-level, sparse vegetation is sometimes found. The channels which lie between the reef and the shore are of great value as shipping lanes, though frequently only for shallow-draught vessels.

The greatest of all the barrier reefs is the Great Barrier Reef of eastern Australia, which extends for more than a thousand miles along the coast of Queensland.

(iii) **Atolls.** These are typical low coral islands, roughly circular in shape, very variable in size, and enclosing a lagoon (diagrams *c* and *d*). The encircling ring is usually broken by one or more gaps which give access to the lagoon. The lagoon is usually shallow, though depths of 300 ft. are known. Beneath the lagoon is a coral floor. Atolls generally rise abruptly from ocean floors, and the coral formation is known to exist at depths far exceeding that at which the

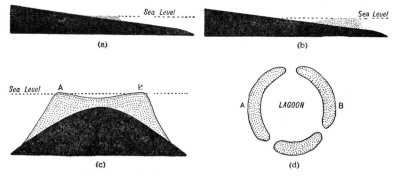

(a) Fringing reef; (b) barrier reef; (c) cross-section, and
(d) plan, of an atoll and its lagoon

polyps can live, suggesting that subsidence has occurred since the
deposition of the coral.

Darwin's Theory of Atoll Formation. The precise mode of formation
of atolls has, therefore, long been a matter of controversy. The most
widely accepted theory is that advanced by Darwin about the middle
of the last century. He assumed that the polyps first built a fringing
reef around an island that was gradually subsiding. The rate of subsidence must be no more than the rate of upward growth of the coral,
otherwise the polyps would be taken into too great a depth of water
for their existence. Because of the abundance of food, the absence of
sediment, and the normal salinity of the water, the coral growth would
take place outwards, that is, along the margin of the free ocean water.
On the landward side of the reef, lack of food, the presence of sediment,
and the probable freshness of the water, would all tend to prevent
growth. The surface layers of the coral already formed there would
decay, and so the fringing reef would develop into a barrier reef. As
subsidence continued the polyps would continue to build outwards and
upwards. In time the atoll as we know it would evolve. The base of
the coral may well have subsided far below the level at which it was first
formed. The lagoon persists because the polyps tend to build outwards
and upwards (that is, where conditions are most favourable) and because there is a certain amount of decay of the coral already formed.

Ingenious as this theory is in its attempt to explain the origin of
certain atolls, it does not succeed in all cases and, as a result, it is not
universally accepted.

Atolls seldom rise more than a few feet above sea-level. In time, soil
forms on the weathered and decayed limestone, and seeds, possibly
carried by birds, possibly drifted there by the sea, and in some cases
planted by man, start a limited type of vegetation, of which the most
typical is the coconut palm.

H

CHAPTER VII

THE OCEANS

THE general form of the ocean basins has already been discussed in Chapter II (diagrams, pp. 29 and 30). It was pointed out there that by far the greater part of these oceans have a depth of from 12,000 to 18,000 ft. (diagram, p. 29). Over relatively small areas these depths are considerably exceeded as, for example, in the Philippines Deep to the east of the Island of Mindanao, the greatest known depth (35,400 ft.), in the Kermadec Deep (31,000 ft.), in the Tonga Deep (30,000 ft.), in the Porto Rico Deep (28,000 ft.), etc. Such depths are comparable to the greatest land heights, such as Mt. Everest (29,000 ft.), Mt. Godwin Austen (28,250 ft.), etc. Also, over relatively small areas, but more particularly around the continental margins, the ocean water is comparatively shallow. Yet, even out in the ocean, well away from land, shallower water is sometimes found, due to the presence of submarine ridges (or **ocean rises**) as, for example, the Challenger and Dolphin Ridges of the Central Atlantic.

The cross-section of a continent and ocean basin on p. 30 immediately suggests a sub-division of a typical ocean basin into five distinctive parts :

(i) **Deep-sea Plain,** an undulating area, devoid of any marked relief, and from two to three miles below sea-level.

(ii) **Ocean Deep,** usually a trough-like depression which plunges steeply to considerable depths.

(iii) **Ocean Rise,** usually taking the form of a ridge rising above the deep-sea plain.

(iv) **Continental Shelf,** really a continuation of the continental land mass ; its surface slopes gently down to a depth of about 600 ft. below sea-level.

(v) **Continental Slope,** a marked slope which falls away from the continental shelf down to the deep-sea plain.

DEPOSITS ON THE OCEAN FLOOR

The deposits on the ocean floor are frequently classified as " terrigenous " (from the Latin *terrigena*, meaning " born of the earth ") if derived from the land, and " pelagic " (from the Latin *pelagus*, meaning " the open sea ") if derived from the skeletons of the many and varied marine organisms.

Terrigenous deposits are usually to be found in belts of varying width round the continental masses. They include rock debris of various kinds (gravel, sand, silt, etc.) which have been eroded from the land and carried out to sea by rivers and currents. The coarser grained of these materials will tend to concentrate in the very shallow waters near the land ; the finer grained will generally extend considerably farther from the land, but seldom more than 200–300 miles unless abnormally strong currents are operating (for example, off the mouths of large rivers). Such deposits are usually termed **muds.** They vary greatly in colour according to their chemical composition, with a tendency towards blue-grey.

Pelagic deposits are often referred to as **oozes.** Such deposits usually form only a relatively thin covering since they accumulate so slowly. Four main types of deep-sea ooze are generally recognized :

(i) **Globigerina Ooze.** This is the most widespread of the oozes, covering very considerable areas in the Atlantic, Indian, and South Pacific Oceans. Globigerina form a class of minute marine animals possessing shells (" tests ") which are perforated by tiny holes. They are found in very great numbers, particularly in the warmer seas. When they die their shells, which consist of calcium carbonate, sink to the ocean floor and so build up a layer of ooze.

(ii) **Pteropod Ooze.** This is found only in the warmer and rather shallower waters, and even there in very restricted areas. Pteropods are a class of molluscs that swim freely by flapping their fin-like appendages. Their shells, also of calcium carbonate, form the oozes occurring on parts of the Central Atlantic Ridge and in the shallower waters to the east of Australia.

(iii) **Radiolarian Ooze.** This is found over a large area lying near the equator in the Pacific, and over an area lying south-west of the East Indies. Radiolarians are somewhat akin to Globigerina, with the important difference that their shells are composed of silica. They are practically confined to tropical waters, but there they have been found alive at depths exceeding 500 fathoms. Their siliceous remains, less soluble than calcium carbonate, form oozes at considerable depths.

(iv) **Diatom Ooze.** This is found in a broad belt near the Antarctic Circle and across the North Pacific. Diatoms are a class of microscopic plants, invisible to the naked eye, of which more than ten thousand species, presenting great variety of forms, have been identified. They flourish in the cooler waters of the oceans and increase rapidly. Their fossil remains consist of silica.

Red Clay. Over very large areas in the Pacific, and in the deeper parts of the Atlantic and Indian Oceans, the typical oozes are missing. Instead a reddish-brown clay is found. This is thought to be largely volcanic in origin. At very great depths the remains of organisms, whether silica or calcium carbonate, dissolve. Thus red clay alone, being insoluble, is left to accumulate, but at a very slow rate. Elsewhere, presumably, it is mixed with the oozes, but to such a small

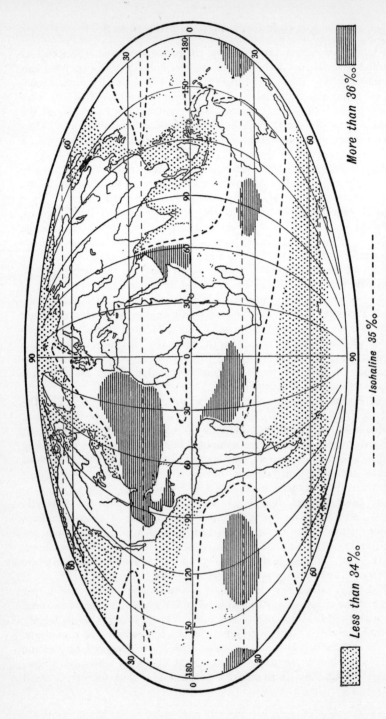

More than 36 ‰

SALINITY OF THE SURFACE WATER OF THE OCEANS

--------- Isohaline 35 ‰

Less than 34 ‰

extent that it does not greatly affect their composition. Similarly, no doubt, oozes are mixed with the terrigenous muds, but in relatively insignificant proportions.

SALINITY

Ocean Waters. Normal ocean water contains very considerable amounts of various salts in solution. It has been estimated that the total amount of dissolved salts in all the oceans would be sufficient to form a crust 170 ft. thick over the surface of those oceans.

It has already been noted that rivers carry varying, though usually comparatively small, amounts of salts which have been dissolved from the rock formations of their basins. The most important of these river salts is calcium carbonate, and it might be thought that, in time, very large quantities of this salt would accumulate in the oceans. This is not the case, for numerous marine organisms extract it to build up their skeletons and shells.

The proportions of the various salts in ocean water have been estimated as follows : Sodium chloride 77·7%, magnesium chloride 10·8%, magnesium sulphate 4·7%, calcium sulphate 3·6%, potassium sulphate 2·5%, calcium and magnesium carbonates 0·3%, magnesium bromide 0·2%, other salts 0·2%. The composition remains remarkably constant except at very great depths, where a slight increase in the carbonates is found. We are, of course, referring to free ocean water well away from land.

The salinity of ocean water is usually expressed as the number of units (by weight) of all salts contained in a thousand units (by weight) of ocean water. The average salinity for all the oceans is about 35 (written 35°/₀₀). Moreover, free ocean water everywhere has a salinity very near the average.

This uniformity (as with the percentage composition of the various salts) is due, in large measure, to the circulation set up in the oceans by " currents " and " drifts ".

Clearly, two factors can affect the local salinity, namely, the rate of evaporation of surface water, and the amount of " fresh " water added by rainfall, rivers, melting icebergs, etc.

The case of the Atlantic Ocean will serve to illustrate these two modifying factors. Near the equator the rainfall is heavy and occurs all the year round ; the air tends to be saturated with moisture, with the result that evaporation is restricted. The salinity, therefore, tends to be slightly, but only slightly, below normal. Between latitudes 15° N. and 30° N. (also 15° S. and 30° S.), approximately, there is a " dry " belt. (Over the land this dry belt gives rise to the Trade Wind Deserts.) There is practically no rainfall; the skies are cloudless; the air is " dry ", and there is rapid evaporation. As a result the salinity rises to more than $36°/_{oo}$, and in parts exceeds $37°/_{oo}$. In the far north, off the coasts of north-east Canada and Greenland, there is much fresh water added from icebergs (while even sea-ice forms relatively pure water), there is little evaporation (due to the colder air and generally cloudy skies), and there is a moderate precipitation (that is, rain, snow, etc.). We therefore find a large area with a salinity less than $35°/_{oo}$, and smaller areas even below $32°/_{oo}$. Some of this water of low salinity is carried southwards along the coasts of eastern America by the Labrador Current, with the result that, so far south as the New England coast, we find water with a salinity rather below normal. But, extending past the coasts of Britain and Norway, there is a tongue of water with a salinity slightly above normal, carried there by the North Atlantic Drift, a surface drift which gathers up some of the water brought by the Gulf Stream from the region of high salinity off Florida to the neighbourhood of Newfoundland. Here it comes under the influence of the prevailing " westerlies " and so " drifts " across the Atlantic.

Off the mouths of really large rivers like the Amazon and Mississippi, the salinity is lowered appreciably, possibly for two or three hundred miles out to sea.

The variation in salinity over the surface of the oceans is indicated, in simplified form, in the chart on p. 106.

Wholly or Partially Enclosed Seas. Here quite another set of circumstances is encountered, for the waters of enclosed seas do not mix freely with those of the oceans. We are concerned, therefore, with a purely local salinity.

Caspian Sea. This sea, wholly enclosed, is an area of inland drainage and, in general, may be classed as a salt lake. In the north, off the mouth of the Volga, however, its waters are relatively fresh ; but in the almost detached Gulf of Kara Bugaz, which has no rivers flowing into it, and is situated in a semi-desert region, the salinity reaches $180°/_{oo}$. (In the Dead Sea, in Palestine, another area of inland drainage, the salinity is even greater, $240°/_{oo}$.)

Baltic Sea. This sea is only partially enclosed, having outlets into the North Sea through the narrow Kattegat and Skagerrak, but it is, to all intents and purposes, land-locked. Numerous large and well-watered rivers flow into it, and as evaporation is restricted, its salinity is generally low, dropping to $2°/_{oo}$ in the north of the Gulf of Bothnia. (Mean salinity about $7°/_{oo}$.)

Mediterranean Sea. With an area of just over a million square miles and an extreme length of 2,300 miles, the Mediterranean Sea might almost be compared with the ocean basins from which it is virtually cut off by a submarine sill, about 1,000 ft. below the surface, across the Strait of Gibraltar. It is situated in a region of " summer drought ", and, in relation to its size, has **very** little fresh water added. Evaporation is rapid, particularly in summer when the air is dry, the temperature high, and the sun shining from an almost cloudless sky. The salinity is therefore high, averaging about $38°/_{oo}$. (In the Red Sea these conditions are emphasised to an even greater extent, the salinity averaging about $39°/_{oo}$.)

When representing the change in the salinity from one part of the ocean to another on a map, areas of different salinity are usually separated by lines called isohalines (lines of equal salinity). Thus, the isohaline $35°/_{oo}$ separates an area in which the salinity is more than $35°/_{oo}$ from one in which it is less than $35°/_{oo}$.

TEMPERATURE OF OCEAN WATER

The mean annual temperature (that is, the average temperature taken over the course of a whole year) of the surface water of the oceans is shown in the chart on p. 110.

It is, of course, a well-known fact that surface temperatures vary appreciably from one season to another, particularly in higher latitudes, though considerably less so than air temperatures. The mean annual temperature shows a general decrease from equatorial regions towards the poles, as is only to be expected. But, superimposed on this general distribution of temperature, we can clearly see the influence of ocean currents and drifts. The " cold " Labrador Current effectively reduces surface-water temperatures off the North American coast as far south as New England ; the " warm " North Atlantic Drift, on the other hand, pushes a " gulf of warmth " past the shores of Britain and Norway towards the Arctic Ocean. A number of other instances of the same kind are to be found, but they will be understood more fully when the subject of ocean currents generally has been discussed.

As also might be expected, the temperature of ocean water decreases with increasing depth, at first fairly rapidly and then more slowly. In the deepest parts of the ocean basins, the temperatures are consistently low no matter what the latitude—only a little above $32°$ F. with occasional " pockets " dropping as low as $30°$ F. (Ocean water under normal atmospheric pressure freezes at about $28°$ F., the actual figure depending on the degree of salinity.)

The Mediterranean Sea furnishes an example of the temperature conditions prevailing in an enclosed basin. Not only has this sea an area of almost ocean extent, but also it has depths approaching the same order. Its western basin descends to about 14,500 ft. in the deepest part ; its eastern basin descends to more than 13,000 ft. ; over its entire area it has a mean depth estimated at nearly 5,000 ft. It is thus a very considerable body of water. But it is cut off from the Atlantic Basin by a submarine sill across the Strait of Gibraltar, little

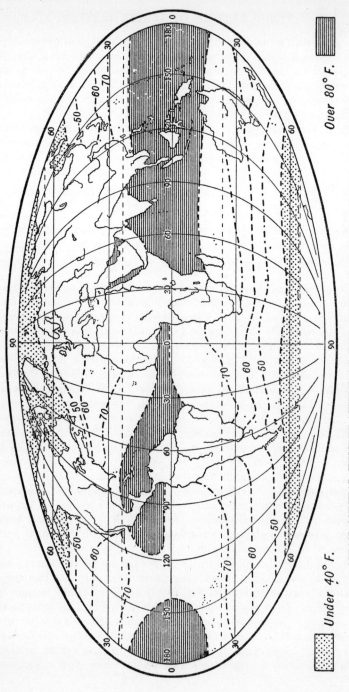

Under 40° F.

Over 80° F.

MEAN ANNUAL TEMPERATURE OF THE SURFACE WATER OF THE OCEANS

more than 1,000 ft. below the surface. This sill prevents the circulation of all but the surface water between the Atlantic and Mediterranean Basins. Even the movement of surface water is restricted by the narrowness of the Strait, which varies from 9 to 23 miles, a very small opening in relation to the areas involved.

The mean surface temperature in the vicinity of the Strait, both in the Atlantic and in the Mediterranean, is about 65° F. At the level of the top of the sill, the temperature, both in the Atlantic and in the Mediterranean, has dropped to about 55° F. Below this level the temperature of the Atlantic water continues to fall until, at a depth of 14,000 ft., it is no more than about 35° F. The temperature of the Mediterranean water, on the other hand, does not fall appreciably below 55° F. (the temperature at the top of the sill) no matter what the depth. Thus, at the bottom of the Mediterranean Sea the temperature of the water is some 20° F. warmer than the Atlantic water at a corresponding depth on the other side of the sill—a very considerable difference.

Conditions in the smaller Red Sea are even more marked. Here, again, there is a sill, at about 1,200 ft. below the surface. The surface temperature over much of the Red Sea is about 80° F., and in places even higher. At a depth of 1,200 ft. it has dropped to about 70° F., but below that level it remains practically constant at that figure. On the other side of the sill, the temperature of the water in the Indian Ocean continues to fall.

A similar set of influences is at work in the interchange of water between the Arctic and North Atlantic Basins. Extending from the north of Scotland to Greenland is a submarine ridge (the Wyville-Thompson Ridge) on which stand The Faeroes and Iceland. This ridge prevents the draining of the very cold bottom water from the Arctic into the North Atlantic, and so allows the warm water of the North Atlantic Drift to exert a much greater influence on north-west Europe than would otherwise be the case. Cold water from the Arctic Basin does drain into the North Atlantic, however, through Davis Strait (Labrador Current), and into the North Pacific, through the Bering Strait (the Bering Current or Kamchatka Current).

OCEAN CURRENTS

It has been seen that differences both in temperature and salinity exist over the ocean basins, particularly in their surface waters. An increase in salinity produces an increase in the density of the water; an increase in temperature (provided the temperature is not lower than 39° F.) produces a decrease in density. In both cases the converse is also true. Thus increased salinity will tend to cause surface water to sink. Similarly, decreased temperature will tend to cause surface water to

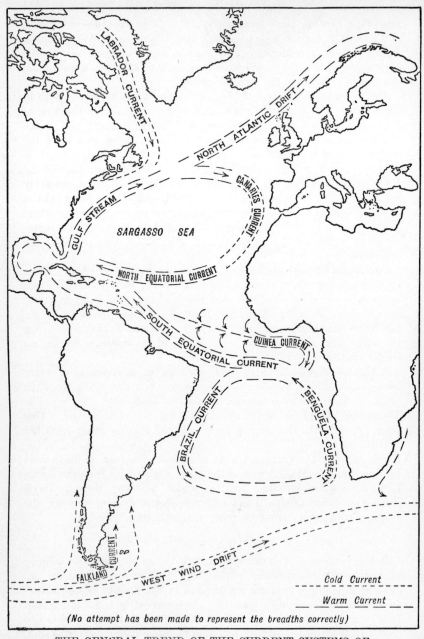

LABRADOR CURRENT

NORTH ATLANTIC DRIFT

CANARIES CURRENT

GULF STREAM

SARGASSO SEA

NORTH EQUATORIAL CURRENT

SOUTH EQUATORIAL CURRENT

GUINEA CURRENT

BRAZIL CURRENT

BENGUELA CURRENT

FALKLAND CURRENT

WEST WIND DRIFT

Cold Current ------

Warm Current -- -- --

(No attempt has been made to represent the breadths correctly)

THE GENERAL TREND OF THE CURRENT SYSTEMS OF
THE ATLANTIC OCEAN

sink. It may well happen, of course, that increased temperature (tending to decrease the density) will be accompanied by increased salinity (tending to increase the density). Such factors would clearly tend to counteract one another, and whether, on balance, the density actually increased or decreased would depend on local conditions.

However, in certain parts of the ocean basins there is a tendency towards a **vertical movement** of water in comparatively localised areas. Such vertical movements tend, in turn, to set up **horizontal movements** —a surface current and a return under-current. These " convection currents " undoubtedly do play a part in the circulation of water in the ocean basins. But the problem is complicated by a number of other factors, of which winds, the rotation of the earth, the shape of the land-masses, and the shape and depth of the ocean basins are probably the most important. These various factors, operating collectively, are responsible for the origin and behaviour of ocean currents and drifts, and any one of the factors may, apparently, assume local predominance. Reviewing the subject as a whole, however, winds appear to be the predominant motive force.

Atlantic Ocean. Within the tropics, the Trade Winds blow fairly steadily throughout the year, in the Northern Hemisphere from the north-east, and in the Southern Hemisphere from the south-east. These winds, in effect, drift two streams of water across the ocean from east to west—the **North Equatorial Current** and the **South Equatorial Current**. A constant drift of water in one direction without replacement would, in time, lead to a serious diminution in the water off the western coast of Equatorial Africa. So the **Equatorial Counter Current**, a return surface current flowing between the other two, comes into being to maintain the normal level. Off the coast of West Africa it is known as the **Guinea Current.**

The South Equatorial Current flows towards South America, where the pronounced shoulder of Brazil (Cape St. Roque) causes it to split. (Note the influence of a land-mass.) One part turns south to form the **Brazil Current**, a " warm " current since equatorial water is moving into the colder water of higher latitudes. While flowing south, this current, partly due to the rotation of the earth, and partly due to the trend of this particular coastline, tends to swing away from the Brazilian coast. Farther south, in about lat. 35° S.–40° S., the current does, in fact, swing away to merge with an expansive drift which is being driven towards the coast of South-West Africa.

This very expansive west-east drift lies in the belt of prevailing westerly winds, the " Roaring Forties ", and, as the **West Wind Drift**, sweeps round the southern oceans so far south as about lat. 60° S.

Off the coast of South-West Africa a powerful stream, the **Benguela Current**, swings away from the West Wind Drift and sweeps into the

South Atlantic. This current, bringing the colder water of higher latitudes towards the equator, is a " cold " current. As it moves northwards off the coast of West Africa it tends to swing away from the coast, and eventually does, to merge with the South Equatorial Current. In effect, therefore, it restores to the area off the coast of West Africa some of the water removed by the South Equatorial Current.

Thus there is a continuous ring of currents moving in an anti-clockwise direction round the South Atlantic. Over a vast area in the middle of the ocean there are no perceptible currents.

Twice, so far, in the case of the Brazil and Benguela Currents, reference has been made to the tendency on the part of certain currents to swing away from the coast. This is due to the earth's rotation. In the Northern Hemisphere all bodies moving under natural laws tend to swing to the right ; in the Southern Hemisphere to the left. In the case of the currents referred to above, this tendency has an important consequence. When surface water swings away from the coast, an " upwelling of bottom water " takes place to maintain the level of the off-shore water. This bottom water is normally considerably colder than surface water. A current that tends to swing away from the coast is therefore a direct cause of the belt of " cold " surface-water usually found off such coasts.

Now let us return to Cape St. Roque where we left a part of the South Equatorial Current. This part is turned northwards and follows the coast of South America towards the West Indies. On the way it merges with, and reinforces, the North Equatorial Current. There is thus an abnormally large mass of " equatorial " water moving towards the south-east of North America. Some of this water passes through the Caribbean Sea and into the land-locked Gulf of Mexico ; another branch passes to the east of the West Indies (that is, outside the island-belt). Now just as water cannot be drained away from an open basin without replacement (that is, counter-currents) so water cannot drift into a basin without setting up compensating outlet currents. From the Gulf of Mexico, therefore, water moves out through the Florida Strait as the Gulf Stream. Augmented by the water which has passed outside the West Indian island-belt, the Gulf Stream, off the coast of Florida, becomes probably the most powerful of all the ocean currents. It has a mean velocity of about 3 knots ; in parts its velocity is as high as 5 knots. As it flows northwards the Gulf Stream tends to swing away from the American coast. This enables the Labrador Current, coming from the north and hence swinging into the coast, to flow between the Gulf Stream and the coast for a considerable distance. Just south of Newfoundland the Gulf Stream apparently comes into " conflict " with the Labrador Current, and there the true Gulf Stream ends.

But the " warm " Gulf Stream, coming from warmer to colder latitudes, has brought a very considerable amount of warm water which is
left on the surface in the track of the prevailing westerly winds. This
warm water drifts across the North Atlantic at a rate of about 10 miles
a day. The more southerly branch of the drift swings away to the
south, off North-West Africa, to form the Canaries Current (a " cold "
current) which eventually merges with the North Equatorial Current.
Here, again, the complete cycle is seen—but now it is clockwise. In
the middle of this " ring of currents " is another vast area in which
there are no perceptible currents. Large quantities of " Gulf Weed "
(Sargassum), drifting out from the Gulf of Mexico, are swept into
this slack area, and there they remain. In consequence the area is
known as the Sargasso Sea.

Returning to the West Wind Drift of the North Atlantic, the course
of its more northerly branch, the North Atlantic Drift, must now be
followed. Under the influence of prevailing south-westerly winds, and
probably because of the special configuration of the land-masses and
ocean basins in this portion of the earth, the North Atlantic Drift
swings away to the north-east between Britain and Iceland, past
the coast of Norway, and into the Arctic Basin. (Branches of the
North Atlantic Drift penetrate the narrow seas around the British
Isles.)

The Arctic Basin differs from the other great oceans in being largely
land-locked. Since water is flowing into the basin over the Icelandic-
Faeroe ridge, there must necessarily be compensating outlet-currents
elsewhere. One such passes through the Bering Strait into the North
Pacific ; another passes through Davis Strait into the North Atlantic
as the Labrador Current. This " cold " current skirts the coast of
Labrador, rounds Newfoundland, and swings in towards the American
coast, producing, in effect, a " cold wall " between the Gulf Stream
and the coast as far south as New England.

Pacific and Indian Oceans. The main features of the currents of
the Pacific and Indian Oceans are shown on p. 116.

In the Pacific, there is no land-form comparable to Cape St. Roque.
The Kuro Siwo has not, therefore, the prominence of its Atlantic
counterpart, the Gulf Stream.

The configuration of the North Pacific is very different from that of
the North Atlantic. There is no North Pacific drift comparable to the
North Atlantic Drift ; the British Columbia Current is the nearest
approach, but its influence is not nearly so great.

In the Indian Ocean is seen some of the most convincing evidence
possible concerning the current-generating effect of winds. During the
northern summer, the South-West Monsoon blows over India ; during
the winter the winds are completely reversed (the season of the North-

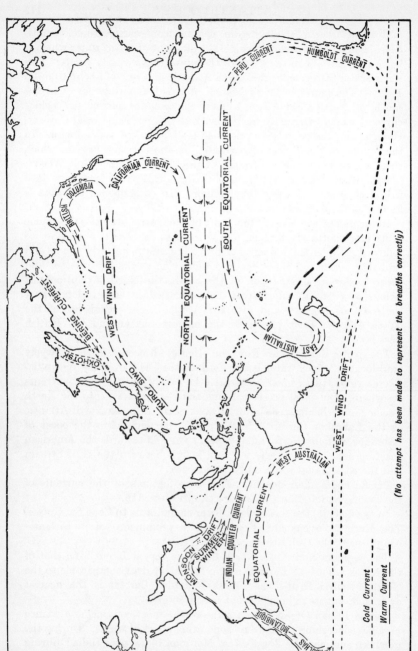

THE GENERAL TREND OF THE CURRENT SYSTEMS OF THE INDIAN AND PACIFIC OCEANS

(No attempt has been made to represent the breadths correctly)

Cold Current ------

Warm Current —

East Monsoon). During the summer the movement of the water in the Indian Ocean north of the equator is generally clockwise ; during the winter it is anti-clockwise. This, of course, is a generalisation, for large masses of water in motion do not easily have their directions reversed. Over large areas very variable currents must inevitably result, and a symmetrical arrangement will only become evident after a steady driving force has been operating for a considerable time.

Before leaving the subject of currents and drifts we must briefly examine one other effect due to winds. When winds are " on-shore " they tend to drift surface water towards the shore. When, however, the winds are " off-shore " they tend to remove surface water from the shore. Such an effect is accompanied by the upwelling of bottom water, which is generally colder than the surface water. In effect, therefore, the influence of off-shore winds is similar to that of currents that swing away from the shore. It sometimes happens that the two influences which cause upwelling reinforce one another. The Benguela Current, for example, tends to swing away from the African coast ; but over much of this same coast the prevailing winds are the off-shore South-East Trades. Both influences will tend to cause an upwelling of bottom water, producing an off-shore belt of cold water, quite apart from the relatively cold water of the current itself.

Ocean currents and drifts have important effects on the climate of the lands off the shores of which they flow, but consideration of this effect will be deferred (pp. 144-6).

THE TIDES

It is a well-known feature of coastal areas, bordering the open sea, that " sea-level " varies, both from hour to hour and from day to day. On cliff coasts such variations are marked by the heights reached at different times by the sea ; on gently shelving shores the variations are marked, more particularly, by the breadth of foreshore covered. We speak of the " tide coming in " when the sea-level is rising. (This is sometimes referred to as the **flood-tide,** or the tide is said to be " flowing ".) When the sea-level is falling we speak of the " tide going out ". (This is often referred to as the **ebb-tide,** or the tide is said to be " ebbing ".) Twice a day (actually, on the average, twice in 24 hours 51 minutes) the tide " flows ", and twice a day it " ebbs ". At many seaside resorts this is a matter of some concern to those interested in bathing.

But it is also a familiar fact that the ebb-tide does not always " go out " the same distance ; nor does the flood-tide always " come in " the same distance. Twice a month (at new moon and full moon), flood-tides are higher, and ebb-tides are lower, than the average. These **are** called **spring tides.** Also twice a month, and midway between

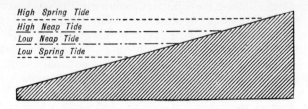

successive spring tides (at the first and last quarters of the moon) flood-tides are lower, and ebb-tides are higher, than the average. These are called **neap tides**. The difference between spring tides and neap tides is shown in the accompanying diagram.

Tide-generating forces. Tides are slight " swellings " or " bulges " of perhaps two or three feet (with compensating and similar " flattenings " elsewhere) in the water " envelope " of the earth. They are produced by the gravitational attraction of the moon and sun on the earth. Certain investigators claim to have observed tidal movements in the atmosphere as well. Such effects, even if actually present, are apparently very slight. Of the tidal effects in the great water masses, however, there can be no doubt and attention will be confined to these.

Although recent careful investigation has done much to determine the precise nature and extent of the various processes involved in the generation of tides, our present knowledge is still far from complete. Nevertheless, for our purposes, certain features do stand out unmistakably.

Suppose that we have two *rigid* bodies in space, of masses M and m respectively, their centres a distance D apart. These two bodies will exert a mutual gravitational attraction on one another of $k \cdot \dfrac{Mm}{D^2}$, where k is a constant.

The mass of the sun is about 332,800 times that of the earth ; its mean distance from the earth is about 93 million miles. The mass of the moon is only about $\frac{1}{80}$ that of the earth ; its mean distance is only some 240,000 miles. If these values are substituted, in turn, in the above formula, we find that the sun exerts on the earth a pull about 180 times as great as that exerted on the earth by the moon.

It has been stated above that the gravitational pull varies inversely as the square of the distance. Points on the surface of the earth show an extreme difference of 8,000 miles (the diameter of the earth) in their distance from an external body (for example, the sun or the moon). Now 8,000 miles, for most practical purposes, is an insignificant distance when compared with 93 million miles (the distance of the sun), but it assumes much greater significance when compared with 240,000 miles (the distance of the moon).

It is not difficult to obtain an approximate evaluation of this difference in gravitational pull for, say, points situated at the centre of the earth and on its surface, 4,000 miles nearer the sun (or moon). It is then found that the difference in gravitational pull (which is the actual tide-generating force) is no longer inversely proportional to the square of the distance, but inversely proportional to the cube of the distance. It is still directly proportional to the product of the masses concerned. The result is that the tide-generating effect due to the moon is about two and a half times that due to the sun. If the earth were perfectly *rigid* it would not yield to these tide-generating forces; for purposes of gravitational attraction, we could imagine its whole mass concentrated at its centre, so that the question of differences in gravitational attraction over its various parts would not arise. In fact this is almost the case with the " solid " earth; it yields very little. With fluids, however, it is otherwise; they yield readily.

The tide-generating effect of the moon on the great water masses is, then, our first consideration; that of the sun is of lesser, but still considerable, importance.

Another very important consequence of this tide-generating effect (much more difficult to explain in an elementary treatment such as this, but no less important for all that) is that two tidal swellings are produced at the same time.

Just as water is " pulled into a bulge " on the side of the earth nearest to the moon, so it is " thrown into a bulge " on the side farthest from the moon. Midway between these diametrically opposed bulges the water is drawn away to leave a flattened zone. Thus do the high tides and low tides start, as gentle swellings and flattenings on the surface of the oceans. As the moon revolves round the earth these high tides and low tides, in effect, " follow " it. This movement of the tidal swell (strictly a tidal wave) is produced by a vertical movement of the water. In front of the advancing " wave " the particles of water are moving upwards; behind the " wave " particles are moving downwards. (" Wave " is here used in the sense of the " crest of the swell ".) Thus the " wave-form " moves on horizontally. Only when the tides come into shallow water is there any horizontal movement of the actual particles of water. (We are, of course, ignoring the influence of currents.)

The moon revolves round the earth in the same direction as that in which the earth is rotating, completing its revolution in approximately 28 days. For this reason the interval between consecutive high tides (or low tides) is longer than 12 hours.

Suppose that the moon is in the position M_1 (p. 120). There will then be high tide at A. Ignoring the earth's revolution round the sun (it has no bearing on this particular point), the point A will rotate once in 24

I

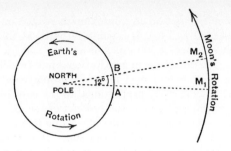

hours, returning to its original position with reference to space. But in one day the moon has moved forward in its orbit $\frac{1}{28}$ of a complete revolution—a little more than 12°. The point A has therefore to rotate farther (about 12°) before it becomes vertically below the moon again, now in the position M_2. High tide will therefore occur in the position B, not A, after the earth has completed its rotation. On an average it takes the point A about 51 minutes to rotate through this extra angle to B. But during this period of 24 hours 51 minutes the point A has also experienced the high tide thrown up on the side farthest from the moon, for the earth has made one complete rotation. Thus the average interval between consecutive high tides is about 12 hours $25\frac{1}{2}$ minutes, but for various reasons this is subject to some variation. When tides arrive early they are said to prime; when late, to lag.

Spring Tides and Neap Tides. We are now in a position to understand how spring tides and neap tides come into being. Spring tides are caused when the tide-generating effect of the sun reinforces that of the moon; that is, when the earth, sun and moon are in alignment. This happens at new moon and full moon. Neap tides are caused when the tide-generating effect of the sun is opposed to that of the moon; that is, when their forces of gravitational attraction are at right angles. This happens at the first and last quarters of the moon.

On the average, the relative heights of spring and neap tides are in the ratio of 7 to 4. It will be at once evident that the greater the amount of water *heaped up* in one place to form a high tide, the greater must be the amount drawn away from elsewhere to form the low tide. Thus spring tides are both higher at high tide, and lower at low tide, than neap tides.

Tides in Shallow Waters. So far we have been considering the purely theoretical case of an earth uniformly covered with deep water. But, to a large degree, what has been said is also applicable to the deep ocean basins. There the difference between high tide and low tide (range or amplitude of the tide) is a matter of perhaps 2 or 3 feet. This is because the tidal wave (or tidal swell), always maintaining the

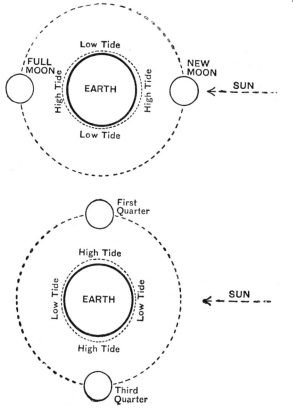

Formation of tides ; spring (above) and neap (below)

same position with reference to the moon, travels round the earth with uniform velocity.

When, however, the tidal wave enters shallow water, quite another set of circumstances operates. The shelving sea floor exerts, as it were, " friction ", with the result that the velocity of the front of the " wave " decreases. But while the front is being retarded the remainder of the wave-form, still in deep water, is moving with its greater initial velocity. This leads to a piling up of the tidal water, particularly noticeable when the tidal wave enters the shallow waters over the continental shelf. A further piling up results when the tidal wave enters a narrowing gulf or estuary, for then friction of the sides is added to friction of the floor, retarding the wave front more and more and accentuating the whole effect.

For these reasons the range in certain places is very large. Thus, at

Avonmouth (Severn Estuary), the range of ordinary spring tides is about 40 ft. At certain times, around about the equinoxes, the spring tides (called **equinoctial springs**) are rather higher. Then Avonmouth may have a range of 50 ft. Similarly an extreme range of 100 ft. is claimed for the Bay of Fundy (Eastern Canada). In most places around the British Isles the range of ordinary spring tides varies from 10 ft. to 20 ft. Gibraltar, on the other hand, shows an extreme range of little more than 3 ft., due to the fact that the Mediterranean is an enclosed sea.

Where there is a large range of the tide, strong tidal currents are set up. Then a decided horizontal movement of the water results; the tide becomes a "stream". Such streams are a feature of certain straits; for example, Menai Strait, Pentland Firth, etc. When a strong wind blows in the opposite direction to a strong stream, a very violent sea may result; this is usually called a tidal race; for example, Portland Race (off the "Isle" of Portland).

A strong wind, by blowing towards the shore over a flowing spring tide, may well cause tides considerably above the average. In certain circumstances, when such a tide is flowing up a narrowing and shallowing river estuary, a rather extraordinary phenomenon may result. This is the bore or eiger (also aegre). The front of the flowing tide becomes a "wall", several feet above the level of the upstream water. It is most common during equinoctial springs; for example, "bore" (Severn), "eiger" (Trent), "mascaret" (Seine).

The tidal scour due to a large range of the tides is an important factor in keeping river mouths and estuaries free from silt. As the outgoing stream, reinforced by the river current, is generally stronger than the ingoing stream, the silt is usually carried out to sea well away from the opening. Under such conditions a river is prevented from building a delta.

Special Features of Local Tidal Action. The main tidal wave of the British Isles approaches from the south-west. One branch proceeds up the English Channel and another round the north of Scotland and into the North Sea. Meanwhile lesser branches weave in and out among the numerous islands and into the many estuaries.

London. Off the Thames Estuary a high tide advancing eastwards from the Channel "meets" a high tide advancing southwards from the North Sea. (They are not strictly two parts of the same high tide, because the branch which has passed round the north of Scotland has taken 12 hours longer to reach the Thames Estuary than has the branch passing along the Channel.)

Thus reinforced "doubly high" tides flow up the estuary, giving very high water. But 6 hours later, the two "lows" also coincide, producing unusually low tides. The Thames Estuary has therefore a strong tidal scour, but docks are necessary to accommodate shipping. Further, all but the very smallest vessels must wait for the tide before entering or leaving the port.

Southampton. In Southampton Water, two high tides follow one another in succession, so causing a prolonged high-tide period of about four hours. This " double-tide " phenomenon, which is also discernible elsewhere on the nearby coast and in the vicinity of St. Malo, on the coast of France, is apparently caused, as in the case of the tides of the Thames Estuary, by the super-position of the two main branches of the Atlantic incoming tide, one upon the other. The actual differences observed depend upon the phase between the two branches of the tidal wave at the particular place in question. The northern branch, after rounding the north coast of Scotland into the North Sea, passes through the Strait of Dover, and meets the next incoming tide from the west, after the latter branch has reached the high-water mark. The problem is still further complicated by the fact that the tide moving along the Channel towards the Strait of Dover is being forced into a rapidly-narrowing outlet at the Strait. The port of Southampton has an unusually long period of high water, and a correspondingly short period of low water ; equally important is the fact that the water is never really low. Yet there is adequate tidal scour to prevent silting in the port. These factors are of great value to a passenger port, for even the largest liners can enter and leave with the minimum delay. This largely explains why Southampton became the leading passenger port of Great Britain.

Liverpool. The " bottle-necked " estuary of the Mersey ensures a good tidal scour in the neck, where stands Liverpool. The port is not, therefore, greatly troubled by silt. Outside the estuary, however, silting does occur, and there are sand-banks. The navigable channel has therefore to be carefully buoyed. Further, with a range of ordinary spring tides amounting to about 30 ft., vessels frequently have to wait before they can enter the port. This partly explains why Southampton is preferred to Liverpool as a passenger port.

Rhine Delta. It is unusual on an open tidal sea to find a river delta. In this case slack water results from the coincidence of a North Sea " high " with a Channel " low " (and vice versa). Notice how markedly this case differs from that of the Thames.

Dogger Bank. Conditions here are comparable to those prevailing off the mouth of the Rhine. The Dogger Bank is an extensive sand-bank in the North Sea, some 50-100 miles from the Yorkshire coast. In the generally slack water, deposition takes place readily. Over most of the area the depth of the water is only from 10 to 20 fathoms, while in some places it is no more than 6 fathoms.

CHAPTER VIII

THE ATMOSPHERE

THE atmosphere is the layer of air that envelops the earth to a height of perhaps 200 miles.

As man, like the other animals, evolved on the surface of the earth at a height not very far above sea-level, his organs have naturally become adapted to the conditions prevailing in the lower atmosphere. This makes it all the more difficult for him to investigate the conditions existing in the upper atmosphere. He has not even adapted himself to the atmospheric conditions found at the highest parts of the earth's " solid " surface—at the relatively small height of some five miles above sea-level. True, modern science has enabled him to maintain life at considerably greater heights than this, but only under artificial conditions and for limited periods. The tremendous difficulty experienced in reaching the summit of a mountain such as Everest lies, not so much in attaining any exceptional skill in mountaineering and rock-climbing, as in maintaining anything approaching normal activity at such high altitudes. Several well-organised Everest Expeditions have been beaten back, not from any lack of skill on the part of the highly trained members, but from the sheer inability of the climbers to find sufficient physical endurance to complete their formidable task within the comparatively short time suitable for climbing.

Constituents of Air. Confining our attention to the lower atmosphere, where our information is well founded and reliable, we can say that dry air is a mixture of several gases, of which two—nitrogen (78 per cent. by volume) and oxygen (21 per cent. by volume)—predominate. Oxygen is the gas that sustains life ; nitrogen serves to " dilute " it to a " strength " suitable to the needs of living organisms. Also present in the air are traces of carbon dioxide—perhaps 3 parts in 10,000. In respiration, carbon dioxide is breathed out by animals and oxygen is taken in ; carbon dioxide is also set free by the combustion of carbon compounds. If it were allowed to accumulate in the atmosphere, animal life would soon cease. Fortunately, however, there are opposing influences at work. All plants with green colouring matter are able to absorb carbon dioxide, retaining the carbon to build up their tissues, and releasing oxygen. A kind of balance is therefore preserved. Animals use oxygen and release carbon dioxide in respiration ; green plants need carbon dioxide with which they build up their tissues, and release oxygen. The process by which green plants utilise carbon dioxide takes place only in the presence of light and is therefore known as photosynthesis; it must not be confused with respiration, which is going on continuously in plant tissue just as it does in animal tissue.

Of the other gases present in ordinary air we shall refer only to water vapour. This is found in very varying proportions over different parts of the earth's surface and is noteworthy for its important effects on the human body. Water vapour is water in the form of a gas; for our present purposes we may regard it as behaving like a normal gas. It mixes freely with the air and is invisible. It must not be confused with the so-called "steam" which forms a cloud just above the spout of a kettle. (That cloud, like the clouds in the sky, is composed of droplets of water.) When the temperature of the air is low, the presence of considerable quantities of water vapour gives rise to a very "raw" feeling. In a "dry" atmosphere much lower temperatures may be quite comfortable. It is not uncommon for a Canadian, acclimatised to the cold, dry winters of the Prairie Provinces, to complain about the rawness of a British winter when, in actual fact, the British temperatures are far above those of his native home. Similarly, the white man experiences far more discomfort in a damp heat (for example, Equatorial West Africa or the Amazon Lowlands) than he does in a dry heat (for example, Egypt or the mining settlements in the West Australian Desert).

In addition to these gases, air normally contains many impurities. Dust derived from decayed rocks is to be found everywhere, carried along by the wind. Relatively large amounts of soot and gaseous compounds of sulphur and nitrogen are common over industrial areas; particles of salt are generally to be found over seaside places. Tiny seeds, pollen from plants, and countless bacteria of all sorts are widespread. Observation shows, however, that such impurities are confined to a comparatively thin layer near sea-level.

Weight of the Atmosphere. Air is a material substance; it has weight. A column of air, one square inch in cross-section, extending from sea-level to the upper limits of the atmosphere, would weigh approximately 14·7 pounds. We therefore say that the average "atmospheric pressure" at sea-level is about 14·7 lb. per square inch. Wherever the atmosphere has free access, this pressure is distributed equally in all directions. (This is one of the properties of fluids.) Thus, under normal conditions, our bodies have an "internal pressure" which exactly balances the "external pressure", and we are not, therefore, conscious of the great weight pressing on us. (In the same way fish that live in the ocean depths are adapted to the much greater pressures found there.) If, however, the air is evacuated from a fragile vessel, we are at once aware of the reality of atmospheric pressure. When the internal pressure has been sufficiently reduced, the vessel will collapse under the weight of air which presses on it from all sides.

Because the atmospheric pressure at any level is due to the weight of air above that level, it follows that atmospheric pressure must necessarily decrease with increase of height above sea-level. Further, because air consists of a number of gases which yield very readily to changes of pressure, the layer nearest to sea-level will be compressed the most and the layer nearest to the upper limit will be the least dense. Thus the pressure decreases with increasing height, rapidly at first, and then more slowly. At a height of about $3\frac{1}{2}$ miles, atmospheric pressure is reduced to one half its sea-level value. The next $3\frac{1}{2}$ miles show a much smaller reduction ; the succeeding $3\frac{1}{2}$ miles a smaller reduction still ; at a height of about 200 miles, atmospheric pressure is probably reduced to a figure closely approaching zero. Our knowledge of the upper atmosphere, however, is far from complete, and it is only in very recent years that determined attempts have been made to reach very considerable heights. Even now, by the use of specially constructed balloons, oxygen respirators, electrically heated clothing, etc., a height of only some 14 miles above sea-level has been achieved.

The lower layers of the atmosphere are sometimes called the _tropo-sphere_ ; within this zone, temperature, in general, decreases with increasing height. Above a height of rather more than seven miles is the **stratosphere**. Its base is not everywhere at the same height above sea-level, nor does it remain, apparently, always at the same height over any particular place. Rather does it appear to " hover ", lifting a little and falling a little at different times. Between the troposphere and stratosphere is the _tropopause_, a transition belt some two miles thick.

Certain electrical phenomena are possibly associated with the position of the base of the stratosphere. In recent years the stratosphere has assumed some importance in view of the possibilities it offers for a revolutionary mode of flying. It is quite possible that we must look to the stratosphere for satisfactory explanations of many other factors, including some which affect our everyday life. Certain aspects of the weather, for example, are not adequately explained in the light of our present knowledge. Perhaps the stratosphere will one day yield the answers that have long baffled investigators.

CLIMATE AND WEATHER

It is quite customary to speak of " cold weather ", " hot weather ", " wet weather ", " windy weather ", " frosty weather ", etc. Yet these and many other types of " weather " may, at different times, all occur at one place. Weather, then, is the _state of the atmosphere at any_ *given moment.* It is very important to realise this, particularly in the case of a place which is subject to varied, and apparently haphazard, changes in its weather.

When we refer to climate, on the other hand, we think of the sort of weather that may be expected at any given time. It is, in some respects, an average of the customary weather.

We are very apt to compare the climate of one place with that of another. But, if we are to compare climates fairly, we must have some accepted method of measuring and averaging the various weather factors, and we must lay down general principles which shall be consistently observed.

The study of phenomena associated with the atmosphere is known as **meteorology,** and observation posts specially set up to facilitate this study are known as meteorological stations. At the most important of such stations continuous records or hourly readings are taken of all weather factors; for example, pressure, temperature, rainfall, wind, sunshine, cloud, etc. At rather less important stations similar observations are made, but at specified hours each day, and with certain adaptations to meet the particular requirements of the individual place.

(*a*) **Measurement of Pressure.** Pressure is measured by means of a barometer. In Britain the official type of instrument used in meteorology is the **Kew Pattern Barometer.** In principle it is exactly the same as the simple mercury barometer, but several refinements are embodied in its construction to make it more suitable for its particular purpose. The actual mechanism of the barometer falls rather within the scope of physics and will not, therefore, be discussed here. However, for the present purpose, some aspects of the simple mercury barometer will be examined.

The pressure of the atmosphere on the open surface XY "balances" the column of mercury CD in the barometer. Should atmospheric pressure increase, the surface XY will be depressed and mercury will be forced from the vessel LM into the tube AB, raising the level of C. A greater vertical height of mercury is thus necessary to balance the increased atmospheric pressure. Should atmospheric pressure decrease, mercury will flow from the tube AB into the vessel LM, lowering the level of C. A smaller vertical height of mercury is thus necessary to balance the decreased atmospheric pressure. The vertical height of the level at C above the surface XY is therefore a measure of the atmospheric pressure. Hence the pressure of the atmosphere is often referred to as x in. (or cm.) of mercury. What is really meant is that the atmospheric pressure exactly balances a vertical column of mercury x in. (or cm.) high.

At sea-level the height of the balancing column of mercury is usually about 30 in. (or 76 cm.). At a height of 1,000 ft. above sea-level the height of the column will normally drop to about 29 in. At a height of $3\frac{1}{2}$ miles above sea-level, the height of the column will normally drop to about 15 in.

When atmospheric pressure is measured in terms of the height of a column of mercury, we are using a gravitational unit, for the balancing pressure—due to the weight of the mercury in the column—clearly depends on the force of gravity, which is not everywhere the same. For many purposes this variation is of no consequence. However, to remove the uncertainty resulting from the use of a gravitational unit, an absolute unit, which is constant under all conditions, has been introduced into precise meteorological measurements. This unit is the **bar,** and the pressure of the atmosphere is usually given in **millibars** (1,000 millibars = 1 bar). 1,000 millibars (mb.) are equivalent to a sea-level reading in latitude 45° N. or S. of 29·53 in. of mercury, after due correction has been made for the temperature of the mercury in the barometer. (Since mercury expands with increase of temperature —considerably more so than the glass tube containing it—the height of the mercury column will depend, to some extent, on the temperature. For many purposes this, again, is of no consequence. For very accurate work, however, a correction must be made. In the case of the Kew Pattern Mercury Barometer the " standard temperature " is taken as 12° C. (about 54° F.), and all readings are " reduced " to this temperature.)

For first-class meteorological work, therefore, the reading of the mercury barometer must be corrected for: (*a*) altitude, (*b*) latitude, and (*c*) temperature. Then the pressure is recorded in millibars.

Since the barometer is an instrument of great precision it should be kept indoors and it should always be handled carefully. It should be kept well away from fires, radiators, etc., and should always be shielded from direct sunlight. To read the scales, however, a good light is necessary.

The mercury barometer is not really a portable instrument; it needs to be set up carefully and left undisturbed. For many purposes, therefore, the **aneroid barometer** is useful. It is compact and portable, but, like all delicate instruments, it should be handled with care. Essentially it consists of a flat metal box with corrugated ends, from which some of the air has been evacuated. If the pressure of the atmosphere increases, the free end of the box is pressed slightly in; if the atmospheric pressure decreases, the natural resilience of the light metal casing causes the end of the box to move out again. These movements of the free end of the metal box are transmitted through a system of levers to a pointer moving over a graduated scale. The instrument must be calibrated by comparing its readings with those of a standard mercury barometer. The aneroid barometer is invaluable where a compact, light, portable instrument is to be preferred to great precision. In the aeroplane it forms the basis of the **altimeter.**

Where a continuous record of the pressure is required, and where great precision is not essential, the **barograph** is frequently employed. An aneroid barometer, by operating a system of levers, moves an inked pen which is brought into contact with a piece of graph-paper attached to a rotating drum. As the graph-paper moves, the pen marks any changes in the pressure by moving up or down at right angles to the direction of movement of the paper, so tracing a zig-zag line. When the speed of rotation of the drum is known, time lines can be drawn on the graph paper. The instrument must be calibrated by comparing its readings with those of a standard mercury barometer.

(*b*) **Measurement of Rainfall.** Rainfall is recorded as the average *depth* of water (in inches in Britain) which would accumulate on an impervious surface in a given time. It is measured by means of a **rain-gauge.** The Meteorological Office has approved an instrument of specific design, details of which are shown below.

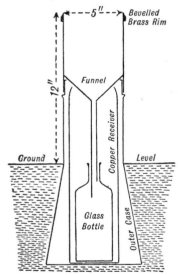

The Rain-gauge (based on the Meteorological Office 5 in. pattern)

The Taper Measure calibrated in inches for use with a particular rain-gauge

Gauges are generally made of copper, a metal noted for its durability under varying conditions. Two standard sizes are in use ; the diameter of the funnel should be either 5 in. or 8 in. Essentially the gauge consists of an outer case, a receiving vessel, a funnel, a clear-glass bottle and a calibrated measure. The upper rim of the funnel is reinforced with a stout brass ring to prevent deformation. This brass rim is then bevelled so that the exact area of the funnel can be determined and splashing avoided. Below the rim the sides of the funnel are in the form of a cylinder for 4–6 in. This also minimises the effects of splashing and so increases the accuracy of readings. The sloping sides of the funnel taper until only a comparatively small opening remains. Below this point, a long tube leads down to the glass bottle which stands inside the copper receiving vessel. Normally the bottle is removed during a reading and its contents emptied into the calibrated measure. Should there be exceptionally heavy rainfall, however, the collected water may overflow from the bottle into the copper receiving vessel. Then the receiver must also be removed and emptied. Should water overflow from the receiver into the outer case it, too, must be emptied, but this is a rare occurrence. (In the 5-in. gauge a pint bottle is used and this holds about " 1¾ in. of rain " ; in the 8-in. gauge a quart bottle is used and this holds rather less than " 1½ in. of rain ").

The rain-gauge is set up on level ground well out in the open. If there are buildings, walls, trees, bushes, etc., in the vicinity, the gauge must be placed at a distance from them of at least twice the height of the object concerned. Further, the rim of the gauge must be horizontal and should be exactly 1 ft. above the ground. Around the gauge the surface should be either closely cut grass or sand according to circumstances. This again minimises the effects of splashing. In a very exposed site sweeping ground-winds may make readings unreliable. Then some form of wind-screen should be erected, subject to the condition given above. A distant belt of trees or a wall is often helpful, or a turf wall, about 1 ft. high and surrounding the gauge at a distance of 5 ft., may be employed.

When a suitable site has been found, the outer case is sunk into the ground and made secure against even the most violent of gales, care being taken to ensure that the prescribed conditions are observed. This is most important if readings taken in several different places are to be strictly comparable. For this reason a roof should not be used on account of the variable wind eddies encountered in such situations. These eddies, the result of purely artificial conditions, may so disturb the normal distribution as to give an entirely wrong impression.

The rain-gauge is, in effect, a method of " magnifying " the amount of rainfall, as the following simple calculation will show.

Let the area of cross-section of the funnel be A sq. in. and that of the measuring cylinder a sq. in. Now suppose that " 1 in. of rain " falls. The volume of water collecting in the bottle will thus be A cub. in. When poured into the measuring cylinder, this water will rise to a height of $\dfrac{A}{a}$ in. By making a much smaller than A the " 1 in. of rain " will rise to a considerable height in the measuring cylinder, and the accuracy of the reading will be much increased.

In practice a **taper measure** is used, so that even small amounts of rainfall can be measured to the nearest hundredth of an inch. For a mere trace, the bottom division marked is $\frac{1}{200}$ in.

Even during dry weather the gauge should be examined every day, as dew sometimes gives rise to appreciable precipitation.

In the case of snow, special precautions are usually needed. The snow should be melted either by warming the funnel carefully (for example, by wrapping a cloth soaked in hot water around the outside) or by adding a known quantity of warm water. (This quantity of added water must, of course, be subtracted from the total in the bottle when the reading is taken.) Approximately 10–12 in. of newly settled snow are equivalent to 1 in. of rain.

The gauge should be examined regularly for defects (for example leaks), and the bottle and receiver should be kept clean. Although simple in construction, the rain-gauge is an instrument of precision and must be treated as such.

(c) **Measurement of Temperature.** The characteristics of the various types of thermometers and the general procedure adopted in measuring temperature may justly be considered as coming within the scope of physics. Here we shall examine only those points which are of special importance in meteorology.

Maximum and Minimum "Shade" Temperatures. In Britain the approved **maximum thermometer** is a mercury-in-glass instrument with a constriction about one inch from the bulb. When the temperature rises, the mercury expands and is forced past the constriction into the stem. When the temperature falls, the thread of mercury breaks at the constriction and the detached part remains in the stem as a self-recording index. To re-set the thermometer it is necessary to swing it briskly, but carefully, with the bulb outermost.

The **minimum** thermometer is a spirit-in-glass instrument (for example, alcohol). A small index is immersed in the spirit in the stem. When the temperature falls and the spirit contracts, the index is drawn along the stem towards the bulb by the surface tension of the meniscus. When the temperature rises, the spirit flows past the index, which remains in the position it occupied at the minimum temperature.

For use in the British Isles, the maximum thermometer should be graduated from 0° F. to 130° F.; the minimum thermometer from -30° F. to 100° F.

Both these thermometers are mounted in a nearly horizontal position, with their bulbs slightly lower than their other ends. In this position the risks of the index slipping are minimised.

To ensure strictly comparable conditions from one place to another, a special design of screen, known as the **Stevenson Screen,** has been approved. Essentially it consists of a " box ", mounted on a stand, the inside of which is always in the shade, but through which fresh air can circulate freely. This is achieved mainly by the double louvred sides—strips of wood mounted one above the other in the form of a series of inverted V's. The height of the screen above sea-level should be determined so that the necessary corrections can be made for altitude when plotting the readings of different stations on the same chart. The screen should be freely exposed to sun and wind, and should not be shaded by buildings or trees, etc.

Earth Temperatures. For some purposes the temperature of the ground at various depths is required. Thermometers are suspended in iron tubes which have been sunk into the ground. The usual depths for comparative purposes are 1 ft. and 4 ft., but for agricultural purposes observations are frequently made at 4 in., 8 in., and 2 ft. The thermometers are enclosed in glass tubes and their bulbs are embedded in paraffin wax to render them less sensitive to sudden changes of temperature. (Underground changes of temperature are very gradual, so that there is no loss of accuracy as a result of the coating of paraffin wax, but the observer is enabled to withdraw the thermometer from the tube in order to read it, before the temperature of the bulb has had time to change appreciably.) These thermometers are usually graduated from 20° F. to 100° F. Care must be taken to see that water does not collect in the tubes.

For shallow depths (for example, 4 in. and 8 in.) another type of thermometer is sometimes used. This has the stem bent at right angles so that the bulb is at the required depth and the stem resting on the surface. The great advantage is that the thermometer can be read without moving it from the ground.

Grass-minimum Temperature. Readings in this class are important in connection with ground-frosts. A minimum thermometer is mounted horizontally on two Y-supports with its bulb just touching the tips of some short grass, 1–2 in. high. In general, damage does not occur to growing plants until the temperature has dropped rather below 32° F. For this reason a ground frost is considered to have occurred when the grass-minimum thermometer records a temperature of 30° F. or below.

(*d*) **Measurement of Humidity.** Air contains a certain amount of water vapour (water in the form of a gas). For the present it is sufficient to note that, at a given temperature, a given quantity of air can hold so much water vapour and no more ; in that state the air is said to be saturated. But the amount of water vapour a given quantity of air is capable of holding depends on its temperature. Warm air can hold more water vapour than cold air. This brings us to an important definition. The amount of water vapour actually present in a given volume of air, at a given temperature, expressed as a percentage of the amount of water vapour that same air could hold (if saturated), at the same temperature, is known as the **relative humidity.** If the relative humidity is very high (for example, nearly 100 per cent.) the air is "moist"; if the relative humidity is very low, the air is "dry".

To determine the relative humidity, **wet-bulb and dry-bulb thermometers** (or the **wet- and dry-bulb hygrometer**) are used. These are two identical, standardised thermometers, mounted vertically and side by side in the Stevenson screen. One is left as an ordinary thermometer (dry-bulb). The other has its bulb covered with muslin which is kept moist by means of a wick dipping into clean water. Unless the air is saturated, evaporation will take place from the moist muslin ; the drier the air, the greater will be the rate of evaporation. But evaporation produces cooling ; the greater the evaporation, the greater the cooling. Hence, normally, the wet-bulb thermometer gives a lower reading than the dry-bulb. Tables have been prepared which give the relative humidity from an observation of the dry-bulb temperature and the difference between the dry-bulb and wet-bulb temperatures.

(*e*) **Measurement of Sunshine.** The **Campbell-Stokes Sunshine Recorder** (the Meteorological Office approved pattern) consists essentially of a glass sphere which focuses the rays from the sun on to a specially prepared card mounted in a metal bowl also forming part of a sphere with its centre at the centre of the glass sphere. The instrument must obviously be set up in such a position that no obstacle can come between it and the sun. Because the apparent course of the sun can be accurately calculated for any day and in any latitude, a time chart can be marked on the card. While the sun is shining, a burnt trace appears on the card ; when direct sunshine is cut off, the burnt trace ceases. Using the time chart, the separate lengths of burnt trace can therefore be totalled.

(*f*) **Measurement of Wind.** The direction of the wind is given by the **weather-cock** or **wind vane.** This consists of a pointer with a large "tail", free to rotate about a vertical axis so that, when the wind blows, the tail swings round and the pointer looks into the wind. The directions north, east, south and west are marked on the fixed support of the vane.

The speed of the wind is determined by means of the anemometer. This usually consists of four (or three) hemispherical cups attached to the ends of two crossed horizontal metal arms mounted on a vertical spindle. As will be seen from the diagram, the cups will cause the arms to rotate because the concave sides of the cups offer more resistance to the wind than the convex sides. The speed with which the arms rotate will bear some relation to the speed of the wind. The rotation of the arms is transmitted through accurate mechanism to an inked pen which traces a mark on paper attached to a rotating drum.

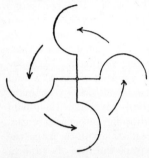

Thus, knowing the speed of rotation of the drum, time lines can be drawn on the paper, and at any given time the speed of rotation of the anemometer arms is known. When the instrument has been once calibrated, it can be used to read off directly the speed of the wind.

Since the presence of trees, buildings, etc., causes wind eddies of a most uncertain nature, the exposure of an anemometer is of the utmost importance. The best situation is one that is open and flat for a considerable distance. Then the instrument should be mounted on top of a mast or lattice tower, some 30–40 ft. high.

Beaufort Wind Scale. This is a system, originally devised by Admiral Beaufort early in the nineteenth century, of wind classification by reference to a specific number on a scale according to the effects produced by the wind. In his original specification, Admiral Beaufort was concerned with the effects of wind on ships of war of a type now obsolete. A revised version, however, has come into use for inland areas as a result of long and careful observation. The main features of this classification, together with the appropriate scale numbers, are set out below.

Beaufort Scale No.	Description	Effects	Speed
0	Calm	Smoke rises vertically	Less than 1 m.p.h.
1	Light Air	Smoke drift indicates wind direction ; wind vanes usually unaffected	1–3 m.p.h.
2	Light Breeze	Wind vanes affected ; leaves rustle ; wind noticeable on face	4–7 m.p.h.
3	Gentle Breeze	Leaves and small twigs in constant motion ; light flags extended	8–12 m.p.h.

Beaufort Scale No.	Description	Effects	Speed
4	Moderate Breeze	Dust and loose paper raised; small branches moved	13–18 m.p.h.
5	Fresh Breeze	Small trees in leaf seen to sway; small waves form on inland water	19–24 m.p.h.
6	Strong Breeze	Large branches sway; whistling in telegraph wires	25–31 m.p.h.
7	Moderate Gale	Whole trees in motion; wind resistance noticeable when walking	32–38 m.p.h.
8	Fresh Gale	Twigs break off trees; progress generally impeded	39–46 m.p.h.
9	Strong Gale	Structures slightly damaged; chimney pots and slates removed	47–54 m.p.h.
10	Whole Gale	Considerable structural damage; trees uprooted; seldom experienced inland	55–63 m.p.h.
11	Storm	Very rare on land; widespread damage	64–75 m.p.h.
12	Hurricane	Very rare except in certain tropical areas; widespread devastation	More than 75 m.p.h.

It must be remembered that the wind seldom maintains a uniform speed for more than a comparatively short time. Usually gusts of varying intensity are interspersed with frequent lulls.

CLIMATIC " MEANS "

In countries such as Britain, weather records have been kept for very many years; further, a large measure of international collaboration has been achieved since 1873, when the International Congress of Meteorology assembled in Vienna.

From personal impressions, no less than from careful meteorological observations, it is obvious that the weather experienced in a limited locality may be very variable. For this reason observations must be made over a considerable period before we can begin to speak about the climate. Detailed analysis of meteorological records suggests that a minimum period of 35 years is necessary before reliable averages can be determined. This does not mean that the weather repeats itself every thirty-five years; but it does mean that, over such a period of years, we can reasonably expect all the different types to occur. The longer the period taken, of course, the more trustworthy will be the *average*. When the average has been determined we know what may reasonably be expected; we are not at all sure that, in any particular year, the actual weather will bear any *close* resemblance to this average. The average is, in fact, nothing more than a probability.

K

Mean Monthly Temperature. In the case of a minor meteorological station the Stevenson screen is visited daily (at, say, 9 a.m., when it is most unlikely that the temperature would be either at the maximum or minimum) and the maximum and minimum thermometers are read and re-set. Thus, at each visit, maximum and minimum temperatures for the past 24 hours are recorded, and the mean temperature for that period can be determined, by halving the sum of the two readings. (The " minimum " usually occurs at about 3 or 4 a.m. (G.M.T.) and the " maximum " at about 2 or 3 p.m.) This process is continued for a particular month, when an average of the daily " means " for that month is determined. This gives the average temperature for that particular month. The same process must be repeated for at least thirty-five years, when it will be possible to determine a grand average for any given month. This grand average is known as the **mean monthly temperature.** When determined in this way the mean is usually slightly different from that determined by averaging the hourly readings, but for the present this difference can be neglected.

Similarly, by taking the average over the whole year, instead of over just one month, the **mean annual temperature** is obtained.

Subtracting the lowest mean monthly temperature (usually for January in Britain) from the highest (usually for July in Britain) gives the **mean annual range of temperature.** Subtracting the mean of the " minima " from the mean of the " maxima " gives the **mean diurnal (daily) range.** Similarly the diurnal range for any particular month can be calculated, and the diurnal range for one month can be compared with that for another. The diurnal range is important in that it emphasises the difference between day and night temperatures.

Mean Monthly Rainfall. The rain-gauge is emptied daily and the total rainfall for any particular month determined. (In some places, especially those difficult of access, monthly gauges, fitted with larger bottles, are used.) The total rainfall for this same month is then determined for at least thirty-five consecutive years, and an average of these monthly totals found. This monthly total, based on the average for at least thirty-five years, is known as the **mean monthly rainfall.** Similarly, by finding the total for the whole year and averaging at least thirty-five consecutive yearly totals, the **mean annual rainfall** is obtained.

When studying the different types of climate that are to be found over the earth's surface, it is often instructive to ascertain the seasonal distribution of rainfall. Thus, it may be helpful to compare the summer rainfall with that of winter. This can be done very easily provided the mean monthly rainfall is known throughout the year.

Climatic data for atmospheric pressure, relative humidity, hours of sunshine, wind direction, etc., can also be obtained, and such valu-

able information as the mean frost-free period, the mean period available for cereal growth, etc., calculated. In short, observations of the
weather can be organised in such a way as to give invaluable climatic
data. But, important as *means* undoubtedly are, they must not be
emphasised unduly. In some regions *extremes* exert a controlling
influence ; a killing frost, for example, might well negative a favourable mean temperature.

Diagrammatic Representation of Temperature and Rainfall. Temperature is very conveniently represented by means of a graph. If
temperature is plotted along the y-axis, and time along the x-axis, we
can see at a glance the change of temperature with time. The following
mean monthly temperatures for a particular place are plotted in this
way on diagram (i).

Jan.	Feb.	Mar.	April	May	June	July	Aug.	Sept.	Oct.	Nov.	Dec.	
39	40	43	48	53	57	60	60	56	50	45	42	°F

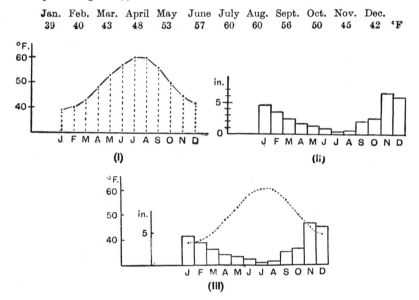

(I)   (li)

(III)

Although rainfall could also be represented by a similar type of
graph, a more appropriate and striking method is shown in diagram
(ii). The amount of rainfall is plotted along the y-axis, and time is
plotted along the x-axis, but the mean monthly totals are indicated by
block columns, not by the line graph ; one reason for doing this is
that rainfall does not vary continuously with time, as temperature does.

The following mean monthly rainfall figures are plotted in diagram
(ii) and refer to the same station as do the temperatures given above.

Jan.	Feb.	Mar.	April	May	June	July	Aug.	Sept.	Oct.	Nov.	Dec.	
4·5	3·5	2·5	1·7	1·3	0·9	0·4	0·6	?·0	2·5	6·5	5·9	in.

It is often very helpful, when studying climatic data, to combine the mean monthly temperature and rainfall figures in one diagram. Diagram iii (a combination of diagrams i and ii) shows how this may be done. The advantages of such a diagram are at once evident. At a glance we can see the mean temperatures month by month, the range of temperature, the monthly rainfall totals, and the seasonal distribution of rainfall. The combined diagram gives a concise and instructive summary of two of the most important features of climate.

THE MAPPING OF CLIMATIC DATA

When dealing with climate we are usually more concerned with "areas" than with a host of separate "points". Thus we need a method of mapping data applicable to a particular area.

It has already been seen how climatic records are compiled at a number of specimen stations scattered over a country. The closer the network of meteorological stations the more detailed will be our knowledge of the area as a whole. In a country such as Britain, with a close network, truly representative records are available for every physical sub-division of the entire area. In certain parts of the earth, on the other hand, for example, parts of Canada and Australia, Antarctica, etc., climatic records are very scanty, and detailed information, over large areas, is not available.

As will be seen later, the climate at any particular place depends partly on the position of the place (that is, latitude, relation to land and water, etc.) and partly on its own individual local physical form. When comparing the climate of one place with that of another, it is often convenient to eliminate, so far as possible, the influence of local physical form. To do this, we must "correct" the actual readings to their sea-level value. Such readings are said to be *reduced to sea-level*. It is not possible to do this with all climatic data. For example, if a certain place has a mean annual rainfall of x in., it is not possible to say that the place would have a reading of y in. if it were at sea-level; no such precise relation between rainfall and height exists. True, rainfall does, very often, depend on height, but not in such a simple way.

In the case of atmospheric pressure, however, it has already been seen that the pressure decreases with increasing height above sea-level. This rate of decrease due to height can be readily calculated. But atmospheric pressure varies from one place to another for reasons very different from a mere change in height. Such variations in pressure are of great climatic importance and have a marked effect on winds and rainfall. It is often convenient, therefore, to eliminate the influence of height and to reduce the pressure to its sea-level value. Temperature also is greatly influenced by height, and here, again, it is often convenient to reduce to sea-level. (On the average, the temperature of the air decreases at the rate of about 1° F. for every 300 ft. of ascent above sea-level. This rate is only an approximation and is subject to certain local variation. See also p. 155.)

When mapping weather readings or climatic data for some particular area, a specific time must be chosen. Thus we might map temperature conditions over the British Isles at some definite hour (*weather*) or we might map the mean temperatures for some definite month (*climate*). When weather observations extending over an area are plotted for some specific time, the resulting map is known as a synoptic chart. (See p. 180.) To facilitate the plotting of weather observations and climatic data on maps we make use of certain special lines.

Isotherms. An isotherm is a line drawn on a map to separate two areas of different temperature, on one side of the line the temperature being above, and on the other side below, that of the line. Very often, in the case of air temperature, isotherms are reduced to their sea-level value ; by eliminating the influence of local relief the resulting map is greatly simplified. (Isotherms are not necessarily restricted to air temperatures ; for example, the surface temperature of ocean water may be mapped in the same way.) Isotherms can be drawn either to depict temperature conditions at some specified time (*weather*) or to represent the mean conditions over some definite period (*climate*).

Isobars. An isobar is a line drawn on a map to separate two areas of different " sea-level " atmospheric pressure, on one side of the line the pressure being above, and on the other side below, that of the line. Here, again, isobars may be drawn to depict either weather observations or climatic mean data.

Isohyets. An isohyet is a line drawn on a map to separate two areas having different amounts of rainfall over some prescribed time, on one side of the line the rainfall being above, and on the other side below, that of the line. No reduction to sea-level can be made, but the isohyets may refer either to weather readings or to climatic data.

The accompanying diagram shows the general method of using isotherms. The same general method can be used equally well for isobars and isohyets.

When drawing temperature, pressure, or rainfall maps, it is instructive to choose a style of shading or a range of colours

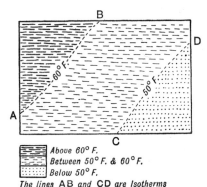

Above 60° F.
Between 50° F. & 60° F.
Below 50° F.
The lines AB *and* CD *are Isotherms*

which emphasises the transition from smaller to greater. If the intensity of the shading or colours is gradually increased from one area through successive areas, and the map is carefully drawn, the main features of the distribution stand out very clearly.

FACTORS AFFECTING AIR TEMPERATURE OVER THE EARTH'S SURFACE

The heat of the atmosphere is derived almost entirely from the sun. Solar energy (radiant heat, light, etc.) enters the earth's atmosphere, a material substance. If this atmosphere were " pure " throughout, the solar energy would reach the land and water surfaces with very little loss. What actually happens is that the numerous impurities (dust, soot, water particles, water vapour, etc.) stop a certain amount of the energy and so become heated themselves. As they float through the air this heat is given up to the atmosphere by conduction from the heated impurities. Taking the earth as a whole, quite an appreciable amount of heat is given to the atmosphere in this way. Even so, the greater proportion of the solar energy does actually reach the land and water surfaces, which are thereby heated. The effects, however, are confined to a layer comparatively near the surface, particularly in the case of the solid crust. This surface layer then, in effect, becomes a " radiator ". The layer of air touching this earth radiator is heated by conduction, with the result that it expands and rises, thereby setting up convection currents. In this way the lower layers of the atmosphere are heated; these convectional heating effects are, in general, confined to a relatively shallow layer wholly below the stratosphere. In addition to this convectional heating, the earth radiator sends some heat into the atmosphere by radiation.

Thus, although the sun is the original source of heat reaching the atmosphere, the earth-radiator is the *effective* source for by far the greater part of the heat.

If all the heat which reached the earth from the sun were to remain in the atmosphere, there would clearly be a steady accumulation of heat with a gradually rising temperature. This, of course, does not occur, for the heat is gradually dissipated into space, thereby maintaining a balance.

(a) Latitude. It has already been seen (p. 16) that the greater the angle of elevation of the sun the greater the amount of solar energy reaching the earth at that particular place. Over the course of a whole year, the average angle of elevation will be greatest at the equator and least at the poles. We should expect, therefore, that the temperature of the air would decrease from the equator towards the poles. In general, and with certain modifications, this is the case.

(b) **Altitude.** As the earth radiator is the chief source of the heat given up to the atmosphere, the nearer air is to that radiator the more we should expect it to be heated. Thus temperatures at sea-level should be greater than those at heights above sea-level, and the decrease in temperature with increasing height should continue, at least for a considerable distance. This, again, is generally true, a feature which is emphasised by a physical property of the air itself. Near sea-level the air is more dense (due to the weight of air above that level) than at greater heights (where there is less air above the particular level). Thus, in a given volume, the mass of air will decrease with increase in height above sea-level. As the height increases, therefore, there will be less and less air to hold heat; there will also be fewer impurities present. In general, the temperature of the air within the troposphere decreases at an approximate rate of about 1° F. for every 300 ft. of ascent, but the actual rate is subject to a certain amount of local variation. (See also p. 155.)

Although elevated land areas do exert some influence on the temperature of the air above them (for example, an extensive plateau, when heated by the sun, does warm the air above it to some extent, appreciably more so than a typical mountain, in fact) they do not greatly alter the case. This is largely due to the decreasing density of the air, but partly to the fact that by far the greater proportion of the impurities are confined to the lower layers. Heat from elevated areas is merely dissipated more rapidly; it does not remain in the atmosphere to anything like the same extent as does heat from land areas near sea-level, and its influence is therefore not so lasting.

(c) **Distance from the Sea.** Here we encounter a factor which modifies to a marked extent the influence of latitude. A land surface, when heated, behaves very differently from a water surface. In the case of a land surface, solar energy does not penetrate to any considerable depth; in the case of water, solar energy is able to penetrate to an appreciably greater depth. (This difference is due to the " opaque " and " transparent " natures of the two substances.) In the case of a land surface, the heat can travel to another part of the surface only by conduction, and the rocks of the earth's surface are generally bad conductors; in the case of water, the heat can travel to another part because the water itself can move, giving rise to convection currents. (This difference is due to the solid and fluid natures of the two substances.) The specific heat of water is considerably higher than that of any rock; hence, if 1 lb. of water and 1 lb. of any rock are each given the same *amount* of heat, the temperature of the rock will increase more than that of the water. (It must be remembered, however, that the surface rocks have a density two to three times that of water, a fact which tends to offset the influence of specific heat.)

The result of all this is that, when land and water surfaces each receive the same amount of heat per unit of surface area, the temperature of the land surface rises more rapidly, and reaches a higher point, than that of the water surface. But the converse is also true ; a land surface cools more rapidly, and reaches a lower temperature, than does a water surface. Thus, in summer the continental land masses become considerably hotter than the oceans in corresponding latitudes ; in winter the land masses become considerably colder than the oceans.

These same general characteristics will also be true of the air over land and water areas. Thus air temperatures near the oceans tend to be cooler in summer and warmer in winter than those prevailing over areas in corresponding latitudes far from the sea. A few examples will illustrate the extent of these differences.

Victoria, on Vancouver Island (Western Canada), has a mean January temperature of 39° F. and a mean July temperature of 60° F. Halifax, in Nova Scotia (Eastern Canada), has a mean January temperature of 24° F. and a mean July temperature of 65° F. These two stations are at almost identical heights above sea-level (less than 100 ft.) In the heart of the North American continent we find Winnipeg (at a height of about 750 ft.) with a mean January temperature of $-4°$ F. and a mean July temperature of 66° F. ; an approximate reduction to sea-level of Winnipeg's temperatures gives $-1°$ F. for January and 69° F. for July. Yet these three stations are all in approximately the same latitude (Victoria, 49° N. ; Winnipeg, 50° N. ; Halifax 45° N.). Notice that the greatest difference is experienced in *winter*. The reason for the difference between the January temperatures of Victoria and Halifax (one on the western seaboard and the other on the eastern) will appear later (see p. 145).

The following figures for European stations illustrate the same features. The places selected are all in latitude 52° N. (very nearly) and at heights above sea-level varying from 18 ft. to 390 ft., so that temperature differences due to altitude are almost negligible.

Valencia (S.W. Ireland)—January 44° F.   July 59° F.

London	-	-	-	,,	39	,,	63
Berlin	-	-	-	,,	31	,,	66
Warsaw	-	•	ʊ	,,	26	,,	66
Saratov	-	-	-	,,	12	,,	72

Over large areas in the heart of Asia the winter air temperatures drop well below zero on the Fahrenheit scale ; for example, Tomsk (January, $-3°$F.), Irkutsk (January, $-6°$ F.), Yakutsk (January, $-46°$ F.), Verkhoyansk (January, $-58°$ F., the earth's lowest recorded mean).

In summer, air that comes off a land mass will be " warm " ; air that comes off the ocean will be " cool ". In winter, air that comes off a land mass will be " cool " (and frequently cold), whereas air that comes off the ocean will be " warm ". We shall return to this point when discussing the influence of prevailing winds (p. 144).

In a similar manner, but to a lesser degree, large lakes (for example, the Great Lakes of North America) exert an influence on temperature conditions. Thus in the Lake Peninsula (between Huron, Erie, and Ontario), and elsewhere near the Great Lakes, " fruit belts " are possible because the prevailing winds, blowing off the large bodies of water, minimise the risks of late frosts.

(d) **Rainfall and Cloud.** When the sun shines from a clear sky, land surfaces in particular are rapidly heated. The air above them also soon becomes heated (by the earth radiator). Over the hot deserts, for example, shade temperatures of 120° F. are not uncommon during the day when the sun is nearly overhead. But the absence of a cloud cover enables the heat from the earth radiator to escape from the lower layers of the atmosphere very rapidly. At night the temperature of the land surface falls considerably ; so does that of the air in the lower atmosphere. A large **diurnal range** of temperature is thus a characteristic of " hot " desert climates.

In Britain a cloudless summer's day gives rise to a decidedly warm land surface (for example, the dry sands by the sea) and high air temperatures (frequently exceeding 80° F. in the shade). Should a cloudless night follow, the ground may become quite " cold ", air temperatures may become quite " chilly ", and there would probably be a heavy fall of dew. In winter a cloudless day, though sunny, is usually " fresh " rather than " warm " ; a cloudless night is brilliantly starry and " keen ", and generally frosty.

The **Monsoon Lands** provide some interesting data concerning the influence of dense cloud and heavy rainfall on temperature. Study the following figures for Bombay.

	April	May	June	July	Aug.	Sep.	Oct.	Nov.	
Mean temp.	82	85	82	80	79	79	81	79	°F.
Mean rain	0	0·7	20	26	16	11	2	0·4	in.

Monsoon rainfall is restricted to the summer months when, in the case of places such as Bombay, it is very heavy. Notice how the heavy rains of June (when the monsoon " breaks ") are accompanied by a lowering of the mean monthly temperature. The rainfall for July is even greater ; the temperature continues to fall. This is due partly to the cloud cover and partly to the greatly increased evaporation. When the " wet season " ends, in October, the temperature rises again ; it is hotter in October than in any of the months of July, August, or September ; it is as hot in November as it is in August. Usually, in the northern hemisphere, we expect July or August to be the hottest month.

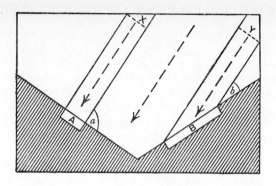

(*e*) **Aspect.** Slopes that face the sun (that is, south-facing slopes in the northern hemisphere) are generally warmer than slopes that face away from the sun. The diagram shows how this comes about. Two equal beams, containing equal amounts of solar energy, are incident on the two surfaces *A* and *B* at very different angles *a* and *b*. Where the angle of incidence is greater (*a*) the concentration of solar energy per unit area will clearly be greater also (*A*) (cf. p. 16). But another factor must also be considered, namely, shelter. South-facing slopes (northern hemisphere) are sheltered from cold northerly winds; north-facing slopes are exposed to them.

In the Alps, for example, aspect is of great importance in many of the valleys. To a marked extent it controls the distribution of settlements and the whole economy of agriculture.

(*f*) **Ocean Currents.** Ocean currents are important in that they produce local differences in the temperature of off-shore ocean surface water (p. 111 *et seq.*). They therefore modify the influence of the ocean. How this influence is extended to the land areas will now be seen.

(*g*) **Prevailing Winds.** Consider first the case of the British Isles. The prevailing winds are westerly or south-westerly, that is, from the Atlantic Ocean. In summer, therefore, they tend to be cool winds; in winter, warm. As a result, air temperatures over Britain seldom cause distress, either in summer or winter. (Mean July temperatures, reduced to sea-level, range from 64° F. in the London area to 55° F. in the north of Scotland; mean January temperatures range from 44° F. in south-west Ireland to 38° F. in eastern England.) The oceanic (or maritime) influence is particularly valuable in winter, when Britain is 20°–30° F. warmer than the average for its latitude; it is said to have a "*positive anomaly of temperature*" of 20°–30° F. The warmth of the ocean, and the additional warmth of the North Atlantic Drift, is brought to the land area by the prevailing winds.

But experience also shows that the British Isles do not always have westerly winds; sometimes winds blow from the European mainland,

and occasionally for considerable spells. In winter such easterly and north-easterly winds are " cold ", for they are coming from a cold land mass, and they bring about a marked fall in temperature. These influences give a characteristic course to British isotherms in winter. When the westerly winds blow they produce a greater warming effect in the west than in the east ; when easterly winds blow they chill the east more than the west. Both influences, therefore, tend to make the west warmer than the east, that is, the isotherms run generally north-south. The ocean is, in effect, Britain's winter source of warmth ; the prevailing **Westerlies** are the " transporting agent ". In summer, when the direct influence of the sun is so much greater, the isotherms take a generally east-west direction, the south being warmer than the north because of the effects of latitude (see p. 16).

Off the eastern shores of North America, in the same latitude as the British Isles, we find the *cold* Labrador Current and very different temperature conditions. In winter the winds generally experienced in this region are the Westerlies ; that is, they blow from the *cold* land mass of North America. The temperatures along this coast are therefore low (Nain, in latitude 56° N., has a January mean of −7° F. ; cf. Christiansund (Norway), in latitude 63° N., with a January mean of 35° F. Even Halifax (Nova Scotia), in latitude 45° N., has a January mean as low as 23° F., while Boston, in latitude 42° N., has one of only 28° F.*)*. In summer, on the other hand, the winds are largely on-shore, that is, blowing from the *cool* ocean, and over the *cold* current. The current thus intensifies the cooling effect of the ocean at this season (Nain has a July mean of only 46° F., whereas Christiansund has one of 56° F.).

Here, then, we find a substantial difference between the winter temperatures of the western and eastern margins of land masses in temperate latitudes, due to the influence of the ocean and the prevailing winds (cf. Victoria (Vancouver Island) and Halifax, as mentioned on p. 142. In eastern Asia this winter cold is even more pronounced : Vladivostok, in latitude 43° N., has a January mean of only 7° F., but an August mean of 69° F.

Now turn to the southern part of the North American Continent. Off its eastern shores is the Gulf Stream, a distinctly *warm* current, at least as far north as Cape Hatteras ; off its western shores is the *cold* California Current. In summer the winds over the eastern coastlands tend to be on-shore, that is, they blow from the ocean over the Gulf Stream before reaching the land. These winds are cooling winds, but the current diminishes the cooling influence of the ocean. In winter, on the other hand, the winds tend to be off-shore ; clearly neither the ocean nor the current can then have much influence on coastal temperatures. The latitude of this region is such, however, that winter temperatures remain fairly high : Charleston, January 50° F., July 81° F.

Off the western coast we find very different conditions. During the summer the winds tend to be on-shore ; that is, blowing from the ocean, over the *cold* California Current. Summer temperatures along the coast are therefore low, partly due to the cooler air flowing in, and partly due to the formation of fog which decreases insolation ; San Francisco has a July mean of only 57° F. (cf. Lisbon, in nearly the same latitude, 70° F.) Inland, the cooling effect diminishes rapidly ; Sacramento has a July mean of 73° F. By September the prevailing wind is no longer on-shore (that is, the ocean and the cold current can have little effect), and the latitude is such that the sun is still capable of considerable heating effect. Thus the September mean at San Francisco is 60° F., that is, higher than the July and August means. Even in November the mean is no lower than 56° F., which is the same figure as that recorded at Lisbon during that month.

These examples must suffice to illustrate the general effects of prevailing winds, of oceans, and of ocean currents, on temperature conditions over the margins of the land masses.

Summary of Major Factors. Generally, *in higher latitudes*, western coastlands are warmer than eastern coastlands in winter. (For example, British Columbia is warmer than Labrador in winter ; north-west Europe is warmer than eastern Siberia.) *In the vicinity of the tropics*, on the other hand, eastern coastlands are warmer than western coastlands in summer ; for example, Rio de Janeiro, January 78° F. ; Iquique, January 71° F. ; Durban, January 77° F. ; Port Nolloth, January 60° F.

A description of the various belts of prevailing winds, with reasons for the general arrangement, will appear in a later section (pp. 165 *et seq.*). For the present we may say that winds tend to blow into the land masses in summer, and away from them in winter. This tendency helps to determine the prevailing winds for many of the coastal areas, and the prevailing winds tend to modify the temperature conditions of such areas.

Local Winds. Similar in effect, but purely local in their influence, are the land and sea breezes. During the day, especially in summer, land areas may become quite " hot ", while water areas may remain comparatively " cool ". These very different heating effects may well give rise to local differences in atmospheric pressure ; over the heated land, low pressure will tend to develop, whereas over the water the pressure will tend to remain relatively high. Air will therefore tend to flow from the high-pressure area to the low-pressure area ; that is, from the water to the land. This is the sea breeze, which is usually cool and fresh ; it is often a feature of coastal areas (and lake-side areas) during hot summer days. During the night the land cools rapidly, while the water remains relatively warm. Now the pressure over the land may become relatively high compared with that over the water. Thus air will tend to flow from the cool land to the warm sea. This is the land breeze. These alternating land and sea breezes are often confined to a comparatively narrow zone bordering the water area. Long spells of calm, fine weather are favourable to their development.

RANGE OF TEMPERATURE

The range of temperature at any place is the difference between some specified maximum temperature and the corresponding minimum. Here we shall confine our attention to the mean annual range, that is, the difference between the highest monthly mean and the lowest monthly mean.

The mean annual range of temperature at different places over the earth's surface is subject to influences very similar in nature to those already discussed in connection with temperature conditions generally.

(a) Latitude. At the equator the noon elevation of the sun is never less than $66\frac{1}{2}°$; for long periods, round about the equinoxes, it is never far from the vertical. Thus the climate is always hot (except at considerable heights), with very little difference between the monthly means, and with a tendency towards slightly higher temperatures just after the time of the overhead sun and slightly lower ones round about the solstices. The mean annual range of temperature is extraordinarily small, and there is no "summer" and "winter". (Singapore: 81° F., May; 78° F., January; range, 3° F. Para: 80° F., November; 77·0° F., February; range, 3° F. Akassa (West Africa): 80° F., April; 76° F., August; range, 4·0° F.)

In general, the mean annual range of temperature increases away from the equator, but other factors modify this simple arrangement. In temperate latitudes there is a definite summer (with high temperatures) and a definite winter (with low temperatures), with the result that there is a considerable range. In the polar regions one would normally expect the range to reach its maximum, for there is one season during which the sun never sets and one during which it never rises. The winter temperatures are very low, but the summer temperatures are not very high, partly because the elevation of the sun is never high, and partly because so much of the summer heat is spent in melting part of the permanent snow-cover.

Records for the polar regions are very incomplete, but it would appear that the mean temperature of the warmest month everywhere inside the Antarctic Circle, for example, is appreciably below 32° F. Over large areas on the Antarctic Plateau the mean temperature of the coldest month has been estimated at well below −35° F.

Although latitude clearly exerts a powerful influence on the mean

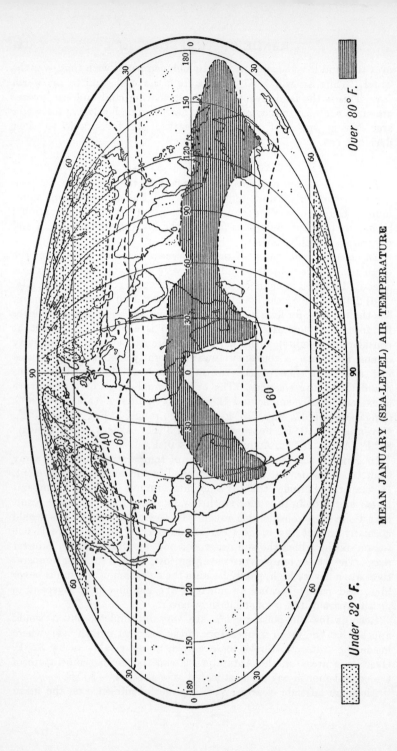

MEAN JANUARY (SEA-LEVEL) AIR TEMPERATURE

Over 80° F.

Under 32° F.

annual range of temperature, the following figures indicate that other forces are also at work.

The following are the ranges for certain selected places :

Lisbon (lat. 39° N.)	Aug. 71° F.	Jan. 50° F. ;	range	21° F.
Rome (lat. 42° N.)	July 76°	,, 45°	,,	31°
San Francisco (lat. 38° N.)	Sept. 60°	,, 49°	,,	11°
New York (lat. 41° N.)	July 75°	,, 30°	,,	45°
Omaha (lat. 41° N.)	,, 77°	,, 21°	,,	56°
Nairn (lat. 58° N.)	,, 57°	,, 37°	,,	20°
Christiansund (lat. 63° N.)	,, 56°	Feb. 34°	,,	22°
Nain (lat. 57° N.)	Aug. 47°	Jan. −7°	,,	54°
Dawson City (lat. 64° N.)	July 60°	,, −23°	,,	83°
Tomsk (lat. 57° N.)	,, 64°	,, −3°	,,	67°
Yakutsk (lat. 62° N.)	,, 66°	,, −46°	,,	112°
Verkhoyansk (lat. 67° N.)	,, 59°	,, −58°	,,	117°

(b) **Altitude.** Altitude, considered quite apart from other possible accompanying factors, also exerts an influence on the mean annual range. If the decrease in temperature, resulting from increase in height, were constant in all circumstances, altitude could clearly have no effect on the mean annual range, for all the monthly means would be lowered by the same amount. But one of the effects of altitude is to increase insolation by day and radiation by night. Reduced to sea-level, day temperatures (that is, maxima) tend to be higher, and night temperatures (that is, minima) lower, than is the case for places in corresponding positions actually at sea-level. A larger diurnal range is therefore to be expected, but this need not necessarily affect the mean temperature. (The mean of 80 and 40 is the same as the mean of 70 and 50, namely 60.)

There is a tendency, however, for the higher day temperatures to be influenced by altitude more than lower day temperatures, due to the rarity of the air and its consequent inability to retain, for long, the heat made available by the increased insolation. Further, precipitation and cloud-cover tend to increase over elevated areas, and the effects of this, assuming a fairly uniform degree of cloud-cover throughout the year, will be most noticeable during the hotter months (that is, when there is greater insolation to counteract). These factors tend to lower the mean temperature of the warmer months to a greater extent than that of the colder months. Very often, therefore, we find that altitude tends to decrease the mean annual range, but frequently to an almost negligible degree.

It is not always easy to isolate the effects of altitude from the combined effects of such other influences as *aspect in relation to local physical form, distance from the sea*, etc., but see p. 155.

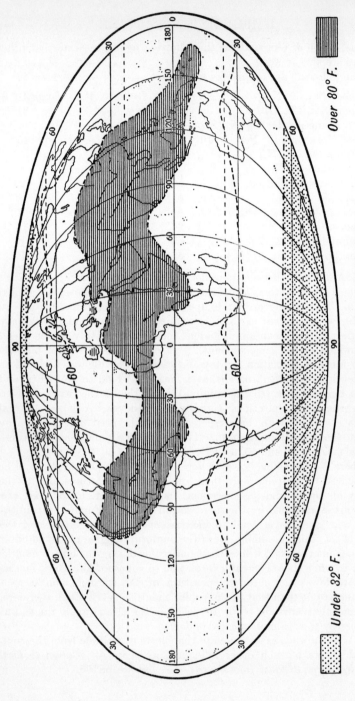

Over 80° F.

Under 32° F.

MEAN JULY (SEA-LEVEL) AIR TEMPERATURE

The following are the ranges at certain selected places.

Simla (7,200 ft.)	June	67° F.	Jan.	39° F.;	range	28° F.
Delhi (700 ft.)	,,	92°	,,	58°	,,	34°
Sao Paulo (2,700 ft.)	Feb.	69° F.	July	58° F.;	range	11° F.
Rio de Janeiro (200 ft.)	,,	78°	,,	68°	,,	10°
Quito (9,350 ft.)	Sept.	55° F.	Nov.	54·3° F.;	range	0·7°F.
Manaos (150 ft.)	Oct.	82·9°	March	80·4°	,,	2·5°
Para (30 ft.)	Nov.	79·7°	Feb.	77·0°	,,	2·7°
Pike's Peak (14,100 ft.)	July	40° F.	Jan.	2° F.;	range	38° F.
Denver (5,300 ft.)	,,	72°	,,	30°	,,	42°
St. Louis (550 ft.)	,,	79°	,,	31°	,,	48°
Nairobi (5,450 ft.)	March	65·2°F.	July	58·5° F.;	range	6·7°F.
Mombasa (50 ft.)	,,	81·8	,,	75·3	,,	6·5

(c) **Distance from the Sea.** Distance from the sea gives rise to higher summer temperatures and lower winter temperatures, that is, to an increase in the mean annual range. A climate such as that of the British Isles, which is said to be of the oceanic or maritime type, has a small annual range for its latitude; one such as that over eastern Europe, or the interior of North America, is said to be of the continental, or extreme type. Near the equator the effects of distance from the sea are often scarcely noticeable (cf. Manaos and Para). In temperate latitudes, on the other hand, the effects are clearly apparent, as the following figures will show. They refer to places which are in approximately the same latitude, and all are less than 600 ft. above sea-level.

Valencia	July	59° F.	Jan.	44° F.;	range 15° F.
London	,,	63°	,,	39°	,, 24
Berlin	,,	66°	,,	31°	,, 35
Warsaw	,,	66°	,,	26°	,, 40
Saratov	,,	72°	,,	11°	,, 61
Semipalatinsk	,,	72°	,,	3°	,, 69

Farther north the effect is even more pronounced, as the following figures show:

Christiansund	July	56° F.	Feb.	34° F.;	range 22° F.
Yakutsk	,,	66°	Jan.	−46°	,, 112°

Moreover, as maritime areas usually have greater precipitation and a more extensive cloud-cover than continental areas, they generally have a smaller diurnal range, particularly in summer.

(d) **Rainfall and Cloud.** We have already seen that dense cloud and heavy rains tend to depress the mean monthly temperatures during summer. This is partly due to the fact that much of the solar energy is taken up by the cloud-cover, and partly due to the very considerable

L

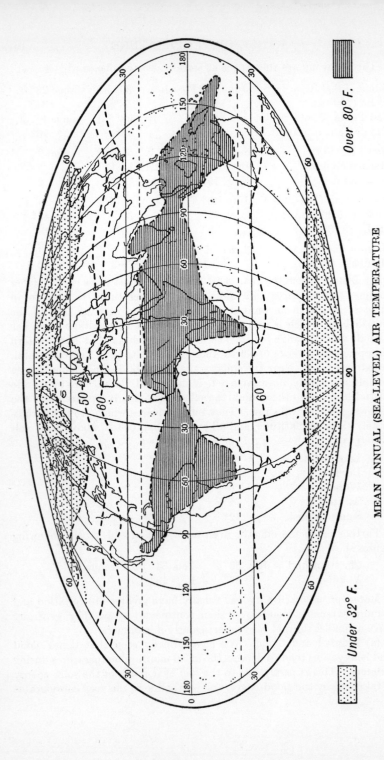

MEAN ANNUAL (SEA-LEVEL) AIR TEMPERATURE

Over 80° F.

Under 32° F.

amount of heat spent in evaporating the abundant surface moisture. But dense cloud-cover, by retarding radiation, tends to raise mean monthly temperatures during winter. In general, therefore, dense cloud-cover and heavy rainfall tend to decrease the mean annual range of temperature. The very small range experienced in the British Isles, for example, is partly due to this influence.

(e) **Aspect.** Slopes that face the sun generally experience both warmer summers and milder winters than slopes that face away from the sun. The greater summer warmth is due to the greater insolation on the former slopes ; the greater winter warmth is due to the shelter afforded. The effect on the mean annual range of temperature will depend on the relative influence of these summer and winter factors, often a purely local characteristic. Frequently, too, the influence of aspect is closely associated with that of altitude, concerning which more will be said later (p. 155).

(f) **Ocean Currents and Prevailing Winds.** A few specific examples will help to explain the general principles involved under this heading.

As a result of the cold current and the generally on-shore winds, the summer temperatures along the coast of California are appreciably lower than would otherwise be the case. The cooling influence of the current in winter is negligible, for at that season the whole tendency of ocean water is to " warm " the land ; at most, the current slightly decreases this warming effect. Thus at San Francisco the means are : September 60° F. ; January 49° F. ; range 11° F. This, it will be noticed, is a very small range for the latitude (38° N.).

In other cold-current coastal areas we find similar influences at work ; for example, Walvis Bay (lat. 23° S.) January 63° F. ; August 55° F. ; range 8° F. Port Nolloth (lat. 30° S.) January 60° F. ; August 54° F. ; range 6° F. Iquique (lat. 20° S.) February 69° F. ; July 60° F. ; range 9° F.

Cold currents chill on-shore winds and so cause much fog, an important factor in the lowering of summer temperatures in such areas, for example, San Francisco.

Summary. Generally, it may be said that the mean annual range of temperature is least in equatorial areas, small in maritime areas, particularly those on the west of continents, and large in the interior areas of land masses, particularly in the northern hemisphere, where the land masses are so extensive.

In the southern hemisphere the relatively small land masses do not give rise to very large ranges. The greatest ranges recorded in Australia are : Bourke, January 84° F. ; July 51° F. ; range 33° F. Charleville, January 83° F. ; July 51° F. ; range 32° F. Nullagine, January 90° F. ; July 59° F. ; range 31° F. William Creek, January 83° F. ;

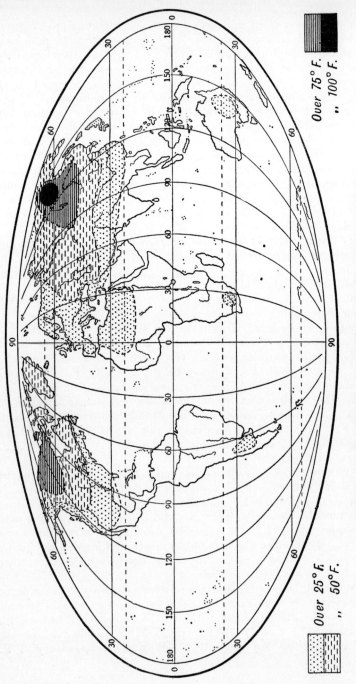

Over 75° F.
„ 100° F.

Over 25° F.
„ 50° F.

MEAN ANNUAL RANGE OF TEMPERATURE (GENERALISED)

July 52° F.; range 31° F. In South Africa the greatest ranges are found on the plateau: for example, Kimberley, January 76° F.; June 50° F.; range 26° F. Hanover, January 69° F.; July 43° F.; range 26° F. In South America the greatest ranges are found in Argentina: for example, San Juan, January 78° F.; June 47° F.; range 31° F. Rosario, January 77° F.; June 52° F.; range 25° F. Santa Cruz, January 59° F.; July 35° F.; range 24° F.

FURTHER CONSIDERATIONS OF THE EFFECTS OF ALTITUDE ON TEMPERATURE

An analysis of many careful observations shows that the rate of decrease in temperature with increase in height above sea-level, varies according to the season, being greatest in summer (that is, when insolation is greatest) and least in winter. Further, it depends, to some extent, on the aspect of the particular place.

The following figures have been arrived at for the Eastern Alps :

Fall in temperature for a rise of 300 ft.
(mean values)

	Summer	Winter	Year	
South-facing slopes	1·1	0·8	1·0	° F.
North-facing slopes	1·0	0·6	0·85	
Enclosed valleys	0·8	0·4	0·75	

These figures certainly show that summer temperatures are depressed more than winter temperatures with increase of height, resulting in smaller annual ranges at higher levels. Thus Catania, near sea-level, has a mean annual range of 29° F., while the summit of Etna, more than 10,000 ft. above sea-level, has a range of only 19° F. But the question does not end there, as the figures given earlier (p. 151 (b)) clearly suggest. There is, in fact, no simple relationship between temperature and height. Enclosed valleys and " intermont " basins, for example, tend to experience a more extreme type of climate than the plains below. Even the diurnal range is not subject to any close relationship, although it is usually greater in valleys and basins at high altitudes than at lower levels. Thus, at Geneva the mean diurnal range is 21° F., while at Chamonix, 40 miles distant and more than 2,000 ft. higher, it is 26° F. At the summit of Mont Blanc, however, only 20 miles distant from Chamonix, the mean diurnal range is only about 6° F.

Inversion of Temperature. The problem is still further complicated by a phenomenon known as inversion of temperature. Sometimes in mountain areas, particularly during prolonged periods of calm, cold, clear weather and high atmospheric pressure, cold air drains down the mountain slopes as katabatic winds (a purely gravitational control of heavier air) and collects in the valley-bottoms, which become progressively colder. In such circumstances the temperature often increases from the valley-bottom up the mountain slopes ; that is, the direction of the normal temperature gradient is reversed. This is inversion of temperature. It is commonly experienced in sheltered valleys and enclosed basins.

In some places the phenomenon is so prevalent that its effects are apparent even in the *mean* figures for the winter season. A notable example is the valley of Klagenfurt, in Carinthia (Eastern Alps), where it has been observed that the mean winter temperature is 24° F. at 1,500 ft., 25° F. at 1,800 ft., 25° F. at 4,500 ft., and 21° F. at 7,500 ft. Thus the first 300 ft. of ascent produce a *rise* of 1° F.—and this refers to the winter mean. Between 1,800 ft. and 4,500 ft. the mean shows little variation, and 3,000 ft. above the valley floor the rise of 1° F. is still evident. Higher still, a fall in temperature does occur, but 6,000 ft. above the valley floor the total fall in the mean is only 3° F. This case, however, is exceptional, and must not be taken as typical of all mountain and valley regions. Yet, inversion of temperature is a very real feature of mountain climate, and settlements avoid the valley-bottoms wherever possible. Hill-slopes, provided they are not too steep, are always preferred ; then the cold air drains past the settlements.

For the same reason much of the cultivation in such areas is subject to a similar control ; the vineyards of Switzerland, Alsace and the Moselle Valley are generally to be found on hill slopes, which have sometimes been specially terraced for the purpose ; the coffee plantations of Brazil, Colombia, etc., are similarly to be found on hill-slopes, at a considerable height above the valley-bottoms.

WATER VAPOUR

Whenever water surfaces are freely exposed to the atmosphere there is a tendency for evaporation to take place ; that is, water passes into the air in the form of vapour (gas). This vapour must not be confused with the " clouds " of minute particles of liquid water which are also present, from time to time. The so-called " steam " which forms a " cloud " round the spout of a kettle really consists of particles of *liquid* water ; it is not vapour.

Water vapour is invisible and mixes freely with the air. Under certain conditions the vapour may change back into water ; this process (the reverse of evaporation) is known as condensation. A given quantity of air cannot go on taking up water vapour indefinitely, but the limit, known as the saturation point (or dew point), depends on the temperature. The graph on p. 157 shows the mass of water vapour which a cubic metre of air at normal pressure (760 mm. of mercury) is capable of holding at various temperatures ; in other words, it shows the saturation value at various temperatures.

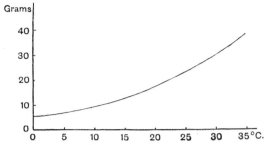

Graph to show the mass of water vapour contained in a cubic metre of saturated air at different temperatures

Study the shape of this curve ; it is most important. Now study the following figures :

Rise in temperature		Increase in mass of vapour contained in 1 cub. metre of " saturated air ".
From 0°C. to	5°C.	1·92 gm.
5	10	2·57
10	15	3·38
15	20	4·41
20	25	5·68
25	30	7·24
30	35	9·14

These figures show that, as the temperature increases, the capacity of the air for holding vapour increases, and at an increasing rate. Thus, if we increase the temperature of 1 cub. metre of air, which is saturated at 0° C., from 0° C. to 5° C., that air is capable of taking up an additional 1·92 gm. of water vapour, but if 1 cub. metre of air, saturated at 25° C., has its temperature raised from 25° C. to 30° C., it will be able to take up an additional 7·24 gm. of water vapour. (Normal pressure is assumed.)

Now consider the converse. If 1 cub. metre, saturated at 5° C. has its temperature lowered to 0° C., its capacity for holding water vapour will be reduced by 1·92 gm. ; that is, 1·92 gm. of the vapour present will condense into liquid water. But if 1 cub. metre, saturated at 30° C., has its temperature lowered from 30° C. to 25° C., its capacity for holding water vapour will be reduced by 7·24 gm. ; that is, 7·24 gm. of the vapour present will condense. This is a most important point in connection with the formation of rainfall. A slight lowering of the temperature of warm, moist, tropical air may well produce very heavy precipitation, whereas a considerable lowering of the cold, if saturated, polar air may produce only a small precipitation. Thus temperature conditions play an important part in the formation of rainfall.

Relative Humidity. The diagram on p. 157 indicates how much water vapour air is capable of holding at different temperatures between 0° C. and 35° C. (32° F. and 95° F.). The amount of vapour in the air, however, is often considerably less than the saturation value.

The amount of water vapour actually present in a given volume of air, at a given temperature, expressed as a percentage of the amount of water vapour that same air is capable of holding (that is, its saturation value), at the same temperature, is known as the **relative humidity.** When the relative humidity is very high (nearly 100 per cent.) the air is said to be "moist"; when the relative humidity is low the air is said to be "dry" (cf. p. 133). "Dry", used in this sense, does not necessarily mean that the air contains no moisture. Over parts of the Sahara Desert, for example, the mean relative humidity during summer is about 25 per cent., rising to about 50 per cent. in winter. Over the same region, the mean summer temperature is above 90° F., and the mean winter temperature rather less than 60° F. With a mean summer temperature well above 90° F., and a relative humidity of only 25 per cent., we should have no hesitation in calling the air "dry". But that same amount of water vapour would be sufficient to saturate air at 50° F. (the mean temperature for May in Britain). It is, therefore, important to understand that "relative humidity" involves, not only a ratio, but also the temperature to which that ratio refers.

FORMATION OF RAINFALL

If air is cooled sufficiently, condensation will ultimately take place, provided that the air is not absolutely dry. This is the essential feature in the formation of rainfall and other types of precipitation (snow, sleet, etc.). We shall now consider, therefore, the various means by which large masses of air are cooled to produce the rainfall which is so essential to life.

(a) **Relief (or Orographical) Rainfall.** Let us first examine the physical processes involved when moist air from the sea encounters an area of strong relief, such as a line of hills or a range of mountains.

Because there is a relief barrier, the air is forced to rise. As it rises this air is subjected to a gradually decreasing atmospheric pressure (the influence of increasing altitude), with the result that it expands. This expansion is practically **adiabatic**, that is, there is no appreciable transference of heat either into, or out of, the mass of ascending air. Consequently the temperature of the rising air falls; in other words, expansion is accompanied by cooling.

This means that the capacity of the air for holding water vapour decreases (see p. 157). But the total vapour content of the air will remain practically unchanged, except where conditions enable restricted evaporation to increase it slightly. The ratio of the total vapour content to the saturation value therefore increases; that is, the relative humidity *increases*. These processes will continue until, in due course, the relative humidity reaches 100 per cent. At this level the air will be saturated. But above this level, expansion and cooling will continue. Now, after saturation point (or dew point) has been reached, further cooling will produce condensation; that is, some of the vapour will change into liquid water.

In general, such condensation takes place on the numerous impurities in the atmosphere, the minute specks of dust, soot, etc., forming the nuclei of the tiny water droplets. (Under certain conditions, for example, in " ionised " air, condensation may take place independently of any solid nuclei.) These tiny droplets form clouds which float in the atmosphere at, and above, the saturation level.

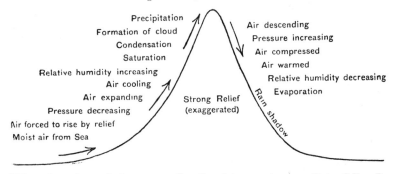

When first formed, however, the droplets are too small to fall. In time, as a result of collision and coalescence, large drops come into being. When their weight is sufficient to carry them downwards through an atmosphere which continually exerts resistance to their motion, these drops reach the land and water surfaces of the earth as rain, snow, sleet, etc. The precise form of the precipitation will depend on temperature and a number of other factors; see pp. 162 and 163.

Suppose that the air stream has reached the top of the relief barrier, and has started to descend on the other side. The pressure will steadily increase, and the air will be compressed. Again the process will be practically adiabatic, with the result that the temperature of the air will rise. Consequently the relative humidity will decrease, tending to promote evaporation. The leeward side of a relief barrier, therefore, tends to be much drier than the windward side. This drier side is said to be in a rain shadow. Thus the western slopes of the Pennines and the Plain of Lancashire, both on the windward side in respect of the prevailing moist westerlies, are generally wetter than the eastern slopes and the Vale of York, which are in a rain shadow so far as the prevailing westerlies are concerned. (How rain-shadow areas come to receive any precipitation at all will be seen later; see pp. 162, 174 *et seq.*

The various processes involved in the formation of relief rainfall are illustrated in diagrammatic form on p. 159. On the windward side the diagram is to be read from the bottom upwards; on the leeward side, from the top downwards.

(*b*) **Convectional Rainfall.** Now consider an area which is being intensely heated by the sun; for example, a tropical area, or a land mass in summer. The surface of the land becomes hot, with the result that the layer of air touching it is heated by conduction (that is, by contact). This heated air expands and, becoming less dense, rises. As it rises, more air flows in across the surface to replace it, and this, in its turn, also rises. Again we have rising air.

Broadly, the subsequent processes are very similar to those operating in the case of relief rainfall; namely, decreasing pressure, further expansion, cooling, and ultimately precipitation. Yet, largely because of the difference in the driving forces involved, differences are usually to be observed in these two types of rainfall. Relief rainfall, though frequently heavy, is usually " steady ". (The rising air is being driven up an incline.) Convectional rainfall, on the other hand, is usually more fitful, often " torrential " or " showery ", and frequently accompanied by thunderstorms. Convectional air currents ascend almost vertically, and they will clearly attain their maximum upward velocity after a period of intense and prolonged heating. For this reason convectional rainfall is most common during the afternoon or early evening; that is, after the convectional system has been working for some time. Further, because the air is ascending vertically, its rate of cooling, once the convectional system is working freely, will be more rapid than if it were moving up an incline. Such rapid cooling will give rise to " sharp showers ".

But there is another important consideration; the air, before its ascent, is relatively hot. Its capacity for holding water vapour is therefore considerable. If, then, the air is also moist, we may expect torrential rainfall. This is frequently the case in equatorial regions (hot, moist, and rapidly ascending air). In the interior regions of land masses the air in summer may also be hot, but it is generally much drier, due to the great distance from extensive water surfaces. Over the continents, therefore, the summer convectional rainfall tends to be rather in the nature of sharp showers.

Sometimes (very infrequently and most sporadically) these same causes bring rainfall to the true deserts. Such rainfall is generally very " local ", but it may be a torrential downpour. The thunderstorms and the tendency towards torrential downpours are associated with the very unstable nature of the atmosphere, brought about by the

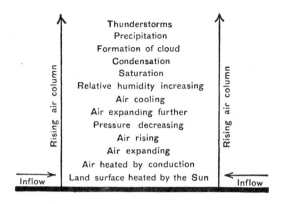

Thunderstorms
Precipitation
Formation of cloud
Condensation
Saturation
Relative humidity increasing
Air cooling
Air expanding further
Pressure decreasing
Air rising
Air expanding
Air heated by conduction
Land surface heated by the Sun

Rising air column

Rising air column

Inflow

Inflow

rapidly ascending currents. This type of rainfall is not uncommon even in such small land areas as Britain (particularly south-east England, where the heating is rather more intense) in summer. The various processes involved in the formation of convectional rainfall are illustrated above in diagrammatic form. The diagram should be read from the bottom upwards.

Thunderstorms. These are of common occurrence during periods of intense convectional heating. Clouds become charged with electricity and then discharge either to the ground or to another cloud. The source of the electric charge is thought to be the breaking up of rain-drops. It has been found that raindrops cannot exceed a diameter of about a quarter of an inch. Any tendency to grow beyond that size is counteracted by the breaking up of the drops, during which process the cloud becomes electrically charged. Further, it has been found that drops cannot fall with a velocity greater than about 24 ft. per second. Hence, if the ascending air stream has a velocity of 24 ft. per second, or more, the drops cannot reach the ground. It often happens during fitful convection that the drops fall for a certain dis-tance and then get carried up again, and this alternate falling and rising may continue for a considerable time before the drop eventually reaches the ground. While this is happening raindrops may " grow " and " break up " many times. Eventually an electrical discharge will occur. Then there may well be a temporary lull in the ascending cur-rent, when the drops will be able to reach the ground in a torrential downpour (in exceptional circumstances sometimes styled a **cloudburst**).

In the case of a thunderstorm accompanied by torrential downpours, it is necessary that the ascending air should start both hot and moist. Equatorial regions are therefore favourable to their development. Unless the heating is intense, there is not sufficient updraft ; unless the air is moist, there is not sufficient condensation of vapour to promote the repeated growth and breaking-up of the drops.

Hail. This is a form of precipitation which frequently accompanies thunderstorms, but many thunderstorms occur without hail falling. In Britain the stones are usually small, but in equatorial regions a weight of 2 lb. and a diameter of 4 in. are known. A diameter not exceeding about half an inch is the usual size, but even then hailstones are capable of doing considerable damage. The stones consist of concentric layers of ice, alternately clear and opaque, and are formed by the freezing of drops of water at considerable heights in the upper parts of towering cumulus clouds. The opaque layers are the result of rapid freezing, when air is imprisoned ; the clear layers are due to a much slower freezing, when the air is excluded.

This concentric shell arrangement suggests how hailstones are formed. The frozen drop of water (the nucleus) falls through the cloud and " collects " a coating of water, which freezes slowly as the drop is descending. Then the drop is carried up again by the convectional updraft and " collects " another coating of water, which freezes rapidly as the drop is ascending. This process may be repeated many times before the hailstone eventually reaches the ground.

(c) **Cyclonic Rainfall.** The temperate cyclone (or depression) will be discussed more fully in a later section (see p. 174). Here we shall examine the processes involved in the actual formation of the rainfall.

The cyclone is a moving low-pressure system, into which air flows from all directions. For our present purpose we shall confine our attention to two of these inflowing air streams—the " polar " and " tropical " air streams. The terms " polar " and " tropical " refer to direction rather than to place of origin, although in certain cases they may well refer to the place of origin with equal exactness. The polar air stream is, therefore, that stream which comes from the general direction of the cold polar regions ; the tropical air stream comes from the general direction of the warm tropics.

These two converging air streams will clearly be at different temperatures. When they meet in the cyclone, the warm tropical air will tend to rise over the cold polar air. This, in effect, is exactly what does happen. The cold polar air remains close to the ground, presenting an inclined upper surface (somewhat like a wedge) to the warm tropical air, which then flows up the incline. Once again, therefore, an ascending air current is set in motion. The relatively warm (and often, as in the case of Britain, moist) tropical air stream ascends into regions of steadily decreasing atmospheric pressure, with the result that it expands and cools, and eventually gives rise to condensation and precipitation.

Such precipitation, it will be noticed, depends *only* on cyclonic activity ; it will be independent of the relief of the land, and of temperature conditions, except in so far as these and other factors may help to determine that activity. Areas that receive little or no relief rainfall may yet receive adequate cyclonic rainfall. Associated with the cyclone, however, there may be a certain amount of relief rainfall, for some of the inflowing air streams may encounter relief barriers. In general, cyclonic rainfall is steady, and may persist for a whole day, or even longer.

OTHER FORMS OF PRECIPITATION

Snow. When water vapour condenses at a temperature below 32° F. snow is formed. In its initial stage this takes the form of minute ice crystals. These gradually coalesce into large flakes, which may " grow " to be as much as an inch across. If the flakes are to reach the ground, the temperature of the air, down to surface-level, should be below, or only a very little above, freezing-point. Mountains which face prevailing moist winds are favourable to heavy snowfalls, for there, especially in the temperate latitudes (for example, British Columbia), are found, during part of the year at least, both abundant condensation and the necessary cold air.

Dew. When water vapour condenses on relatively cold surfaces which are, however, at a temperature above freezing-point, dew is formed. Rapid radiation from a surface during the night may so lower its temperature as to facilitate this process. The layer of air touching the surface is chilled, and condensation occurs. Warm, sunny days, with moist air, followed by clear, cool, cloudless nights, are favourable to the formation of dew. On occasions dew may give rise to an appreciable precipitation which is invaluable for plant growth.

Hoar Frost. When atmospheric vapour condenses, with both the air and the earth's surface at a temperature below freezing-point, hoar frost results. When the condensation takes place on trees, wires, etc., it is usually called **rime**. The vapour is deposited as ice particles. Although the temperature of the ground, and that of the layer of air touching it, must be below freezing-point, hoar frost has been known to form when the temperature of the air only 4 ft. from the ground has been above 32° F.

Glazed Frost. When there has been a considerable period with generally low temperatures and very keen frosts, the ground temperature may fall well below 32° F., and the air may be thoroughly chilled. If, now, warm moist air flows into the area, light rainfall may result. The raindrops will immediately freeze on reaching the frozen ground, to form " glazed frost ". The layer of ice may, in exceptional circumstances, exceed a quarter of an inch in thickness.

Fog. When a mass of air cools (without rising) as a result of rapid radiation by night, a mist develops, which gradually thickens into a fog. The same phenomenon is observed when a moist air current crosses a cold ocean current (for example, at the Golden Gate, San

Francisco), and when a mass of warm moist air mixes with a mass of cold air. In some respects fog resembles the rain clouds, but the latter are formed in ascending air currents; fog remains on the surface, and is not associated with ascending air.

On land, fog often forms during periods of cold, clear, calm weather. The air is chilled by contact with the ground and after saturation point (or dew point) has been reached the condensation appears as fog. On calm evenings the process can often be seen. First a thin white mist forms, which rolls downhill to settle in valleys and low-lying areas. Gradually the mist thickens into a fog. During winter the sun may be unable to disperse it during the day. Then, night after night, it becomes thicker and thicker, a definite menace to practically all forms of transport. In the vicinity of large towns, fogs may become notorious (for example, the " London Fog "). This is due to the large amount of smoke, etc., which mixes with the water particles. Such fogs may be positively harmful to health, partly because they cut off practically the whole of the sun's radiation (and particularly the ultra-violet rays), and partly because of the injurious impurities (products of combustion such as sulphur oxides, etc.) that are trapped in the lower layers of the atmosphere. The reduction during recent years in the amount of smoke emitted in the London area, due to increasing use of electricity and gas, has had a noteworthy effect in reducing the severity of the " London Fog ".

ATMOSPHERIC PRESSURE AND AIR MOVEMENT

The distribution of pressure over the earth's surface is a most important factor of climate, in that it controls the winds. We shall examine this distribution, and the underlying causes, later (see p. 165). Here we shall merely note that there are regions over which the pressure tends to be rather above the average, and other regions over which it tends to be rather below. It must be stressed, however, that *these differences are sea-level differences*; that is, altitude has been allowed for (or, the pressures have been reduced to their sea-level values). When pressure differences exist (or, when there is a barometric gradient) air flows from the region of higher pressure to the region of lower. But, because of the earth's rotation, the air does not flow along the direction of steepest gradient.

Ferrel's Law. All bodies moving over the earth's surface under natural laws are deflected, to the right *in the northern hemisphere*, and to the left *in the southern hemisphere*. This is of particular importance in relation to the movement of air. To a lesser degree the same influence is noticeable in the movement of ocean currents.

It will be noticed that the direction of the wind is oblique to the isobars. The amount of deflection depends on a number of factors, but,

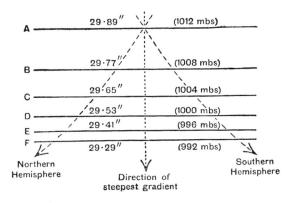

A ———————— 29·89" ╲╵╱ (1012 mbs) ————————

B ———————— 29·77" (1008 mbs) ————————

C ———————— 29·65" (1004 mbs) ————————

D ———————— 29·53" (1000 mbs) ————————

E ———————— 29·41" (996 mbs) ————————

F ———————— 29·29" (992 mbs) ————————

Northern
Hemisphere

Direction of
steepest gradient

Southern
Hemisphere

in general, it is least at the equator and greatest at the poles. Surface friction, however, is also an important factor, decreasing both the velocity and the angular deflection. (Mountains and heavily forested areas offer considerable friction, but the expansive oceans offer very little.) Altitude also plays an important part; at a height of 2,000–3,000 ft., in the latitude of Britain, the direction of the wind is almost parallel to the isobars, that is, the deflection is very pronounced, much more so than at ground-level.

Distribution of Pressure and Accompanying Wind Systems. The major wind systems exert a direct control on the climates of most regions; the wind systems are themselves controlled by the great pressure systems. In a sense, the winds, by transporting large masses of air from one part to another, tend to establish a pressure equilibrium over the earth's surface, but other forces operate to set up inequalities in the pressure distribution, and so the winds never succeed in establishing, for long, anything approaching pressure equilibrium. It should be observed, however, that the pressure differences over various parts of the earth's surface (that is, sea-level values) seldom exceed one inch of mercury—the difference due to an ascent of 1,000 ft. from sea-level; they are frequently much less.

The general arrangement of pressure distribution and winds, averaged throughout the year and approximating to the conditions prevailing at the equinoxes, for an " ideal water globe ", that is, the probable distribution if the earth were completely covered by water, is illustrated in the diagram on p. 166. The actual arrangement will be examined afterwards (see p. 170).

Taking an average through the year, we find that there is a heat belt along the equator, and covering some ten degrees of latitude (approximately 5° N. to 5° S.). Due to the intense heating within this belt the air expands and rises (so producing convectional rainfall). This, then, is a belt of generally ascending air and *low* pressure; it

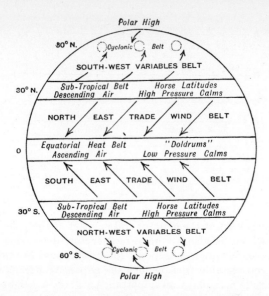

The Planetary Pressure and Wind Systems for an ideal water globe.

is a belt of calms, and is frequently referred to as the **Doldrums**; in the days of sail, ships were often becalmed here for considerable periods.

When the ascending air approaches the upper layers of the troposphere (that is, above a height of about 3 miles) the updraft practically ceases, and the air flows away towards the poles, but, due to the earth's rotation, is deflected. When this **equatorial** air starts on its poleward journey, it is travelling through space at the rate of rather more than 1,000 miles an hour (considering only the earth's rotation). But in higher latitudes the atmosphere at a corresponding altitude is travelling through space with a smaller velocity (for example, in latitude 60° N. or S., it will be half that at the equator). The result is that, as it moves into higher latitudes, this equatorial air becomes more and more deflected to the east (*right :* northern hemisphere; *left :* southern hemisphere).

In effect, we may regard this air, as it moves into the higher latitudes, as " gaining " on the air originally in that latitude. In time, the air ceases to move towards the poles, and becomes two separate gyrating rings. Centrifugal force, developed in these rotating masses, tends to move them back towards the equator (that is, to a zone where the speed of rotation of the earth is more nearly equal to the speed of rotation of the gyrating masses). This leads to a sort of piling up of the upper air (perhaps, more accurately, a compression of the upper air) in about latitudes 30° N. and S.   In these latitudes, therefore, descending air currents are set up and the pressure at sea-level is " high ".

From this sub-tropical high-pressure belt, surface currents flow outwards in both directions, towards the equator and towards the poles. The currents which flow towards the equator are called the **Trade Winds** (N.E. Trades in the northern hemisphere and S.E. Trades in the southern hemisphere).   Here, again, the deflection due to the earth's rotation is clearly shown.   The Trade Winds are relatively shallow systems, extending to no more than 1–1½ miles above sea-level.

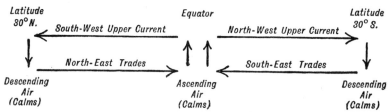

We thus have a complete convection current set up.   It must be remembered, however, that the vertical scale in the diagram is greatly exaggerated.   From the equator to latitude 30° N. or S. the horizontal distance is more than 2,000 miles ; the extent of vertical displacement is a few miles only.

In about latitudes 60° N. and S. there are two further low-pressure belts, which differ markedly, however, from the " equatorial low " These temperate lows are due to the passage of cyclones or depressions. Over the course of a whole year the average pressure in these belts is low, but they are effective as low-pressure areas only when cyclones are passing.   Because these low-pressure belts are " broken ", and because the cyclones travel (in a generally west-east direction) round the globe, the winds which blow into them are *variable* (the variable **westerlies**, with prevailing directions, from the *south-west* in the northern hemisphere, and from the *north-west* in the southern hemisphere).   The variables (or westerlies) are thus very different from the steady Trades (or " track " winds).

In the polar regions, pressure tends to be rather high on account of the persistently low temperatures.   From the polar regions, therefore, air tends to flow into the cyclonic belt (from the *north-east* in the northern hemisphere ; from the *south-east* in the southern hemisphere).

Swing (or Migration) of the Pressure- and Wind-Belts.   The diagram on p. 166 shows the mean positions of the pressure- and wind-belts taken over a whole year ; it also shows the actual positions (ideal, of course) at the equinoxes.

Now consider the conditions prevailing during the Northern Summer (at the northern summer solstice, for example).   The noon **sun**

M

is overhead at the Tropic of Cancer. The equatorial heat-belt ("following" the sun) therefore swings to the north, always lagging behind the overhead sun. Thus, although the overhead sun, in effect, swings through an angle of $23\frac{1}{2}°$ between the equinox and the solstice, the equatorial heat-belt swings only about 5° from its mean position. This northward migration of the equatorial heat-belt is accompanied by a similar migration of the sub-tropical Horse Latitudes belts. The migration of these pressure-belts must clearly affect the wind-belts as well. The cyclonic belt, too, is subject to a certain amount of migration, but in this case the movement is less regular.

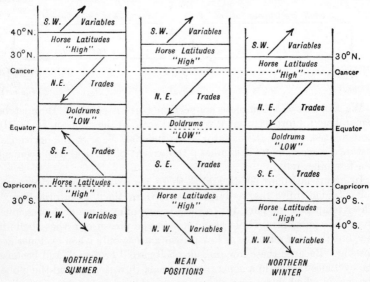

The swing of the Pressure- and Wind-Belts (simplified)

In the Southern Summer a similar migration takes place to the south, for then the noon sun is overhead at the Tropic of Capricorn. Thus, between the two extreme positions (northern summer and northern winter) the equatorial heat-belt swings rather more than 10°, and the Horse Latitudes swing with it, to approximately the same extent. (N.B. The overhead sun "swings" 47° between its extreme positions.)

The seasonal migration of the tropical and sub-tropical belts is indicated in the accompanying diagram. Here, again, for the time being, an "ideal water globe" is assumed. Further, for simplicity, the high- and low-pressure belts have been kept fairly narrow (about 10° of latitude); in actual fact they are liable to spread considerably more than this. This opens up another debatable question. In the diagram the different belts are indicated by clear-cut outlines; in reality, of course, there is a gradual transition from high pressure to low. Yet some sort of outline is obviously necessary to indicate the position and extent of the different belts when they are plotted on a map ; hence the outline drawn will depend on our particular interpretation of " high pressure " and " low pressure ".

In the mean position we find the Equatorial Heat Belt (the Doldrums) " balanced " on the equator ; in June-July (Northern Summer) it moves north of the equator ; in December-January (Southern Summer) it moves south of the equator. Thus a narrow belt along the equator is in the Doldrums all the year round, but away from this belt are two other belts, one north and one south, which experience Summer Doldrums and Winter Trades. (This most important consequence of the swing of the pressure-belts will be referred to again ; see p. 197.)

Farther away from the equator, we move into a belt which experiences the Trade Winds at all seasons; then, near the Tropic of Cancer (and Capricorn), into another which experiences well-developed Summer Trades but Winter Horse Latitude Calms. In the Horse Latitudes Belt the air is not always calm, but such winds as do develop are usually very light ; away from the centre of the belt towards the equator, there is a tendency for light Trades to blow ; away from the centre, towards the poles, the tendency is for light and variable westerlies to develop.

Next we come to a belt which experiences the westerly variables in winter and the Horse Latitude Calms (or the Trades) in summer. (Here, again, is a most important consequence of the swing of the pressure-belts, to which reference will be made later ; see p. 209.) On the poleward side of this belt (that is, polewards of about latitude 40° N. and S.) we move into a belt which is under the influence of the westerly variables all the year round.

Actual Distribution of Pressure. So far only the probable conditions of pressure and winds which would result over an " ideal water globe " have been considered. The actual conditions which exist over a globe consisting partly of water and partly of land will now be discussed.

The diagram overleaf shows, in a generalised way, the distribution of pressure, and the resulting winds, over a land mass and its surrounding ocean. The land mass has been represented triangular in shape to conform more nearly to the actual land masses of the earth.

Several well-developed features of the actual distribution of pressure over a continent and its surrounding oceans stand out prominently. In the northern hemisphere, in January (northern winter), a region of high pressure is found over the northern part of the continent, due to the intense cold. This Continental High over the land mass merges into the Horse Latitudes High over the oceans. Cyclonic activity at

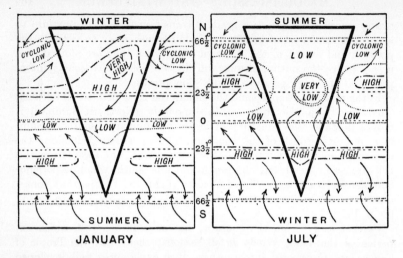

this season is very restricted over the continent, but is very marked over the oceans. The Doldrums Low shows an appreciable southward extension over the continent. The Horse Latitudes High of the southern hemisphere is broken over the continent, for it is summer and the land is hot. In the northern hemisphere, in July (northern summer), a region of low pressure is found over the continent, due to the high temperatures prevailing over the land. This Continental Low merges with the Doldrums Low (now slightly north of the equator), so that the Horse Latitudes High is confined to the oceans. (The effects of extreme continentality, as illustrated in the extensive northern part of the continent, should be carefully compared with the very much smaller continental tendencies found in the southern part of the continent, where the land mass is tapering rapidly.) The Horse Latitudes High of the southern hemisphere now appears as an unbroken belt across both land and water, but somewhat broader over the land. The cyclonic belt of the southern hemisphere shows but little seasonal variation, for the influence of land is here at a minimum.

Due to the swing of the Equatorial Heat Belt (Doldrums) it often happens that winds cross the equator, with the result that they are deflected through practically a right angle ; N–S winds to the *left*, and S–N winds to the *right*.

Monsoon Type of Climate. This type of climate is a direct result of the alternating Continental High (winter) and Continental Low (summer). It is seen at its greatest development in south-east Asia, but monsoonal tendencies are found, in greater or lesser degree, in northern Australia, south-eastern United States of America, and parts of tropical East and West Africa.

The distinctive feature of monsoonal climate is the seasonal reversal of the wind. In summer, the winds blow into the Continental Low; in winter, they blow out from the Continental High. In summer, moist winds blow off the oceans; in winter, dry winds blow off the continents. Summer is therefore a rainy season; winter a dry season.

Since the monsoon type of climate reaches its greatest development in south-east Asia, it is to this region that we should naturally turn to examine the conditioning influences. Here there is not only a vast continent, with a considerable area in tropical and sub-tropical latitudes, but also extensive and lofty plateaux. The effect of all this is to accentuate the difference between the Summer Low and the Winter High. Further, the generally east-west coastline exposes the continent to the greatest possible expanse of equatorial and tropical water.

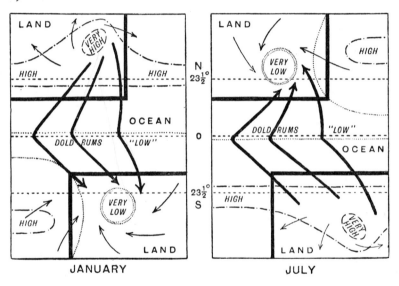

In the diagram two land masses, one north of the equator and the other south, are represented, separated by a broad expanse of tropical ocean. This somewhat ideal arrangement bears some resemblance to the actual conditions found in south-east Asia and northern Australia.

In January an intense high-pressure system develops over the northern continent (winter), and an intense low-pressure system develops over the southern continent (summer). The Continental High is higher than the Horse Latitudes High; the Continental Low is lower than the Doldrums Low. Hence there is a practically continuous pressure gradient from the Continental High over the northern land mass to the Continental Low over the southern land mass; and air, flowing out from the northern continent, tends to cross the equator and flow into the southern continent.

In July the Continental High is over the southern land mass, while the Continental Low is over the northern area. There is now a practically continuous pressure gradient operating from the southern High to the northern Low (that is, in the reverse direction from that of January). Air therefore tends to flow out from the southern continent, across the equator, and into the northern land mass.

The arrows in the diagram indicate the main air streams (very much generalised). In January the winds north of the equator are really "reinforced" North-East Trades, their local direction being modified by their position with reference to the controlling pressure systems. In general, winds will blow out from the northern High in a clockwise direction; and into the southern Low also in a clockwise direction. These winds cross the equator to become generally north-west—the North-West Monsoon of the southern continent. (South of the equator, therefore, the usual South-East Trades have been replaced by north-west winds.) In July the winds south of the equator are really "reinforced" South-East Trades, again, their local direction being modified by their position with reference to the controlling pressure systems. The winds blowing out from the southern High will be generally anti-clockwise in direction; those blowing into the northern Low will also be anti-clockwise. These winds cross the equator to become generally south-west—the South-West Monsoon of the northern continent. (North of the equator, therefore, the usual North-East Trades have been replaced by south-west winds.)

It will now be apparent that the two separate continents, and the intervening expanse of ocean, are "linked" by a somewhat complicated system of pressure distribution. This interdependence is of fundamental importance in the true monsoon type of climate. The inflowing air stream must first cross a wide expanse of tropical ocean, with the result that the winds, by the time they reach the land mass, are both hot and very moist. When these winds are cooled (as, for example, when they rise to cross regions of strong relief) very heavy rainfall usually occurs. In the true monsoon regions such rainfall takes place only during the summer months; in winter, the winds blow off the land and are therefore dry. Thus Bombay has a mean annual rainfall of almost 80 in., of which 75 in. fall during the four months June–September. Hong Kong, with a mean annual rainfall of 80 in., receives more than 60 in. during the five months May–September. Cherrapunji receives 400 in. of its total of 428 in. during the six months April–September.

Some of the characteristics peculiar to the various Monsoon Lands will be examined later (see p. 200).

CHARACTERISTIC FEATURES OF THE MAJOR PRESSURE AND WIND BELTS

(a) **The Equatorial Belt.** Here the air is always hot (the mean for each month is about 80° F. at sea-level and the diurnal range is about 10–15° F.), and usually moist (the relative humidity for places near the ocean is almost invariably more than 80 per cent. all the year round). Over most of the belt convectional currents rise, with the formation of heavy rainfall, which shows well-marked maxima round about the equinoxes (usually just after the time of the overhead sun). The region is often one of calms, and such winds as blow are usually very sluggish. In coastal areas, however, the " sea-breeze " assumes local importance. Occasionally, too, violent tornadoes or thunder-squalls relieve the monotony for a very brief spell. Europeans find conditions there very enervating. In general we may consider the belt as extending between the parallels 5° N. and 5° S.

(b) **The Trade Wind Belt.** Here the air temperatures, as we move away from the equator, become rather hotter in summer and rather cooler in winter, with a lower mean for the year ; there is a definite seasonal influence ; there is at least a part of the year when the white man can become " refreshed " and recover some of his flagging energy. Over the land, mean monthly temperatures during the summer may exceed 90° F., while daily maxima frequently rise above 120° F. ; the winters are pleasantly cool. In the main, these are the **Trade Wind Desert Regions.** The air is dry, the wind often fresh, and the climate is not unhealthy, provided there is adequate water.

The Trades blowing towards the equator (that is, from generally cooler latitudes to warmer), are drying winds. The **North-East Trades** blow strongly and steadily between the Tropic of Cancer and the parallel 5° N. ; nearer the equator, and when they cross the equator, they are usually light and variable. Over the oceans the Trades are the steadiest of all the winds. At St. Helena (South Atlantic), for example, the mean wind direction over the whole year shows 70 per cent. from the south-east, 20 per cent. from the south, and 7 per cent. from the east. Over the land masses the strong heating by day and the rapid cooling by night cause a marked diurnal variation in the wind strength. In coastal areas, land and sea breezes are often very pronounced.

The steadiness of the Trades is sometimes interrupted by very violent storms of wind and rain, often accompanied by thunder and lightning. These tropical storms (hurricanes, typhoons, and tropical cyclones) will be referred to again later (see p. 183).

Just outside the tropics are the **Horse Latitudes.** Here the air is generally calm and dry (descending air currents). On the edge of the belt nearer the equator, " light Trades " usually alternate with periods of calm ; such winds are normally rather variable both in strength and direction. On the edge of the belt nearer the poles, "light Westerlies " usually alternate with the periods of calm ; these are very variable in direction.

(c) **The Westerlies (or Variables) Belt.** This belt extends polewards from the Horse Latitudes, and its limits, both to north and south, are very variable. The winds within this belt are notoriously variable, both in strength and direction, but there is a tendency to a prevailing westerly direction. At Scilly (off south-west England) the mean wind direction shows about 60 per cent. with a westerly component (that is, between north and south, on the west side), and about 40 per cent. with an easterly component (that is, between north and south, on the east side). There are times when the general direction may be easterly for weeks on end.

These very variable winds are due to the nature of the controlling pressure systems. Towards the equator the belt is bounded by the Horse Latitudes High, which may either disappear from over the land (in summer) or extend into the continental high (in winter). Towards the poles the belt is bounded by Temperate Cyclone (or Depression) tracks. Thus, in the case of the British Isles, several influences help to determine the winds : (i) the North Atlantic cyclone track (often referred to as the Icelandic " Low "), (ii) the Horse Latitudes belt (which may develop into a practically detached anticyclone, or area of high pressure, often referred to as the Azores " High "), (iii) the " continental high " in winter, and (iv) the " continental low " in summer.

THE TEMPERATE CYCLONE

Attention will be confined here to the cyclones of the northern hemisphere, and particularly to those of the North Atlantic. It must be remembered, however, that they have their counterparts south of the equator.

The tracks of the major depressions usually lie near latitude 60° N., although they are subject to considerable variation ; so much so, in fact, that it is very unlikely that two cyclones ever follow identical tracks throughout their entire courses.

To understand fully the detailed structure of a cyclone it is essential that observations should extend through the whole depth of the atmosphere. Although observations near the surface of the earth have been made with great care for a very long time, observations in the upper atmosphere have been, and still are, very limited. This lack of information concerning conditions in the upper atmosphere necessarily leaves the whole question of cyclones open to considerable doubt. Nevertheless, great advances have been made in recent years, due largely to the work of two Norwegians, Vihelm Bjerknes and his son Jakob Bjerknes.

The Polar Front. During the World War of 1914–1918, Norway found herself deprived of observations of the weather for areas lying beyond her own shores. This made it extremely difficult for her to make weather forecasts for her important mercantile and fishing fleets. To overcome this handicap, in part, she established a close network of meteorological stations all over the country, and trained volunteers specially to man them. In this way a large amateur organisation came into being for the express purpose of observing and recording meteorological phenomena. One of the great advantages of a close network of stations is that air currents can be traced throughout their entire course. Important details, frequently lost in a more open network of stations, are brought to light by the closer network.

Thus it was that V. and J. Bjerknes were able, in due course, to advance their polar front theory of the cyclone.

This theory assumes that there is, near the major cyclone tracks, a tendency towards low pressure. It has already been seen that in the upper atmosphere, above the Horse Latitudes, the high-pressure belt is due to a centrifugal swirl, which is fed partly by air from equatorial latitudes and partly by air from the higher temperate latitudes. It is quite conceivable, therefore, that low pressure does, in fact, tend to develop over the higher temperate latitudes. Into this low-pressure belt air would naturally flow, both from the high-pressure belt of the Horse Latitudes and from the high-pressure belt of the polar regions. Thus two very different air streams would tend to converge on the same area. The Polar Air Stream would clearly be colder and heavier ; the Tropical Air Stream would be warmer and lighter. Further, these differences would be accentuated in winter, when the polar regions are abnormally cold. The cyclone is supposed to develop as a result of the interaction of these two different air streams. (An analogy may be found in the case of converging or parallel streams in a body of water, when " eddies " are seen to develop between the two streams. It is probable, however, that this analogy is by no means perfect ; yet it does illustrate the eddy effect.)

The distribution of pressure (at sea-level) in a typical well-developed cyclone is indicated in the diagram. The actual pressure and the pressure gradient—indicated by the closeness of the isobars—will depend on the indi-

The distribution of pressure in a cyclone (the lines are isobars : the pressure is given in millibars)

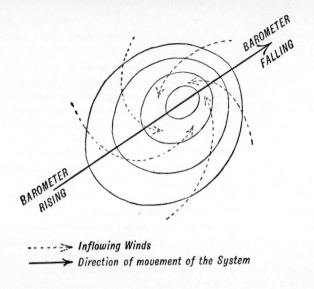

- - - - ⋙ *Inflowing Winds*
⟶ *Direction of movement of the System*

vidual cyclone, and no two cyclones are ever exactly alike. However, all cyclones have this in common—that the isobars are roughly
circular or elliptical, and that the pressure decreases towards the
middle.

Air Movements. Since the pressure is greatest around the outside of
the cyclone and least in the middle, air will clearly flow inwards, the
wind strength depending on the pressure gradient ; that is, in general,
the closer the isobars the greater the pressure gradient, and the greater
the wind strength.

The diagram shows the general direction of the winds flowing into a
cyclone (northern hemisphere), and the direction of movement of the
system.

Reference has already been made to Ferrel's Law relating to wind
deflection. In the case of the cyclone, this same principle is more
conveniently expressed in **Buys Ballot's Law**, which states that if an
observer stands with his back to the wind, in the *northern* hemisphere,
the *low-pressure* area will lie on his *left* side. In the *southern* hemisphere
it will lie on his *right* side. This means that in the northern hemisphere
the winds blow into a cyclone in a generally anti-clockwise direction ;
in the southern hemisphere the general direction is clockwise. This
would seem to suggest that the winds approach the centre spirally and
then blow round and round the centre. Further, this would suggest
the reason for the name " cyclone ". In the temperate cyclone this
circular movement around the centre does not occur, because the
inflowing air streams are not all equally effective. In fact, two air

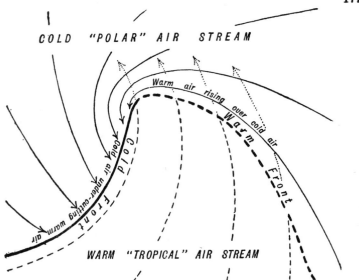

COLD "POLAR" AIR STREAM

Warm air rising over cold air

Cold air under-cutting warm air

Cold Front

Warm Front

Warm air

WARM "TROPICAL" AIR STREAM

Plan of the meeting of the "Tropical" and "Polar" air streams in a cyclone

streams dominate the entire inflow: the Tropical Air Stream and the
Polar Air Stream.

The problem is still further complicated by the movement of the
low-pressure system as a whole. In general, the entire system moves
in an easterly direction (that is, in front of the cyclone the barometer
"falls"; in the rear of the cyclone the barometer "rises"). In the
North Atlantic the major cyclones tend to remain over the warm drift
water, especially in winter, but even this is no safe rule. Careful examination of the courses actually taken by depressions over a long period
shows that generalisation on this subject is most unreliable; it may
well be impossible. The speed of movement of the whole system is
likewise variable, and extraordinarily difficult to anticipate. Sometimes cyclones may remain stationary for a few days; at other times
they may attain a speed of 60 miles an hour; the average speed is
probably between 15 and 20 miles an hour. (This speed of the *entire*
low-pressure system must not be confused with the speed of the
inflowing winds.)

The general directions taken by the two main air streams are shown
above. From this diagram it will be seen that the Tropical Air
Stream (consisting of warm, light air) meets the flank of the Polar Air
Stream (consisting of cold, heavy air). The cold air, hugging the ground,
spreads out like a wedge; the warm air moves up the gentle incline
so formed. Although there must be a certain amount of intermixture

along the plane of separation of these two streams, the Polar and
Tropical currents largely maintain their individual identities. Meanwhile, the Polar Air Stream, swinging round the back of the cyclone,
takes the Tropical Air Stream in the flank, with the result that the
warm air is lifted somewhat sharply off the ground.

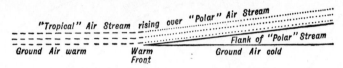

The diagram above shows the warm air rising over the cold. The inclined plane of the wedge usually makes an angle of about ½° with the
horizontal ; it is this very gradual ascent that produces the continuous
steady rain or drizzle, which is such a feature of cyclonic rainfall.

As will be seen from the diagrams (pp. 177 and 178), the ground air on
the south side of the cyclone is mainly warm (the Tropical Air Stream).
The front edge of this mass of warm air is known as the **Warm Front**.
As the cyclone moves to the east the Warm Front moves too, bringing
generally warm temperatures to the areas over which it passes. When,
however, the warm air is lifted off the ground and replaced by cold
surface air, there is a sudden drop in temperature. This occurs at the
Cold Front. It will be noticed that a sudden change in the direction of
the wind marks the passing of the Cold Front (from a generally southerly
direction to a north-westerly) ; that is, the Tropical Air Stream gives
place to the Polar Air Stream. But with the passing of the Cold
Front violent squalls may spring up ; for this reason the Cold Front
is frequently called the **squall line** ; the squalls are often called **line
squalls**. Sometimes the Cold Front overtakes the Warm Front
(an *occlusion*) ; that is, the warm air is lifted completely off the ground.

Weather Effect over Britain. In Britain, the passing of the Warm
Front is marked by generally warm and moist southerly winds. As
these winds blow into the low-pressure centre, they may give rise to a
steady warm rain (expansion and cooling). When they rise over the cold
air they will almost certainly produce rain (or snow), but the rain will
fall through the cold air (and in winter through *cold* easterly or
northerly winds) providing some of the most unpleasant weather
experienced in Britain. This steady rain may last for a whole day
or more. When the Cold Front passes there is a sudden drop in
the temperature of, possibly, 10°–15° F. The steady rains cease, to
be replaced by sharp " clearing showers " (due to the somewhat
violent lifting of the warm air). During summer, hail frequently falls
at this stage, while thunder and lightning are not uncommon.

Suppose that we are stationed just south of the line of approach of the
centre of a cyclone. The first warning is a slight and gradual falling of

the barometer.   Then the sky becomes whitish with thin fibrous clouds
(cirrus) at a high level.   These spread over the sky like a veil.   The
sun appears " watery ", and perhaps a halo is seen ; by night similar
phenomena might be observed in the case of the moon.   Then the
clouds thicken, more especially in layers at considerably lower levels
(stratus).   The sun now shines but dimly, as through ground glass ; by
night the moon might be obscured altogether.   Finally dark rain-
clouds (nimbus) appear, and then the rain.   Meanwhile, the winds
have been southerly and warm, but they have been swinging more
and more to the west (that is, veering, or moving round in a clockwise
direction).   Then comes the Cold Front with the sudden drop in
temperature, and probably with violent squalls.   The wind changes
to north-west and sharp showers follow.   Soon the sky breaks and
patches of blue appear, but these may soon be covered over again,
for the cloud formations change rapidly.   After a time the " clearing
showers " cease altogether, the sky clears, the barometer rises, and that
particular spell of cyclonic weather has passed.   Sometimes, however,
three or four cyclones follow one another in quick succession—they
are often referred to as a " family of cyclones "—in which case the
process is repeated.

Should the station lie just north of the centre, the changes in the
weather are markedly different.   The winds will change from easterly
to northerly and then to north-westerly ;   they will all be cold.   (Winds
that change in this direction are said to back, that is, they are " backing "
against the hands of the clock.)   Should any rain (or snow) reach the
ground it would be cold and most unpleasant.   There will be no squall
line, and the weather will gradually clear.

Depressions and the Synoptic Chart.   The synoptic charts on p. 180
illustrate several of the features associated with fronts in depressions.

The isobars are drawn at intervals of 4 mb., and alongside the position of each meteorological station are shown certain aspects of the
weather as actually recorded at the time of observation.   To simplify
the transmission and mapping of this information, the Beaufort Weather
Code has been devised.   The symbols most commonly used in this code
are : **sky**—b cloudless, bc partly cloudy, c cloudy, o overcast ; **visibility**—f fog, m mist, z haze, v unusually good visibility ; **precipitation**—r rain, s snow, h hail, d drizzle, p passing showers ; **thunderstorms**—l lightning, t thunder.   The intensity of certain features of the
weather can be denoted by the use of capitals and the suffix $_0$; thus r_0
light rain, r moderate rain, pr passing showers of moderate rain,
R heavy rain, PR passing showers of heavy rain, RR continuous heavy
rain.   When rain is falling at the time of observation the station is
marked by a black dot.   Wind direction is indicated by an arrow, and
wind strength by barbs on the arrow (a full-length barb represents two

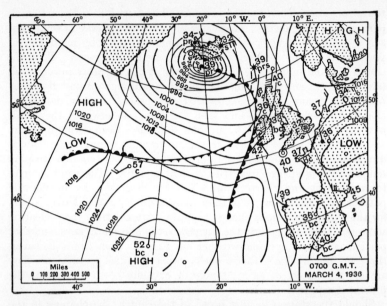

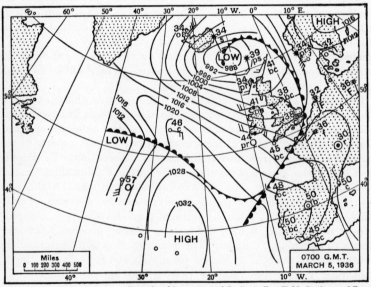

SYNOPTIC CHARTS FOR MARCH 4 AND 5, 1936, FROM
Meteorology for Aviators

units on the Beaufort wind scale, and a half-length barb one unit.) Air temperature is given by a number (° F.) placed near the station. The fronts separating the main air masses are shown on the charts by strongly marked lines ; the warm front is indicated by rounded teeth, the cold front by sharp teeth.

In the chart for March 4 the depression is shown with its centre just south of Iceland. The isobars indicate a pronounced pressure gradient in the vicinity of the centre where the winds reach moderate gale strength, but the fronts show that the depression is largely occluded and therefore well past its prime. This explains the apparent absence of a distinctly warm sector, for the tropical air stream has been under-cut and lifted completely off the ground, a fact shown by the amalga-mation of the two fronts along a line running south-west away from the centre. It is to be expected, therefore, that the decline of the cyclone has definitely set in, and that it will shortly die away. The chart for March 5 confirms this, for the occlusion has spread to the outer edge of the depression ; during the same interval the pressure at the centre has increased appreciably, and only in one small area does the wind strength exceed a moderate breeze.

But the two charts show the existence, farther west in about latitude 50° N., of a second warm front which is progressing eastwards and heralding the approach of another depression. The station marked on the south side of this front (the warm sector) is experiencing southerly winds and a temperature of 57° F., whereas the station on the north side is experiencing easterly winds and the considerably lower tempera-ture of 46° F. This warm front clearly separates two very different air masses—a polar stream and a tropical stream.

In general, the winds blow across the isobars at a relatively small angle, and near the fronts, where the change in wind direction is abrupt, the isobars are bent rather sharply, thereby destroying the symmetry.

Away to the south lies an **anticyclone** (the Azores " High ") from which a tongue or **wedge of high pressure** extends to the north-west between the two depressions. In the chart for March 4 the southern tip of another wedge extending from the north-west is also shown ; between the two wedges lies a **col** (the similarity of this arrangement to that of the col as a relief feature will be at once apparent).

The Secondary Depression. A very important feature of most major depressions is the accompanying " secondary ". This is really a shallow depression within the major low-pressure system, and its presence can be detected on synoptic charts by local bulges in the isobars. Secondary depressions often exert a great influence on the weather in their vicinity, and as they frequently develop rapidly and without **warning,** they complicate the problem of weather forecasting enormously.

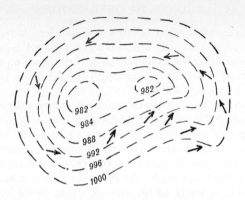

A Secondary Depression (here an elongated trough extending from the major cyclonic depression), and the resulting winds. Note the marked difference in the wind direction on the two sides of the trough. This is a very pronounced secondary depression and gales would probably accompany it

In the case of cyclones approaching the British Isles, secondary depressions frequently come into being off the western shores. The major depression may then pass to the north of Scotland, while the secondary depressions travel across Britain. Very bad weather, including **exceptionally** strong gales, is sometimes associated with these secondary depressions, although they may well appear to be relatively insignificant on the synoptic chart.

When two or more cyclones follow one another in fairly quick succession a wedge of high pressure usually separates the individual depressions. This wedge of high pressure, over which the air is generally descending, feeds the air streams that flow into the rear of the cyclone that has just passed and into the front of the cyclone that is just approaching. Over the centre of the wedge the sky is usually blue and the weather calm and fine. By day, even in winter, the sun may feel quite warm, especially in sheltered places. But the air in a wedge is already cold, due to the polar air left on the ground by the previous cyclone after the passing of the Cold Front, and sharp frosts are to be expected at night during winter and spring. Generally this is an exhilarating type of weather. " Wedges ", however, seldom remain for long ; they form rapidly in the rear of cyclones, and give place, just as rapidly, to succeeding cyclones.

On an average, 30-35 cyclones approach, or pass near, the shores of Britain during the year, winter being the season of greatest activity, and summer the season of least. Some of these cyclones may form part of a low-pressure system that extends from the Mediterranean Sea to Greenland, but usually they are considerably smaller than that (perhaps 500–1,000 miles in diameter). The number of cyclones, **no**

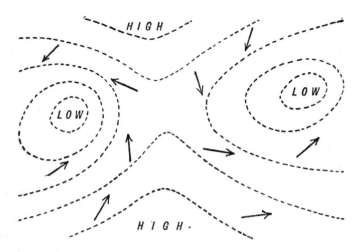

A wedge of high pressure separating two depressions, and the
accompanying winds

less than their size and the weather they produce, is liable to deviate
far from the mean.

From what has now been said, it would seem that cyclones are a very
uncertain factor in the weather of the " Westerlies Belt " (for example,
Britain). In time, after a more thorough and extensive investigation
has been carried out, we may be able to predict their behaviour with
much greater accuracy than is at present possible. The value of
accurate forecasting can scarcely be over-estimated, for it concerns
so much that is of major importance : for example, agriculture,
fishing, shipping, air transport, etc.

Heat Waves and Cold Waves. Before leaving the subject of the
temperate cyclone, brief reference must be made to a phenomenon
which is of particular importance on the continent of North America.
The Tropical and Polar air streams have primarily to do with *direction*.
Under certain conditions, however, they may equally well have reference to the *origin* of the air, which may travel enormous distances to
reach the cyclone. Between the Gulf of Mexico and Hudson Bay
there extends a vast lowland, which is everywhere less than 1,000 ft.
above sea-level. There is thus no effective climatic barrier to north-
and south-moving air streams. In winter a depression over the Gulf
of Mexico may cause cold air (the Polar Stream) to drain right down
to the Gulf Lowlands. Cold waves of this type do great damage to
fruit crops, for example, in Florida. In summer, a depression near
the Great Lakes may cause warm air (the Tropical Stream) to flow
far north, where the heated continent further intensifies the effect.
In the Great Lakes region, heat stroke is not uncommon as a result.

THE TROPICAL CYCLONE

The cyclone of the Indian Ocean, the hurricane of the West Indies and the typhoon of the South China Seas somewhat resemble the temperate cyclone (or depression) in that they are all moving low-pressure systems into which winds blow. The tropical cyclone, however, is usually much smaller in extent (perhaps 100–200 miles in diameter) and normally has much greater pressure gradients, with the result that the winds accompanying it frequently reach hurricane strength while revolving around the centre.

Light and irregular winds, a rapidly falling barometer, and sultry weather usually herald the approach of a tropical storm. In the centre of the cyclone (the " eye of the storm ") there is usually an area of calm, perhaps 20 miles in diameter, over which the pressure is very low. Around this core the winds swirl furiously (*anti-clockwise in the northern hemisphere ; clockwise in the southern*). Away from the core the violence gradually decreases. The sky becomes covered with black clouds, and a torrential downpour, often accompanied by thunder and lightning, adds to the fury. Ships at sea may experience the greatest difficulty in surviving the storm ; coastal areas may be completely devastated (for example, Miami in Florida in 1926, when more than a hundred people lost their lives and structural damage alone cost £15 millions).

THE ANTICYCLONE

The anticyclone is a high-pressure system. In general, the air over an anticyclone is descending to feed the streams that drain away from the high-pressure centre. Around the anticyclone the winds are generally *clockwise in the northern hemisphere* ; they are *anti-clockwise in the southern*.

Much of the fine weather of the British Isles is associated with these high-pressure systems. Clear skies, light winds or calms, and fine weather are typical. During summer, day temperatures may be consistently high for long periods, but rapid cooling at night often leads to a heavy precipitation of dew. During winter, cold bracing weather may result, with keen frosts at night. Seldom is there heavy rain or strong winds, but a continuous drizzle of very fine rain sometimes occurs.

Anticyclones are inclined to be sluggish in their movements. The high-pressure system may drift about slowly, or it may remain practically stationary for long periods. The pressure gradient is usually extremely gentle ; hence the tendency to light winds and calms. The diagram shows the general distribution of sea-level pressure in a typical anticyclone, although the isobars drawn here are far more regular in outline than is usual.

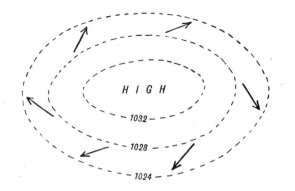

The distribution of pressure in an anticyclone and the accompanying winds. (Northern hemisphere)

SPECIAL TYPES OF LOCAL WINDS AND STORMS

Tornado. The name " tornado " has been given to two distinct
types of storm. The equatorial tornado is a violent thunder-squall of
short duration which is often accompanied by torrential downpours.
The temperate tornado occasionally accompanies the thunderstorms
of a depression (that is, in rear of the squall-line), and may be extraordinarily violent; the zone of devastation is often less than a quarter
of a mile wide. In this zone (the core of the whirl) wind speeds have
been estimated to reach 300 miles an hour.

Temperate tornadoes are probably most common in the eastern and
central parts of the United States of America, but they are not uncommon in Europe, although they are rare in Britain. They are
restricted to land areas, usually in early summer, and most astounding
effects are attributed to them (heavy objects such as vehicles, sheds and
animals have been carried through the air for distances of more than
a mile). The very low pressure in the core (inside the rapidly rotating
whirl, which often assumes the form of a visible column) may produce
explosive effects in closed buildings, which literally burst outwards.
If the column does not reach the ground little damage usually
results.

Sirocco. This is really the Tropical Air Stream that blows into a
Mediterranean depression. Along the southern shores of the Mediterranean Sea such winds, blowing off the desert, are often dry and laden
with dust. In Sicily, southern Italy, etc., the sirocco is usually warm,
moist and enervating, for it has then had time to gather moisture. (In
Egypt the sirocco is known as the khamsim, from the Arabic, meaning
" fifty ", since it blows at intervals for about fifty days, during late
March, April, and early May.) The heat waves of North America are
somewhat similar.

Mistral and Bora. These are local names for polar air streams blowing into Mediterranean depressions in winter, although they may often be characteristically katabatic. Draining from the continent, these winds are especially cold, and they may be violent ; but on account of the trend of the Alpine ranges, they are confined to special tracks. Thus in the Rhone Valley we find the mistral ; at the head of the Adriatic Sea the bora. The " cold waves " of North America are broadly similar.

Harmattan. This is really the North-East Trade Wind, blowing off the Sahara across the lands bordering the Gulf of Guinea during the dry season (that is, in winter). This abnormally dry wind intensifies the effects of the dry season ; vegetation withers ; the relative humidity may fall below 10 per cent. It is usually laden with very fine dust, which only serves to make it all the more troublesome.

Fohn and Chinook. The fohn is a hot dry wind that blows down many of the Alpine valleys during late autumn, winter, and early spring. Its peculiar characteristics are due to the fact that it has crossed the mountains. A rising current of air cools at the rate of about $1\cdot6°$ F. for every 300 ft. of ascent until condensation begins. Then latent heat is liberated and the rate of cooling falls to about $0\cdot8°$ F. for every 300 ft. In the case of a moist wind, therefore, most of the ascent is made under the reduced rate of cooling ($0\cdot8°$ F. per 300 ft.). On the other side of the mountain the descending air will be warmed at the rate of about $1\cdot6°$ F. for every 300 ft. throughout the whole of its course, and it will arrive in the valley considerably warmer than when it previously reached that same level as an ascending current.

Consider a simple example. Suppose that an air stream starts from sea-level with a temperature of 70° F., and with a relative humidity such that condensation would commence at 1,500 ft. During this first ascent of 1,500 ft. the air would cool at the approximate rate of $1\cdot6°$ F. for every 300 ft. Its temperature would therefore fall 8° F. If this air continues to rise for a further 4,500 ft., condensation takes place continuously throughout the 4,500 ft. The rate of cooling will now be at the rate of $0\cdot8°$ F. for every 300 ft., producing a fall for the 4,500 ft. of 12° F. The total fall in temperature for the ascent of 6,000 ft. is therefore 20° F. ; at the top of the mountain the temperature of the air stream will thus be 50° F. Suppose this same air stream descends 6,000 ft. to sea-level. The rise in temperature will be at the rate of $1\cdot6°$ F. for every 300 ft. The rise in temperature during the descent will therefore be 32° F., and the air stream will reach sea-level at a temperature of 82° F., that is, 12° F. warmer than when it originally began its ascent.

The chinook of the " High Plains " in North America (east of the Rockies, in Alberta, Montana, Wyoming, and Colorado) is very similar but far more widespread in its influence. The great value of the chinook is that it melts the snow much earlier than would otherwise be the case, thereby opening up the great grazing-lands ; under very favourable conditions, certain of the grazing-lands may be kept practically snow-free throughout the winter.

Blizzard. Blizzards are very severe snow-storms. In certain parts of the earth (for example, Antarctica, Siberia, Canada, etc.) the precipitation during winter is mainly in the form of dry, finely crystalline snow. When high winds accompany, or follow, such a fall, the powdery snow is swept up into a whirling mass through which it is quite impossible to see. The snow drifts readily, and is driven into the smallest chinks in doors, windows, tents, etc. Travellers who are caught in such a blizzard may lose their sense of direction completely.

In Central Asia the name **buran** is given to these driving storms, whether snow-storms or sand-storms.

Mountain and Valley Breezes. During calm, settled weather in mountain and valley country, breezes may result purely from the nature of the relief. At night a wind blows down the valleys due to the downhill drainage of air that has been chilled by the rapid radiation of heat from the higher areas. This will usually be a cold steady wind, lasting from shortly after sunset until just after sunrise. Winds of this type, which are nothing more than the gravitational control of cold air, are sometimes called **katabatic winds**.

After sunrise a period of calm generally sets in, to be followed later by gentle breezes blowing up the valley. This is the valley **breeze**, as distinct from the downhill **mountain breeze**. The valley breeze is due to the heating by day. The air, confined by the valley, cannot expand as freely as air over a plain, and the pressure gradient is disturbed to such an extent that a generally uphill movement of air results.

Land and Sea Breezes. These have already been referred to (p. 146). During the day low pressure develops over the land, because land heats up more quickly than water, and breezes blow from water to land. During the night low pressure develops over the water, because land cools down more quickly than water, and breezes blow from land to water.

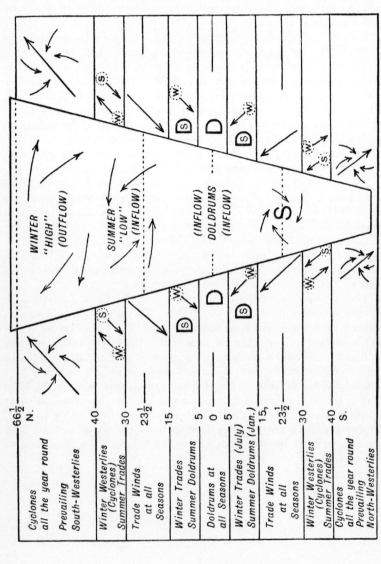

Cyclones
all the year round
Prevailing
South-Westerlies

66½
N.

40

Winter Westerlies
(Cyclones)
Summer Trades

30

23½

Trade Winds
at all
Seasons

15

Winter Trades
Summer Doldrums

5

Doldrums at
all Seasons

0

5

Winter Trades (July)
Summer Doldrums (Jan.)

Trade Winds
at all
Seasons

15,
23½

30

Winter Westerlies
(Cyclones)
Summer Trades

40

Cyclones
all the year round
Prevailing
North-Westerlies

S.

WINTER
"HIGH"
(OUTFLOW)

SUMMER
"LOW"
(INFLOW)

(INFLOW)
DOLDRUMS
(INFLOW)

PRESSURE AND WINDS OVER A LAND MASS AND THE SURROUNDING
OCEAN MARGINS (SIMPLIFIED)

CHAPTER IX

THE NATURAL REGIONS OF THE EARTH

GENERAL PRINCIPLES OF CLIMATIC DIVISION

IN this chapter we shall attempt to show how the various factors so far considered help to determine the climate of a particular area and so enable us to divide the earth into major climatic regions. In making such a division, it will be noted that the climate of an area is reflected in its natural vegetation which, through the ages, has become adapted to the conditions generally prevailing. It must be remembered, however, that one climatic type usually merges into another very gradually; between two distinctive types there is a transitional zone. In maps and diagrams different climatic areas are necessarily divided by sharp lines; unless the conditions are exceptional, such sharp divisions seldom exist in fact.

The diagram opposite represents the pressure and wind conditions over an imaginary land mass and its ocean margins. The land mass is shown tapering southwards to make it conform more nearly to the actual land masses of the earth (for example, North and South America).

The actual distribution of pressure, and the resulting winds, over a land mass and its surrounding ocean margins, depend partly on the planetary system and partly on the control exerted by the unequal heating of land and water. Over the oceans the planetary pressure and wind system is, in the main, by far the predominant control. Over large land masses, on the other hand, the influence of continental control is very evident. The continental high of winter causes a general " outflow "; the continental low of summer causes a general " inflow ". In the heart of a land mass, this alternating " high " and " low " may completely dominate the movement of air, except during periods of weakening in the pressure control (late spring or early summer, and autumn).

Even in smaller land masses the influence of continentality is usually to be seen, particularly in summer; that is, there is a tendency to " summer inflow ", although there may be no marked " winter outflow ". In maritime areas, particularly on the west coasts, the planetary system is usually the predominating influence, but continental influences may take control temporarily; thus the British Isles may experience a spell of weather in winter which owes its origin directly to an extension of the " continental high ". A tongue of high pressure extending westwards from the cold land mass of Eurasia may effectively ward off maritime influences for a period of several weeks in winter.

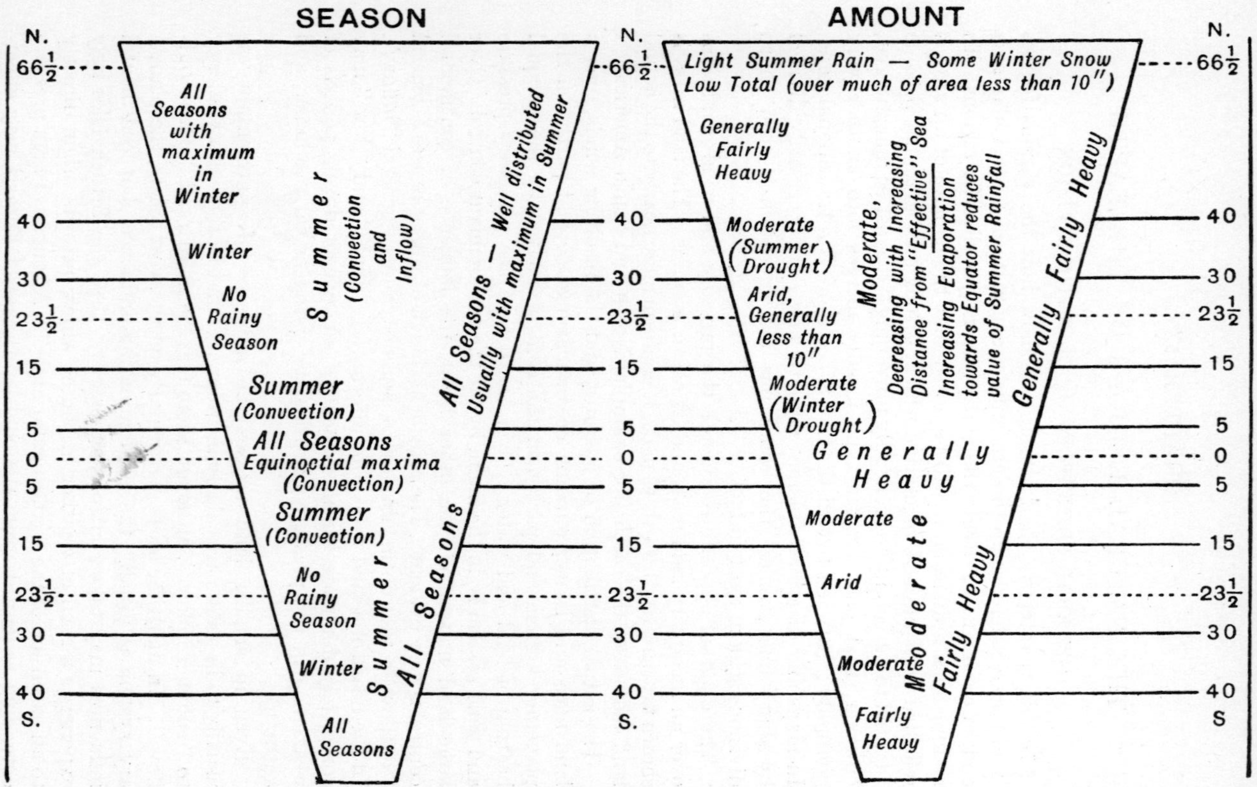

AMOUNT

N. 66½ ---- 40 30 23½ 15 5 0 5 15 23½ 30 40 S.

Light Summer Rain — Some Winter Snow
Low Total (over much of area less than 10″)

Generally Fairly Heavy

Generally Heavy

Fairly Heavy

Moderate

Fairly Heavy

Increasing Evaporation towards Equator reduces value of Summer Rainfall

Moderate, Decreasing with Increasing Distance from "Effective" Sea

Moderate (Summer Drought)

Arid, Generally less than 10″

Moderate (Winter Drought)

Moderate

Arid

Moderate

Fairly Heavy

SEASON

N. 66½ ---- 40 30 23½ 15 5 0 5 15 23½ 30 40 S.

All Seasons — Well distributed Usually with maximum in Summer

All Seasons

Summer (Convection and Inflow)

All Seasons with maximum in Winter

Winter

No Rainy Season

Summer (Convection)

All Seasons Equinoctial maxima (Convection)

Summer (Convection)

No Rainy Season

Winter

All Seasons

Summer

DISTRIBUTION OF RAINFALL OVER A LAND MASS

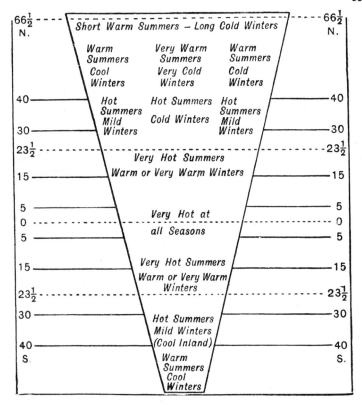

DISTRIBUTION OF TEMPERATURE OVER A LAND MASS

The distribution of temperature over the same imaginary land mass (see diagram above) also shows the influence of continentality Although average temperature tends to decrease from the equator towards the poles, latitude alone is not a sufficient guide to a division of the earth into temperature regions. The long-established classification into the " torrid ", " temperate ", and " frigid " zones is thus of very limited value, although it is still widely and popularly used. In " temperate latitudes ", particularly, it is clearly necessary to distinguish between continental and maritime areas.

The rainfall conditions over the same imaginary land mass are summarized in the diagram opposite. Over by far the greater part of the area, the summer half-year has the heavier rainfall. This is due to the fact that the intense heating of the land during summer is a most important factor in the formation of rainfall, for high temperature usually gives rise to low pressure and inflowing air, which is caught

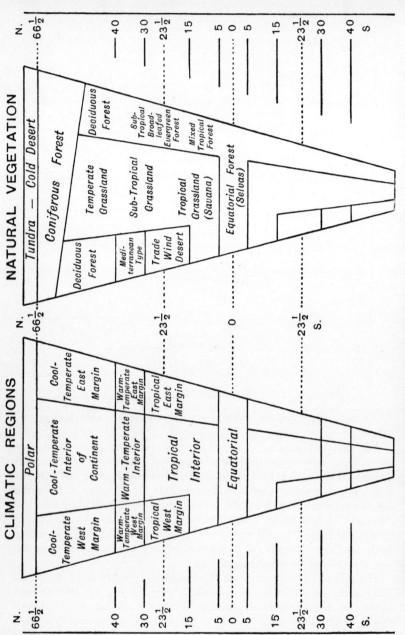

CLIMATIC REGIONS

N. 66½

Polar

Cool-Temperate
Interior
of
Continent

Cool-
Temperate
West Margin

Cool-
Temperate
East
Margin

Warm-Temperate Interior

Warm-
Temperate
West
Margin

Warm-
Temperate
East
Margin

Tropical
West
Margin

Tropical
Interior

Tropical
East
Margin

Equatorial

N. 66½
23½
0
23½
S.

40
30
23½
15
5
0
5
15
23½
30
40
S.

NATURAL VEGETATION

N. 66½

Tundra — Cold Desert

Coniferous Forest

Deciduous Forest

Temperate Grassland

Deciduous
Forest

Mediterranean
Type

Sub-Tropical
Grassland

Trade Wind Desert

Deciduous
Forest

Sub-Tropical
Broad-
leafed
Evergreen
Forest

Tropical
Grassland
(Savana)

Mixed
Tropical
Forest

Equatorial Forest
(Selvas)

N. 66½

40
30
23½
15
5
0
5
15
23½
30
40
S.

DIVISION OF A LAND MASS INTO MAJOR CLIMATIC AND NATURAL VEGETATION REGIONS up in convection currents over the heated area, so producing rainfall. In equatorial regions, air temperatures are generally high, the capacity of the air for holding moisture is great, and convectional ascent is rapid; the heavy rains are a direct result. In polar regions air temperatures are generally low, the capacity of the air for holding moisture is small, and during most of the year there is a tendency for the cold heavy air to settle down rather than rise; the low precipitation, with much of it in the form of snow, is a direct result.

In this generalisation, the possible presence of a major climatic barrier (for example, a mountain range) and the consequent rain shadow effect, have been ignored.

In the diagram opposite a division of our imaginary land mass into major climatic regions is indicated. This division has been arrived at by combining, in convenient form, the data summarised in the diagrams on pp. 188, 190, and 191. Consideration has therefore been given to the distribution of pressure and winds, of temperature, and of rainfall.

It will be noticed, however, that no specific reference has been made to the monsoon type of climate; the imaginary land mass, as represented, would not normally lend itself to the full development of this climatic type. When dealing with the actual continents, it certainly cannot be ignored, for some of the most densely populated regions of the earth are to be found in the monsoon areas.

The major regions of natural vegetation are also shown in the same diagram. That the natural vegetation is a direct result of the climate will be at once evident. It must be remembered, however, that over large areas long settled by man the natural vegetation has been, to a greater or lesser extent, destroyed. In Britain, for example, many of the extensive deciduous forests of pre-Roman days have been cleared, partly to provide agricultural land, partly to provide building material, partly for domestic and industrial fuel, etc. In North America, Australia, Argentina, and elsewhere, to quote another example, large areas of natural grassland have been ploughed up to provide land for the cultivation of cereals.

These general principles of climatic division will now be applied to the actual continents, the main characteristics of each separate region being noted. To illustrate the mean temperature and rainfall conditions, the data for selected stations will be given (as on p. 137). For comparative purposes these diagrams will all be drawn to the same scale.

THE EQUATORIAL REGION

This type of climate, as the name indicates, is found near the equator, mainly between latitudes 5° N. and 5° S. Manaos (3° S.) illustrates the temperature and rainfall conditions over equatorial lowlands; Yaundé (4° N.) the conditions at almost 2,500 ft. above sea-level; Quito (almost on the equator) the conditions at the considerable height of more than 9,000 ft.

The major areas within the equatorial climatic region are the Amazon Lowlands, the coast plains of Colombia, Equatorial West Africa and the Congo Basin, southern Malaya, and the East Indies. The equatorial sectors of the Andes and the East African Plateau have a modified type of equatorial climate.

Within the equatorial region, air temperatures near sea-level are almost exactly 80° F. all the year round (Manaos). Increase in height above sea-level brings about a general lowering of the temperature (Yaundé, Nairobi and Quito). Everywhere the annual range of temperature is small (Manaos, 2·5° F., Yaundé 3·5° F., Quito 0·7° F.). The temperature tends to be slightly higher just after the time of the "overhead sun" (round about the equinoxes) and slightly lower when the "overhead sun" is at its greatest distance from the equator (round about the solstices), but local conditions may modify this simple generalisation. In any event the variation is very small.

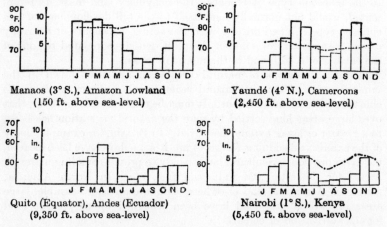

Manaos (3° S.), Amazon Lowland
(150 ft. above sea-level)

Yaundé (4° N.), Cameroons
(2,450 ft. above sea-level)

Quito (Equator), Andes (Ecuador)
(9,350 ft. above sea-level)

Nairobi (1° S.), Kenya
(5,450 ft. above sea-level)

The total annual rainfall is heavy, even in the interior of land masses. Manaos, more than 600 miles inland, has an annual fall of 66 in., while Para, at the mouth of the Amazon, has one of 87 in.; Yaundé, 62 in.; Singapore, 93 in. In the case of Quito (42 in.) the influence of altitude is seen, for the air is generally colder and therefore incapable of holding so much moisture.

On the equator the distribution of rainfall through the year tends to show a seasonal rhythm, rising to maxima at about the equinoxes, and falling to minima at about the solstices. But here, again, local conditions may upset this simple regime. As we move northwards from the equator, the June-July minimum tends to become less and less pronounced, while the December-January minimum becomes more and more pronounced. To the south the reverse is the case; the December-January minimum becomes less pronounced; the June-July minimum becomes more pronounced. This is due to the unequal time intervals between successive appearances of the " overhead sun ". Once again, however, this is only a tendency; local conditions may disturb the theoretical distribution. Yaundé, in latitude 4° N., shows the true equatorial rhythm, whereas Manaos, in latitude 3° S., has a wet season lasting from December to May and a drier season lasting from June to November, with a minimum in August. Quito displays the equatorial rhythm, although the December-January minimum is not very marked.

There are no " seasons " such as are experienced in temperate latitudes, for temperatures are always high, and rainfall is usually spread over the whole year, with possibly one or two rather drier periods. In the true equatorial belt one cannot even speak of a " dry season ", as one can in some other parts of the earth.

Convectional rainfall, with heavy thunderstorms, occurs during most afternoons or early evenings; that is, after the convectional system has had plenty of time to get thoroughly in motion during the great heat of the day. From this it must not be inferred, however, that the nights are cold; in no other part of the earth is the diurnal range so consistently low (10–15° F.). Throughout the whole year the human body can find little relief from the oppressive, damp heat. Thus it is that white people experience so much difficulty in colonising the true equatorial regions. They may live there, provided they take due precautions, for considerable periods, but they cannot undertake the strenuous work required of colonists, and to escape from the monotony of this enervating climate they need long holidays in their native homelands.

The Equatorial Forest. The natural vegetation of such areas is dense equatorial forest (for example, the Amazon Selvas). The whole year is one long growing season, with the result that many of the trees are actually evergreen. Many, however, are deciduous, but they have no prescribed growing, flowering, and fruiting seasons as in temperate latitudes. Thus, although all deciduous trees shed their leaves at some time during the year, it is always possible to find many equatorial deciduous trees in leaf. The forests are therefore always green. A more remarkable characteristic of the equatorial forest, perhaps, is the great variety of trees. On any one acre of land (about half the size of a regulation Association football pitch) it is most unlikely that more than one or two specimens of the same tree would be found. Further, the forest is very dense, and climbing plants (lianas) often mat the trees into an almost impenetrable mass, while the thick canopy of foliage overhead makes the whole region dark, damp, and unhealthy. Where, for some reason, the forest thins out a little and light penetrates, dense tangled undergrowth is found, often in tiers.

These features of the equatorial forest make it of limited economic value. The great variety makes it extraordinarily difficult to collect any one tree which may be in particular demand. Native of the equatorial forests are mahogany, rosewood, and other prized cabinet woods, and the wild rubber and cacao (source of cocoa) trees, together with a great many others of which we may note the cinchona tree, the bark of which yields quinine. Many of the hard woods do not float on water, and so boats or barges are necessary to transport the logs. (The temperate zone soft woods, so widely used in building, are often floated down the rivers to the saw-mills.) The absence of snow entails mechanical transport through a forest, if it is to be developed; and on ground that is often swampy this is not always an easy matter. (In the temperate zone soft-wood forests, the trees grow in " stands ", that is, they are nearly all of the same kind, and the winter snow, by reducing ground friction, enables the logs to be hauled with a minimum of mechanical transport.)

To overcome these many difficulties, **plantations** of certain trees have been developed in selected areas. Clearing an area of equatorial forest, however, is often difficult. Merely to fell the trees and clear the requisite patch would be to expose the soil to frequent torrential downpours. Soil erosion would inevitably result. But the rapid growth of weeds and useless bushes is another problem when the trees have once been cleared. A carefully planned system of clearance is therefore essential. When a plantation has been successfully established the advantages to large-scale production are obvious. All the trees are of the required kind. They are planted in neat rows, and spaced for easy working. Weeds can be kept under control, and the necessary transport can be introduced. Such are the rubber plantations of Malaya, the East Indies, and Ceylon. The commercial rubber tree most generally developed is *Hevea brasiliensis*, native of the Amazon Selvas. In the Gold Coast, similar plantations of cacao have been established.

Development. In the main the equatorial lowlands are relatively undeveloped, largely because white people are unable to work vigorously there. Medical science has made it possible for white people to live in the former " white man's grave ", but it is still necessary to utilize native coloured labour, which is not, as a rule, very enterprising. Even so, certain areas (notably Java, Madura, Malaya) show that great economic development is possible in the equatorial regions.

THE TROPICAL SUMMER RAINS REGION

This type of climate is found mainly between latitudes **5°** and **15°** both north and south of the equator, on the *west* of land masses and in the *interior* regions ; the eastern margins normally have rain all the year round, with a tendency towards a summer maximum. The major areas in this class are the Sudan, the southern part of the Congo Basin, Northern Rhodesia, much of the Brazilian Highlands, and the Orinoco Basin. (South-east Asia and Northern Australia will be discussed under a different heading later ; see p. 200.)

To illustrate the temperature and rainfall conditions, four stations in the Sudan have been selected. They are all in approximately the same longitude and roughly the same height above sea-level. Mongalla (5° N.) is on the edge of the equatorial region ; Khartoum (15½° N.) is on the northern edge of the summer rains belt ; Hillet Doleib (9½° N.) and El Obeid (13° N.) occupy intermediate positions.

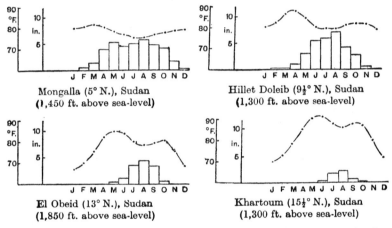

Mongalla (5° N.), Sudan
(1,450 ft. above sea-level)

Hillet Doleib (9½° N.), Sudan
(1,300 ft. above sea-level)

El Obeid (13° N.), Sudan
(1,850 ft. above sea-level)

Khartoum (15½° N.), Sudan
(1,300 ft. above sea-level)

The most striking feature of the temperature is the increase in the mean annual range as we move away from the equator (Mongalla 7° F., Hillet Doleib 9° F., El Obeid 18° F., Khartoum 21° F.). This is due partly to an increase in the highest mean monthly temperature (Mongalla, 83° F. ; Khartoum, 91° F.) and partly to a decrease in the lowest mean monthly temperature (Mongalla, 76° F. ; Khartoum, 70° F.).

Another noticeable characteristic is the slight drop in temperature round about the July-August period. All four stations are north of the equator, and we should normally expect this to be the warmest part of the year, for at this season the noon sun would never be far from overhead, and there would be the cumulative effect of several months of intense heating. The slight drop in temperature occurs, however, during a period of increased rainfall. The greater cloud-cover, which reduces insolation, and the greater amount of heat spent in evaporation, both contribute to the lowering of air temperatures.

With regard to the rainfall, two features stand out very conspicuously; as we move away from the equator, both the length of the rainy season and the total annual rainfall decrease appreciably (Mongalla, 39 in., with 87 per cent. falling in a period of seven months ; Hillet Doleib, 31 in., with 84 per cent. in five months ; El Obeid, 14 in., with 82 per cent. in three months ; Khartoum, 5 in., with 75 per cent. in two months). Mongalla, in fact, approaches very closely to the true equatorial type, but the two equinoctial maxima have converged into one prolonged rainy season, so that the June-July minimum is only just apparent. The December-January minimum, however, is very evident. Khartoum, on the other hand, experiences what can only be described as an arid climate, but its very inadequate rainfall conforms to a definite summer regime.

The summer rainfall is a direct result of the greater heating of the land during that season. Low pressure develops (Summer Doldrums) and a general inflow of air takes place. Such air is hot and often moist ; summer convectional rainfall, with frequent thunderstorms, is therefore to be expected. During the winter the pressure gradient is generally towards the equator, with the result that the normal Trade Winds return to the region. Over the eastern margins the Trades are on-shore, and hence moist, but elsewhere they are dry winds. The marked decrease in the summer convectional rainfall, as we move away from the equator, is clearly seen by comparing the diagrams on p. 197.

The Savana Lands. The natural vegetation of the summer rains region is savana (also savanna or savannah), or tropical parkland (often called grassland). As we move out of the dense equatorial forests the trees gradually thin out and lose much of their variety. In the natural clearings so formed tall tropical grasses grow. Such open wooded country is often styled " park savana ". Still farther away from the forests the trees become less, and the grasses more, conspicuous, until only scattered trees appear in an otherwise grassy area. This is the " grass savana ". Grasses lend themselves to light or seasonal rains, for when there is insufficient moisture to meet the demands of evaporation, the stems and blades merely die down, thereby minimising transpiration, and leaving the roots alive to send up new shoots when favourable conditions return.

Tropical grasses often attain a height of 10–12 ft., or even more, but closely matted turf, so common in temperate latitudes, is not found.

The savana lands are the home of numerous wild animals; they are equally the playground of big-game hunters.

Savana extends across the equatorial regions of the East African Plateau (Nairobi, see p. 194). Here, the general lowering of the temperature due to increased altitude, the relatively light rainfall compared with equatorial lowland areas, and the pronounced minima around about the solstices, all favour savana rather than equatorial forest. It must be remembered that an annual rainfall of 40 in. is not really very heavy for an equatorial region, in view of the amount lost by evaporation.

Provided the rainfall is sufficiently heavy, tropical rain forests will flourish even though there is a pronounced seasonal distribution. This, in the main, is true of a belt extending inland from the Guinea Coast. Freetown (Sierra Leone) has an annual fall of 174 in., of which 130 in. are received in the four months June–September; during the four months December–March, the fall is no more than 3·5 in. Lagos (Nigeria) has an annual fall of 72 in., of which 40 in. are received in the three months May–July; during the four months November–February, the fall is only 6·4 in. Two hundred miles or so inland, and in some places considerably less, savana becomes quite general, because the total rainfall is insufficient to support forest. At Wagadugu (12° N.), some 500 miles from the coast, the total fall is 32 in., of which 26 in. fall during the four months June–September ; during the five months November–March, the total fall is scarcely measurable. At Timbuktu (17° N.) the total fall is only 9 in. ; more than 8 in. fall during the four months June–September.

In the savana regions, therefore, the climatic control is such that a gradual transition takes place, from rich forests on its equatorial margins to poor grass and scrub at the other extreme.

Crops. Like the equatorial regions, the savana lands are capable of considerable development, but this has not, so far, been achieved on any very large scale. In parts of the Sudan, cotton is grown, while in Rhodesia, tobacco is becoming an increasingly important crop. Elsewhere coffee (Kenya), sugar-cane (Queensland, Australia), tropical fruits, etc., attain more than local importance.

With a carefully planned system of irrigation, the savana lands might well become major areas for the production of several important commodities. Even the dry winter season could then be utilised for the growth of crops usually found in temperate latitudes (for example, maize, wheat, etc.). In certain areas which depend exclusively on irrigation for their production, such as Egypt, this " two-crop cultivation " is widely practised. Cotton, rice, sugar, etc., are usual summer crops ; wheat is a most valuable winter crop.

Perhaps the greatest opportunities are offered to the cattle-farmer. Unfortunately, very few animals capable of being domesticated are native of the savana lands. This means that animals of temperate

o

latitudes must be introduced, and these sometimes fall victim to tropical diseases. Modern scientific methods in the prevention of disease, however, have already made cattle-ranching a reality in certain areas, notably the savana lands of Northern Australia and the Orinoco Basin.

THE TROPICAL MONSOON REGION

This may be considered as a special type of the Tropical Summer Rains Region. We have already examined, in a general way, how this type of climate comes into being, and some of its most striking characteristics (see p. 170). Now the discussion will be confined to a more detailed study of the conditions in certain of the more important regions.

The diagrams below illustrate the temperature and rainfall conditions for Bombay and Cape York.

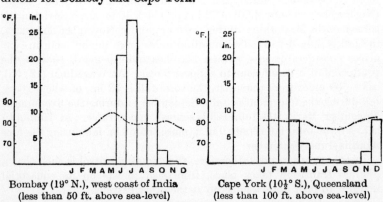

Bombay (19° N.), west coast of India
(less than 50 ft. above sea-level)

Cape York (10½° S.), Queensland
(less than 100 ft. above sea-level)

The monsoon type of climate reaches its greatest development in South-East Asia and Northern Australia although, as will be seen presently, monsoonal tendencies are very marked in certain other parts of the earth.

During the northern summer (July) intense low pressure develops over those parts of Asia which lie near the Tropic of Cancer, namely, Arabia, North-West India, and the lofty plateaux to the north of India. The centre of this low-pressure system is over the Sind Desert and the adjoining area of Baluchistan. (We are, of course, referring to pressures reduced to their sea-level value.) This vast region of low pressure does not, however, operate as one simple low-pressure system, for the Himalayas, on account of their great height, form, in many respects, an effective climatic barrier. This point will be discussed later (see p. 201). At the same time (July) the Horse Latitudes " high " is well developed south of the equator, especially over the land mass of Australia. (The northern Horse Latitudes " high " has disappeared from the land

mass of Asia, and has been replaced by the intense continental " low ".)
The equatorial " low " has something of an intermediate character ;
it is lower than the southern Horse Latitudes " high " but higher than
the northern continental " low ".   In effect, therefore, there is a
general pressure gradient operating from the southern Horse Latitudes
towards the Asiatic " low ", with the result that there is a vast flow of
air towards south-east Asia.

The influence exerted by the Himalayas and other mountain barriers
is, broadly, to " detach " India climatically from the rest of south-east
Asia.   The Indian summer monsoon is controlled by the Sind Desert
" low " ; for the rest of south-east Asia the controlling influence is
the low-pressure area which lies to the north of the Himalayas.   It will
be necessary, therefore, to consider the Indian summer monsoon apart
from the general summer monsoon of South-East Asia.

But one thing is common to all monsoon lands, namely, summer
rainfall, usually very heavy.   During the northern summer (July) the
winds at Bombay are from the sea.   They have blown over many
miles (possibly more than 2,000 miles) of hot ocean, with the result
that they are very warm and very moist.   In rising to cross the
western edge of the Deccan (the Western Ghats) they are the cause of
the very heavy summer rainfall.   At this same time (July) the winds
over Northern Australia are generally from the land, and hence dry.
(During the southern summer (January) the winds at Cape York are
from the sea, and hence moist ; those at Bombay are from the land,
and hence dry.)

Indian Summer Monsoon.   Now return to the Indian summer monsoon.   The low-pressure centre is over Sind.   If, therefore, the law
concerning wind deflection in the northern hemisphere (that is, a
generally anti-clockwise inflow) is applied, we find that (a) in coastal
areas north of the Gulf of Cutch the winds are generally from north and
north-west, and hence dry, because they are from the land or have
crossed but little sea ; (b) south of the Gulf of Cambay the winds
are generally from the south-west, and hence moist, because they
have crossed a wide expanse of ocean ; (c) in Eastern India the
winds will tend to be southerly, and moist when they reach land ;
and (d) in the Ganges Valley the winds will be from the south-
east, blowing up the valley and hence becoming drier as they travel
inland.

All this moist air is flowing into an area confined by a mountain
girdle, which is, in effect, a climatic barrier.   Across the north run the
Himalayas ; to the north-west lie the Sulaiman Mountains ; to the
east lie the Arakan Mountains.   This arrangement has been likened to
a box with one side open.   As more and more moist air is forced into
the " box ", the air already in it can escape only by rising—and rising

air promotes rainfall. The high temperatures, the great expanse of hot ocean traversed by the winds, the " box " arrangement of the northern mountain girdle, all are important contributory factors of the heavy summer rains over India.

The really wet parts of India during the summer monsoon are the western coastal regions south of the Gulf of Cambay, the south-western and central areas of Ceylon, the lower Ganges Valley, the southern slopes of the Himalayas, and the western and southern mountain slopes in Assam and Burma.

The influence of relief is everywhere in evidence. Over much of the Western Ghats, the high western edge of the Deccan, the mean annual rainfall exceeds 100 in., but over the greater part of the Central and Eastern Deccan it ranges from 15 to 30 in. (The Deccan is a tilted plateau that slopes towards the east.) An even more striking example of the influence of relief is seen in the Khasi Hills (Assam), which rise steeply from the plains of the Lower Ganges and the Brahmaputra to rather more than 5,000 ft. Cherrapunji, on the southern (windward) slope, at a height of 4,300 ft., has a mean annual fall of more than 400 in., with about 100 in. in each of the months June and July. Shillong, only 25 miles away but on the northern (leeward) slope, at the greater height of 4,900 ft., has but 80 in.

In the Indo-Gangetic Plain the rainfall decreases from the Lower Ganges towards the Indus. Comparative mean annual figures are : Calcutta, 59 in. ; Patna, 47 in. ; Benares, 41 in. ; Allahabad, 38 in. ; Cawnpore, 32 in. ; Delhi, 26 in. ; Lahore, 18 in. ; Peshawar, 16 in. Over most of the Indus Valley the rainfall is light, or even negligible : Multan, 7 in. ; Jacobabad 4 in. ; Karachi, 8 in.

In the regions of moderate rainfall (say, 20–40 in.) the droughts which occur from time to time bring widespread distress, for the people tend to rely solely on the rainfall. These are the famine areas, but modern irrigation works have done much to offset the uncertainty of the rainfall in such areas. In the " wet " regions the rainfall is almost always certain to be adequate ; in the " dry " regions cultivation never has been possible without some sort of irrigation, however primitive.

Although the summer monsoon does sometimes " fail ", it is, nevertheless, remarkably consistent. At Bombay it " breaks " (or " bursts ") early in June, often with a fall of anything up to 5 or 6 in. in two or three hours ; it reaches the Ganges Delta by the middle of June, and the Punjab by the end of June. By July monsoonal conditions have set in all over India. In the Punjab the season is relatively short, ending just after the middle of September ; in the Ganges Delta and at Bombay the summer monsoon lasts until about the middle of October.

North-East Monsoon. The influence of the northern mountain girdle is equally apparent in winter, when the air flow is dominated by the " continental high ", which has its centre over Mongolia. Cold continental air is prevented from draining into India, where the temperatures remain relatively high as a result. On the other hand, the cold continental air does drain into China, where the temperatures are accordingly lower. Compare the mean January temperatures at Multan and Hankow, both in approximately latitude 30° N., and both on the lowlands : Multan, 56° F. ; Hankow, 40° F.

Over the northern plains of India a " local high " develops, of sufficient intensity to maintain northerly or north-easterly winds over practically the whole of India. This " Indian high " may be compared with the normal Horse Latitudes " high " ; the resulting north-east monsoon with the normal Trade Winds. Over most of India the winter monsoon will clearly be dry, for the winds are blowing from land and over land. In the case of Ceylon and the south-eastern part of peninsular India, however, the winds will have gathered moisture during their passage across the Bay of Bengal, and winter rain will result. At Trincomalee (north-east Ceylon) the four months October–January yield 43 in. out of a total annual fall of 63 in., whereas the four months June-September yield only 12 in. At Tuticorin (in the extreme south of India) the three months October-December yield 16 in. out of a total of 22 in., whereas the three months June–August yield only $\frac{1}{2}$ in.

Indian Seasons. Considering India as a whole, two distinct seasons have so far been recognised : (a) the season of the South-West Monsoon, and (b) the season of the North-East Monsoon. This, however, is not an adequate climatic division of the year.

It must be realised that the complete reversal of a major wind system cannot be effected instantly. The low pressure over Sind (summer) does not suddenly give way to the high pressure over the northern plains (winter). There must be periods of instability intervening between the two different well-established systems.

The India Meteorological Department, which provides the official meteorological service for the Government of India, recognises four " seasons " of the Indian year.

(i) Cool dry season, January and February. The North-East Monsoon is now fully established over the whole of India.

Bombay : Jan. 75° F. and 0·1 in. ; Feb. 75° F. and 0 in.
Calcutta : Jan. 65° F. and 0·4 in. ; Feb. 70° F. and 1·1 in.
Delhi :   Jan. 58° F. and 1·0 in. ; Feb. 62° F. and 0·6 in.

(ii) Hot dry season, March to mid-June. Temperatures rise appreciably, for the " overhead sun " moves northwards across India itself.

Towards the end of the period the north-east monsoon is " breaking down ", gradually giving way to conditions which are to be a necessary prelude to the advance of the south-west monsoon.

Bombay : April 82° F. and 0 in. ; May 85° F. and 0·7 in.
Calcutta : April 85° F. and 2 in. ; May 86° F. and 5 in.
Delhi :   April 86° F. and 0·4 in. ; May 92° F. and 0·7 in.

(iii) **General rains season**, mid-June to mid-September. The south-west monsoon is now fully established over the whole of India, and heavy rains are widespread. This rainfall is not continuous throughout the season, but occurs in downpours, separated by dry and sunny spells. The coming of the rains is accompanied by a drop in the temperature.

Bombay : July 79° F. and 27 in. ; Aug. 79° F. and 16 in.
Calcutta : July 83° F. and 12 in. ; Aug. 82° F. and 11 in.
Delhi :   July 86° F. and 8 in. ; Aug. 85° F. and 7 in.

(iv) **Season of the retreating south-west monsoon**, mid-September to December. Now the south-west monsoon is " breaking down ", first in the extreme north-west (that is, the Punjab), then gradually farther south until it leaves India altogether, to make way for the north-east monsoon. As the temperature falls, the pressure increases over northern India, with the result that the inflowing summer air streams fail to penetrate so far inland. This is particularly noticeable in the case of the stream which flows up the Ganges Valley. Up to the middle of September this inflow reaches the Punjab ; by the end of the month it fails to penetrate much beyond Bengal ; by the middle of October it fails to reach even the Ganges Delta. But during this later period light south-easterly winds, bringing appreciable rain, do manage to reach the coastal areas of Orissa, which is south-west of the Ganges Delta. These successive withdrawals of the summer monsoon mean that the length of the rainy season varies from place to place. Thus the Punjab, which received the summer monsoon last, loses it first ; it has a short rainy season, and, because of the distance inland, the rains are not very heavy (Lahore receives 12 in. during the three months July–September, out of a total of 18 in.).

Bombay : Oct. 81° F. and 2·4 in. : Nov. 79° F. and 0·4 in.
Calcutta : Oct. 80° F. and 4·3 in. : Nov. 72° F. and 0·5 in.
Delhi :   Oct. 79° F. and 0·5 in. ; Nov. 68° F. and 0·1 in.

Another, and possibly more popular, division of the Indian year is as follows :—

(a) The " cool dry " season, from mid-October to March.
(b) The " hot dry " season, from April to mid-June.
(c) The rainy season, from mid-June to mid-October.

Not all the rain that falls within this monsoon region is of the monsoon type. In the Punjab and United Provinces, in winter, a small but valuable precipitation results from the passing of shallow depressions, similar to temperate cyclones, and possibly an extension of the Mediterranean winter cyclonic activity. Lahore receives approximately 1 in. in each of the months January, February, and March, mostly from this source.

Vegetation. The natural vegetation of the monsoon regions depends largely on the amount of the annual fall, since it is almost everywhere characteristically seasonal in its distribution. Where the fall is heavy, monsoon forest abounds. This has some of the features of the equatorial forest, with which it is often grouped in a simple classification. There are valuable hardwoods (for example, sal and teak) and there is considerable variety. But in some important respects the monsoon forest differs from the equatorial. The equatorial forest, considered as a whole, is evergreen, although individual trees may be deciduous; except in those areas where roots can reach moisture all the year round, for example, often on the lower slopes of hills and mountains, where the water table comes near the surface, monsoon forests are wholly deciduous. There is, in fact, a marked seasonal rhythm. During the long dry season the trees shed their leaves, thus conserving moisture by reducing transpiration. During April, May and early June, therefore, they offer little or no protection from the glare of the overhead sun. But with the coming of the heavy rains they soon burst into leaf and grow rapidly. Where the rainfall is less heavy, the forest thins out and savana takes its place; in the drier areas poor scrub and steppe are found. These areas are parched and bare during the hot dry season, but are soon green again after the coming of the rains. Then everything grows quickly.

The Monsoon Lands have long been densely peopled and much of the natural vegetation has been destroyed, sometimes wantonly and with far-reaching consequences. A hill slope, denuded of its natural tree cover, may soon be rendered completely barren as a result of the soil erosion following torrential downpours.

Other Monsoon Areas. This description of the Indian Monsoon Region must serve for all similar regions and we shall here note only the more important of the major characteristics of the other monsoon areas.

For Indo-China and China proper, the controlling " summer low " is situated north of the Himalayas. The summer monsoon for Indo-China is therefore generally from the south (and moist); for China proper it is generally from the south-east (and also moist). In both regions the winds are practically reversed in winter, when they are dry. Reference has already been made to the relatively cold winters

of China, due to the outflow of cold continental air (Peking, Jan. 23° F. ;
Shanghai, Jan. 38° F., Hong Kong, 60° F.). In coastal areas of South
China and Indo-China there is a certain amount of winter rainfall due
to the tendency of the winds to swing back into the land after they
have travelled out over the sea (Hong Kong, Jan. 1·4 in., June 15 in. ;
Foochou, Jan. 1·7 in., June 8 in.)

| | Temp. | | Rainfall | | | |
	Feb.	July	Nov.–Jan.	Feb.–Apr.	May–July	Aug.–Oct.
Hong Kong	58° F.	82° F.	4·5 in.	9·5 in.	41·5 in.	29·0 in.
Hué	68	84	36·5	9·0	10·0	46·5

Certain of the East Indian Islands may be regarded as having a
double monsoon, rather than an equatorial, type of climate. If the
particular place happens to have a northern aspect, it will receive
most of its rainfall from the winds which flow out from Asia (Batavia,
Jan. 13 in., July 2·6 in.). Should the place have a southern aspect it
will receive most of its rainfall from the winds which flow into Asia
(Amboina, Jan. 6 in., July 23 in.). In a similar sort of way, aspect is
responsible for the distribution at Hué (French Indo-China), which
receives 75 per cent. of its 100 in. during the four months September–
December (note the trend of this particular coast line).

| | Temp. | | Rainfall | | | |
	Jan.	May	Nov.–Jan.	Feb.–Apr.	May–July	Aug.–Oct.
Singapore (Lat. 1° 24′ N.)	78° F.	81° F.	30·0 in.	22·0 in.	20·0 in.	22·5 in.
Batavia (Lat. 6° 30′ S.)	78 (Jan.)	80 (Oct.)	27·0	26·0	10·5	9·0
Sandakan (Lat. 5° 50′ N.)	80 (Jan.)	83 (May)	51·0	22·0	19·5	27·5
Amboina (Lat. 3° 36′ S.)	81 (Jan.)	77 (July)	15·0	21·0	67·5	31·0
Penang (Lat. 5° 25′ N.)	79 (Dec.)	82 (Apr.)	20·5	14·5	26·5	45·5
Manila (Lat. 14° 35′ N.)	77 (Jan.)	83 (May)	9·0	2·5	31·0	37·0
Port Moresby (Lat. 9° 25′ S.)	82·5 (Dec.)	78 (Aug.)	13·5	19·5	5·0	3·0

In the case of Japan, winter rainfall is also a characteristic, because
the outflowing winds have first to cross the Sea of Japan (Tokyo,
Jan. 2 in., June 6 in.)

	Temp.		Rainfall			
	Jan.	Aug.	Nov.–Jan.	Feb.–Apr.	May–July	Aug.–Oct.
Kagoshima	45° F.	80° F.	10·5 in.	18·5 in.	34·5 in.	21·0 in.
Nagasaki	42	80	9·5	16·5	30·0	20·5
Hakodate	20	69	9·0	7·5	12·0	16·5

The monsoonal tendency is observed as far north as Manchuria, but these more northerly regions cannot strictly be classified with the tropical monsoon regions (Peking, Jan. 23° F. and 0·1 in.; July 79° F. and 9·4 in.). They are better referred to as the temperate monsoon type, or simply as the **China Type**.

	Temp.		Rainfall			
	Jan.	July	Nov.–Jan.	Feb.–Apr.	May–July	Aug.–Oct.
Shanghai	38° F.	80° F.	5·5 in.	9·5 in.	17·0 in.	13·5 in.
Hankow	40	83	5·0	11·5	23·0	10·0
Peking	23	76	0·5	1·0	14·0	9·5
Mukden	9	76	1·5	2·0	12·0	11·0
Vladivostok	7	69 (Aug.)	2·0	2·0	8·0	10·5

In parts of East Africa, for example, Abyssinia, monsoonal tendencies are very marked (Addis Ababa, Jan. 60° F. and 0·6 in.; July 62° F. and 11 in.).

Reference has been made to the conditions in West Africa under another heading (p. 199), but the monsoonal tendency is marked near the coast (Freetown, Jan. 81° F. and 0·6 in.; July 78° F. and 37 in.).

In the south-eastern States of the U.S.A., these same general monsoon features appear, but to a lesser degree; the winter rainfall is considerably heavier than in the true monsoon regions.

	Temp.		Rainfall			
	Jan.	July	Nov.–Jan.	Feb.–Apr.	May–July	Aug.–Oct.
Galveston	54° F.	83° F.	11·0 in.	8·5 in.	11·5 in.	15·0 in.
New Orleans	54	81·5	13·0	13·5	16·5	14·0
Miami	67	82	7·0	7·0	18·5	23·0
Charleston	50	81	8·5	9·5	15·5	15·0

TRADE WIND DESERT REGION

This type of climate is found mainly on the west of land masses between latitudes 15° and 30°, both north and south of the equator. The major areas in this class are the Sahara, Kalahari, Arizona (and adjoining parts of California and Mexico), Atacama, and West Australia

Deserts. The actual extent of these different deserts, both north-south and east-west, is controlled, in large measure, by the size, shape, and relief of the individual continents. The Sahara, for example, extends over an enormous distance from east to west; so, too, does the West Australia Desert. The Atacama, on the other hand, is confined east-west, but extends from about latitude 30° S. almost to the equator.

The essential characteristics of the climate are due to the prevalence of Trade Winds throughout the year. The Trades are drying winds, except over the eastern margins of the continents. Over the western margins (and often over the interior as well), therefore, there is no appreciable rainfall at any time of the year. There is scarcely ever any cloud; insolation by day is intense; radiation by night is rapid. In summer, during the time of the " overhead " sun, the day temperatures are among the highest recorded anywhere; 120° F. in the shade is not uncommon, though well above the mean. The mean diurnal range is about 30–40° F., so that, in summer, even the nights are seldom really cool. In winter, on the other hand, night frosts do sometimes occur. It is not unknown for day temperatures of well above 80° F., or possibly above 90° F., to be followed by night frosts. By day, particularly during summer, the ground may become unbearably hot; on areas of bare sand, temperatures of more than 170° F. have been recorded. In the hearts of these deserts the annual range is also large for the latitude (30–40° F.). The summers are very hot; the winters comfortably cool.

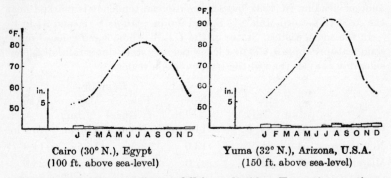

Cairo (30° N.), Egypt
(100 ft. above sea-level)

Yuma (32° N.), Arizona, U.S.A.
(150 ft. above sea-level)

Over the true deserts the rainfall is negligible. From time to time, perhaps at intervals of several years, torrential showers of the convectional type, and of more or less local significance, occur. On the margins nearer the equator light summer rains are to be expected; on the margins farther from the equator a winter rainfall regime is evident. The light summer rains denote convectional influences where the desert is merging into the savana; the winter rainfall regime denotes cyclonic activity where the desert is merging into the " Winter Rains " region.

The vegetation of these desert regions consists entirely of drought-resisting plants (*xerophytes*), such as cacti, thorn scrub, tough wiry grasses, etc. Over large areas bare rock is found ; elsewhere there may be a boulder-strewn waste ; in yet other areas there are expanses of baked clay or loose sand, which is frequently thrown up into dunes. In the oases, where water is readily available, the date palm flourishes and intensive cultivation is practised. In a sense, Egypt is such an oasis, for without the Nile it would be true desert. To illustrate this point Cairo has been selected as one of the stations ; the other, Yuma, is in the Arizona Desert.

The development of desert regions is clearly restricted. In the oases there is often a surplus of such products as dates, vegetables, etc., while in the desert margins there is often enough pasturage to support cattle, sheep, or goats. More important to the outside world, however, are the minerals ; for example, nitrates from the Atacama Desert, gold from Australia, diamonds from South-West Africa, etc.

Provided there is water, the climate is not unhealthy, and in the daily and seasonal rhythm the human body can become refreshed. Of greatest inconvenience, perhaps, is the excessive dryness of the air at times. The dreaded sand-storms are sometimes more than a mere inconvenience ; they may well be a danger to the traveller.

WINTER RAINS ("MEDITERRANEAN") REGION

The so-called Mediterranean type of climate is found on the west of land masses, mainly between latitudes 30° and 40°, both north and south of the equator. Chief among these areas are the coastal margins round the Mediterranean Sea ; but other important areas are the Great Valley of California (San Francisco region), Central Chile (Val-paraiso region), the extreme south of South Africa (Cape Town region), South-West Australia (Perth region), and South Australia (Adelaide region).   North Island (New Zealand) has a similar type of climate, but in a modified form.

In summer these regions are, in a sense, an extension of the Trade Wind Deserts which border them along their sub-tropical margins ; in winter they are, in like manner, an extension of the cyclonic belts which border them along their cool-temperate margins. The " Mediterranean " warm-temperate belt thus owes its characteristic type of climate to the swing of the pressure- and wind-belts.

In summer the Horse Latitudes, or the Trade Winds, are the controlling influence. Calms or light drying winds generally result. Temperatures are high (above 70° F., and in parts above 80° F. during the hottest month) ; sunshine is brilliant and of long duration

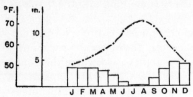

Lisbon (39° N.), Portugal
(less than 100 ft. above sea-level)

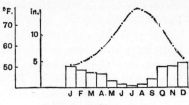

Palermo (38° N.), Sicily
(250 ft. above sea-level)

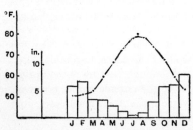

Corfu (40° N.), west of Balkan Peninsula
(100 ft. above sea-level)

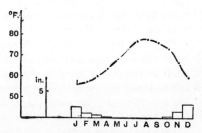

Alexandria (31° N.), Egypt
(100 ft. above sea-level)

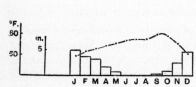

San Francisco (38° N.), California, U.S.A.
(200 ft. above sea-level)

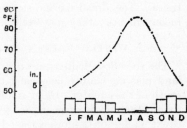

Seville (37° N.), S.W. Spain
(less than 100 ft. above sea-level)

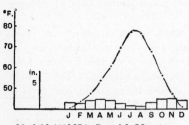

Madrid (40° N.), Spanish Meseta
(2,150 ft. above sea-level)

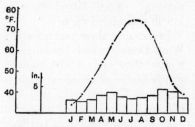

Milan (45° N.), Plain of Lombardy
(500 ft. above sea-level)

(Rome has a mean record of 11 hours sunshine daily during July). Rainfall is negligible in most areas; July and August are often almost completely rainless in the northern hemisphere.

In winter, cyclonic activity predominates, and the prevailing winds are the westerly variables. Winters are mild (above 40° F., and in parts above 50° F. during the coldest month); sunshine is still appreciable, much more so than in Britain (Rome has a mean record of 4 hours sunshine daily during December, the dullest month). Rainfall, though varying considerably from place to place, is generally adequate.

These characteristics may be summarised briefly thus: *hot, dry, sunny summers ; mild, moist winters.*

Although winter is the rainy season (that is, by far the greater proportion of the rain falls in the winter half-year), the rain falls on comparatively few days, and this fact has an important effect on temperature conditions. The mean winter temperatures over many of the Mediterranean coastlands are no higher than those over western Britain. But western Britain has a generally cloudy climate in winter; day temperatures are relatively low, due to the restricted insolation, while night temperatures are relatively high, due to the restricted radiation. In the Mediterranean Region the greater proportion of fine days ensures higher day temperatures (greater insolation) and lower night temperatures (greater radiation). Normally the day temperatures concern us far more than the night; we think of the Mediterranean as having much " milder " winters than Britain. When, therefore, it is stated that the winter temperatures at certain resorts in western Britain are equal to those at recognised winter resorts in the Mediterranean, we must realise the limitations of mean monthly temperatures in describing actual conditions.

Over the northern part of the Mediterranean Basin, frosts occur during a normal winter, but over the southern part, and on the small islands, the temperature rarely falls below freezing-point. Snow, too, though not uncommon along the northern coastlands, is rare over the southern part of the basin.

Reference has already been made to the significance of some of the local winds; for example, mistral, bora, sirocco (pp. 185-6).

To illustrate the varying conditions found within, and near, the " Mediterranean " regions, eight stations have been selected.

Lisbon on the Atlantic seaboard, and Palermo in Sicily, are typical of the popular conception of the " Mediterranean climate ". Corfu in western Greece shows the heavier rainfall over the western margins of the Balkan Peninsula, while Alexandria shows the drier conditions prevailing in the south-eastern part of the basin. Seville illustrates the high summer temperatures experienced in southern Spain, while San Francisco shows the cooling influence in summer of a " cold " ocean current (California Current). Madrid illustrates the continental tendency experienced in the middle of a large peninsula; the range of temperature is greater, and the winter rainfall regime is greatly modified. Milan illustrates this same tendency to an even greater degree; a mean annual range of 40° F. and an all-seasons rainfall regime are not consistent with the true " Mediterranean " type; the Plain of Lombardy, in spite of its popular association with the Mediterranean, belongs, climatically, to Central Europe.

The Mediterranean Basin. The Mediterranean Borderlands, as the cradle of modern civilisation, must always claim unique attention. In Egypt, Crete, Greece, and Rome, advanced civilisations developed early. The genial climate, with its marked seasonal rhythm, was undoubtedly a factor of prime importance in this respect. In the struggle for life, both excessive ease and excessive hardship were absent; but concerted endeavour and careful planning were both necessary if full use was to be made of the seasonal rhythm. Thought was stimulated; man was required to use his ingenuity, and so he progressed.

Vegetation and Agriculture. The mild, moist winters allow of slow growth, but the summer drought has a retarding influence in what otherwise should be the growing season. The natural vegetation, at its richest, is therefore broad-leafed evergreen forest. Such vegetation has become adapted to the prevalent climatic conditions. Roots penetrate deeply, seeking ground-water; leaves are small, glossy, and waxy, bark is generally thick, and stems are usually thickened, thus minimising transpiration during the hot droughty summers. Other special features include the growth of thorns and hairs, and sometimes a bitter taste; slow-growing vegetation does not readily replenish its foliage, so protective devices against both the climate and the ravages of animals are developed. Where the forests have been destroyed, whether by man (for example, for ship-building during the heyday of the Italian " City States "), or by animals (for example, goats are kept in great numbers, and these destroy saplings), the vegetation degenerates into thorn-scrub. This is known as maquis in Corsica and macchia in Italy; in the south of France the name garigue is given to a similar type of degenerate scrub and bush vegetation. Most noted among the Mediterranean trees, perhaps, are the cork oak and the cypresses; of the cultivated varieties, the most outstanding are the olive, fig, orange, lemon, and vine (succulents).

The Mediterranean Region has given to the world some of its most important cereals, notably wheat, the staple bread crop of nearly all white people, though the primitive forms of wheat possibly came from central Asia. To-day wheat is grown over very wide areas, many of which have a climate very different from that of the Mediterranean coastlands, but that is largely due to the fact that science has evolved new types to withstand the different conditions. The typical Mediter-ranean wheat is a " hard " wheat, suitable alike for bread and such other products as macaroni.

The cultivation of wheat in the Mediterranean area provides an interesting illustration of how the seasonal rhythm has been utilised to good advantage. The seed is sown in autumn, and the mild moist winter ensures early growth at the first approach of spring. During its early growth the plant thus has an adequate supply of moisture, and this ensures quantity. As growth proceeds, the rainfall decreases, and the fine sunny weather of late spring and early summer ensures a high quality and a safe harvest when the ears are ripe.

Summer cultivation can only be practised where irrigation is avail-able (for example, the famous huertas of Spain). The intensive culti-vation of a great variety of products is the normal practice.

Cattle are not a feature of the agriculture; the summer drought leads to an absence of good pasture. Goats' milk is widely used in place of cows' milk, and the olive does much to make good the shortage of animal fats.

COOL TEMPERATE (WEST MARGIN) REGION

As we move away from the " Mediterranean " regions towards the poles we find that cyclonic activity dominates the weather throughout the year, and especially in winter.

The climate of the cool temperate (west margin) regions, extending north and south of the equator from latitude 40° to the polar circles is one of warm summers, cool or mild winters, much cloud (particularly in winter), and rain at all seasons, with the winter half-year normally receiving the greater proportion.

These conditions are found over North-West Europe (including the British Isles), the coastal areas of British Columbia, the southern third of Chile, Tasmania, and South Island (New Zealand).

During summer the low-pressure conditions normally prevailing over the land masses allow some degree of maritime penetration in-land, but during winter the high pressure over the continents wards off maritime influences. Here we shall confine our attention to the purely maritime areas.

To illustrate the varying conditions over such extensive regions four stations have been selected. Valencia (or Valentia) Island, off south-west Ireland, portrays the most equable form of this type of climate ; it is not really typical of the whole area. Trondhjem, almost on the Arctic Circle, shows the conditions in the far north ; Bordeaux illus-trates them at almost the other extreme. London, occupying an intermediate position, is more or less typical of the region as a whole.

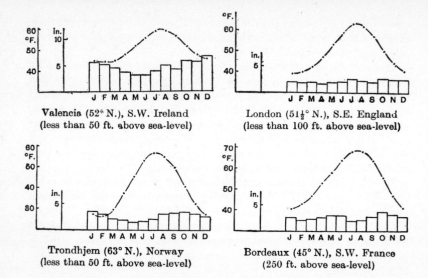

Valencia (52° N.), S.W. Ireland
(less than 50 ft. above sea-level)

London (51½° N.), S.E. England
(less than 100 ft. above sea-level)

Trondhjem (63° N.), Norway
(less than 50 ft. above sea-level)

Bordeaux (45° N.), S.W. France
(250 ft. above sea-level)

The annual range of temperature is small for the latitude (14·6° F. at Valencia; 30·4° F. at Trondhjem), due chiefly to the exceptionally mild winters. The influence of the ocean is also evident in summer, for temperatures are then relatively low.

So far as temperature is concerned, conditions are seldom either uncomfortably hot or uncomfortably cold. The large amount of moisture usually present in the atmosphere, however, frequently causes winter to be a " raw " period.

The winds are notoriously variable, as is only to be expected during cyclonic activity, and gale force is often experienced, especially over coastal areas in winter.

Rainfall varies greatly according to the aspect of the particular place with reference to the westerly and south-westerly winds. The western slopes of Ben Nevis have an annual fall of nearly 200 in., no month having less than about 8 in.; many places lying to seaward of prominent relief experience a total fall of more than 100 in. Even pronounced rain shadow areas usually get a fall of about 25 in., or a little less. Generally therefore, there is no lack of moisture. Further, there is seldom a lack in any particular season. For certain types of cultivation—wheat, barley, etc.—large areas have an excess of moisture, with the result that the growth of such products is restricted.

Cloudy weather is another feature of these maritime areas, and this, too, restricts certain types of cultivation by reducing the possible sunshine.

Natural Vegetation. The natural vegetation, at its richest, is deciduous forest (oak, elm, ash, etc.); it is eminently suited to the climate—a short resting season (winter), and abundant moisture to replenish foliage. It must not be supposed, though, that forest developed everywhere. Exposed situations could often produce nothing better than moorland, while soils, in some parts, encouraged close turf rather than trees. Meadowland, too, developed naturally. Nor were the forests always deciduous; on the higher areas, and towards the polar circles, conifers predominated, due chiefly to the shorter growing season in these less favourable situations.

In Britain particularly, very little forest remains; it has been cleared, partly to provide fuel, partly to provide building material, and partly to make room for agriculture. Rich grassland has largely taken its place, though considerable areas are put under the plough.

It has often been claimed that the climate of these regions is largely responsible for the fact that some of the world's most vigorous and enterprising peoples are to be found there. It is almost certainly true to say that the climate helps to maintain the vigour, even if it was not, in the first instance, actually the cause of it.

COOL TEMPERATE (EAST MARGIN) REGION

These are also regions of cyclonic activity, but maritime influences are less pronounced than over the western margins in similar latitudes. During winter, particularly, the prevailing winds blow off the cold continents, and air temperatures are therefore low (New York, 41° N., January 31° F.; Quebec, 47° N., January 10° F.; Nain, 57° N., January −7° F.). During summer a considerable proportion of the winds are still from the land, but they are now hot, and air temperatures are rather higher than in the west (New York, July 74° F.; Quebec, July 67° F.). Farther north (that is, in the northern hemisphere) the influence of cold ocean currents—the Labrador Current off North America, and the Bering Current off north-east Asia—helps to bring about a lowering of summer temperatures (Nain, July 47° F.)

Rainfall is well distributed throughout the year, and is fairly heavy, though rather less in amount than at corresponding places in the western margins. During winter much of the precipitation is in the form of snow. In eastern Asia there is a marked maximum during late summer, associated with the monsoonal influences over the more southerly parts of that continent (Vladivostok, Jan. 0·3, Feb. 0·3, Aug. 4·3, Sept. 4·4; total 22·4 in.; Okhotsk, Jan. 0·1, Feb. 0·1, Aug. 1·8, Sept. 2·1; total 7·5 in.). In eastern North America this seasonal distribution is scarcely apparent, due to the smaller monsoonal tendencies over this continent, and to the greater cyclonic activity, especially in winter.

P

In the southern hemisphere this climatic type is not found. The only possible locality for it there would be eastern Argentina, southwards from Bahia Blanca. Here, however, the land mass is relatively narrow, and maritime influences prevent very low winter temperatures and large annual ranges (Santa Cruz, 50° S., July 35° F.). Further, the Andes produce a marked rain shadow effect, and the region is largely desert (Patagonia).

Natural Vegetation. The natural vegetation of these eastern margins is mainly forest, but owing to the less favourable conditions, conifers assume much greater relative importance than in the west. North of latitude 50° N. the forests are almost wholly coniferous, but south of this parallel, deciduous forests are also found.

Lumbering thus becomes an important occupation, and the cold winters are turned to advantage, for the frozen snow is utilised to simplify haulage of the "logs", and the flood waters which follow the thaw, carry them away to the saw-mills.

Climatic conditions do not favour agriculture to anything like the same extent as in corresponding latitudes in the west.

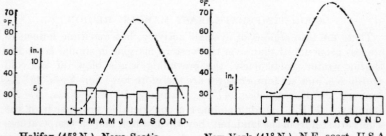

Halifax (45° N.), Nova Scotia   New York (41° N.), N.E. coast, U.S.A.
(less than 100 ft. above sea-level)   (sea-level)

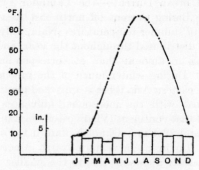

Quebec (47° N.), Lower St. Lawrence
(300 ft. above sea-level)

INTERIOR REGION

As considered here, this region extends from the edge of the savana lands towards the polar circles, occupying a vast area in the middle of the continent.

Far distant from maritime influences, it is essentially a region of temperature extremes. Summers are hot (for the latitude) and winters are very cold. Rainfall is light, resulting from the summer inflow and convection. There is considerably less cloud than in maritime areas in the same latitude, and consequently longer and more intense sunshine.

The following table will give some idea of the transition from a maritime climate to an extreme continental type. The places selected are all in roughly the same latitude, and are all less than 500 ft. above sea-level.

	Jan.	July	Range	Rainfall Oct.–Dec.	Jan.–Mar.	Apr.–June	July–Sept.
Valencia	44° F.	59° F.	15° F.	17·5 in.	15·0 in.	10·0 in.	12·5 in.
London	39	63	24	7·5	5·5	5·5	6·5
Berlin	31	66	35	5·0	4·5	5·5	7·0
Warsaw	26	66	40	4·5	3·5	6·0	8·0
Moscow	14	66	52	4·5	3·0	5·5	8·0
Kazan	8	68	60	3·0	1·5	4·5	6·5
Tomsk	−3	64	67	5·5	2·5	5·0	6·5

The most striking point about these figures, probably, is the great increase in the annual range of temperature as we move away from the influence of the sea. Although there is a difference of only 9° F. in the July temperatures, there is a difference of 47° F. in the January figures. It is in the winters, therefore, that the greatest difference is to be found between the maritime and the continental types of climate.

But the rainfall figures are also instructive. Valencia illustrates the heavy " all-seasons " type of the purely maritime regions ; the winter half-year is appreciably wetter than the summer. In the case of London, continental tendencies are beginning to show ; the winter rain is very little more than the summer. In the case of Berlin, continental tendencies are clearly marked ; the summer rainfall actually exceeds the winter. Still farther inland, the proportion falling during the summer half-year continues to increase. But the proportions at Tomsk, which must be considered as truly continental in type, are comparable with those at Berlin, as presented in the above table, although the period of real winter is relatively drier. Actually, 8 in. of rain fall at Tomsk during the three months June–August, the wettest part of the year ; this is about 40 per cent. of the annual total. In the case of

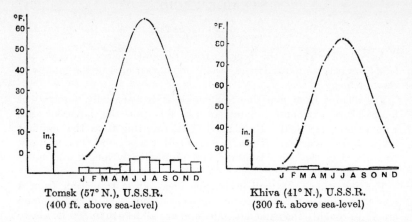

Tomsk (57° N.), U.S.S.R.
(400 ft. above sea-level)

Khiva (41° N.), U.S.S.R.
(300 ft. above sea-level)

Berlin, the figures for the same period, which is again the wettest part of the year, are $7\frac{1}{4}$ in., representing about 33 per cent. of the annual total.

The following stations, which are all less than 900 ft. above sea-level, illustrate conditions in the interior of North America.

	Temp.		Rainfall			
	Jan.	July	Oct.–Dec.	Jan.–Mar.	Apr.–June	July–Sept.
Vicksburg	48° F.	81° F.	11·5 in.	16·0 in.	13·5 in.	10·5 in.
Indianapolis	28	76	9·0	9·5	11·0	10·0
Chicago	26	74	7·0	7·0	10·0	9·5
St. Paul	12	72	4·5	3·0	10·0	10·0
Pt. Arthur	6	63	4·5	2·0	6·0	9·5

Tomsk, in the heart of Siberia, and Khiva, south of the Aral Sea, have been selected to illustrate the temperature and rainfall conditions experienced in the middle of a vast continent.

Natural Vegetation. In the more northerly parts of the "interior region", there is less evaporation during summer, and a greater proportion of the rainfall is thus available for growth. But the growing season is relatively short, and coniferous forest results. These slow-growing trees have become adapted to withstand the very severe winters, and to make the best use of the available summer rainfall. South of the forest are the great grasslands—the North American prairies, the Russian steppes, etc. Still farther south the amount of moisture available decreases (greater evaporation, and generally lighter rainfall), and the rich grasslands give place to "poor steppe", which is comparable to desert grasses.

The rich grasslands are now largely under cultivation, producing enormous quantities of wheat and other food crops. Elsewhere they support numerous cattle.

POLAR REGIONS

Reliable information concerning the true polar regions is very scarce. Over most of Antarctica and Greenland a thick ice-cap persists all the year round. Over many of the lowland areas, however, the ground is snow-covered only throughout the long winter.

Winter temperatures are very low. Dawson City, 65° N., has a January mean of − 23° F. Kola, 69° N., has a January mean of 11° F., but here the moderating influences of the Atlantic Ocean and the North Atlantic Drift have to be taken into account. For long the sun does not rise above the horizon.

As the air is so cold, the winter precipitation is very light, the little that does fall being mainly in the form of snow. Dawson City receives about 2½ in. during the three months December–February; during the same period Kola receives less than 1 in.

Summer days are correspondingly long and the air is then warm; Dawson City has a July mean of 59° F., and Kola one of 55° F.

Since the air is able to hold more moisture, summer rainfall is rather heavier; Dawson City receives 5 in. during the three months, July–September, while Kola receives 3¾ in.

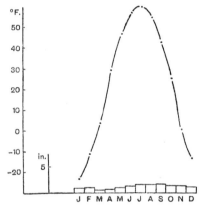

Dawson City (65° N.), Klondike
(1,200 ft. above sea-level)

Natural Vegetation. In the true polar regions the summer temperatures are too low, and the growing season too short, for trees to flourish. The sub-soil is permanently frozen, and only the top layer of soil thaws out in summer. Then marsh is widespread over the lowlands (tundra). The typical vegetation of the tundra consists mainly of mosses and lichens. Here and there stunted birch trees, and willows, are to be found, while on sunny slopes, brightly coloured short-cycle plants of the Alpine type grow in profusion; these plants complete their life-cycle in the space of a few weeks.

Along its temperate margin the tundra gradually gives place to a dwarfed bush vegetation, and then to stunted conifers which slowly merge into the fully developed coniferous forest.

INFLUENCE OF ALTITUDE ON NATURAL VEGETATION

In discussing how the natural vegetation in any particular region responds to the climatic control we have so far touched only very lightly

P2

on the influence of altitude. Yet altitude, through its influence on climate, must clearly play a most important part in the distribution of vegetation.

Generalisation, however, is complicated by the fact that so many factors are involved. Height, alone, helps to determine temperature conditions, but these are greatly modified by the aspect of the particular place. Similarly, aspect must be considered when dealing with rainfall. Temperature, sunshine, frost, humidity, rainfall, all these help to determine the type of vegetation—but they are not controlled by altitude alone, although altitude is of major importance.

Broadly, the vegetation types are distributed in horizontal zones, one type merging into the next, but generalised limits for these zones can only be given for specific areas. Latitude, east, west, or interior regions of continents, north-facing or south-facing slopes, all exert their influence.

Consider first an equatorial region. At sea-level the natural vegetation is normally dense evergreen forest. As the height increases the more delicate varieties gradually disappear, with the result that much of the diversity, so marked a feature at the lower levels, also disappears. However, the forest maintains its essential characteristics up to a height of about 4,000–5,000 ft. in the west and east and 2,000–3,000 ft. in the interior. In the interior and east the forest gives way to savana, but the heavier rainfall in such western areas as the Andes and Cameroons still encourages true forest, but of a sub-tropical type. The next zone is the temperate deciduous forest, which gradually gives way to temperate coniferous forest. At a height of about 8,000–10,000 ft. the forests give place to mountain grasses which, in their turn, 2,000–3,000 ft. higher, are replaced by lichens, mosses, and poor scrub. At 15,000–18,000 ft. is the snow-line (that is, above this level snow covers the ground all the year round). Thus an ascent of 18,000 ft. above the equator reveals a distribution of vegetation not markedly different from that encountered on a sea-level journey from the equator to the poles.

Tracing the vegetation up the southern slopes of the Himalayas, we find sub-tropical jungle, with patches of open savana, extending up to a height of about 3,000 ft. Above this is a broad zone of temperate forest, first deciduous, and then coniferous. The Alpine zone starts at about 12,000–13,000 ft., and extends up to nearly 20,000 ft., above which level there is perennial ice and snow. On the northern slopes, facing Central Asia, the snow-line comes appreciably lower, and the levels of the vegetation zones are altered correspondingly.

The sea-level vegetation of north-west Europe is deciduous forest and grassland. In the Alps this gives place to coniferous forest at a height of about 5,000 ft. At about 7,000 ft. the coniferous forest is replaced by mountain grasses, which are snow-covered in winter but free for cattle grazing in summer. This important feature gives rise to a practice known as transhumance. The cattle are moved up on to the summer pastures (" alps ") round about May, and they are kept there all through the summer. During this time the people tending the cattle live in the little mountain chalets. At the end of the summer the cattle are taken down into the valleys, below the coniferous forest belt. The people move down, too, bringing with them dairy produce and hay. The summer pastures gradually give place to poor scrub, mosses, lichens, etc., and to the characteristic Alpine flowering plants. The snow-line is at about 9,000–10,000 ft.

From these few examples it is clear that altitude, no less than latitude, exerts a powerful control over the distribution of natural vegetation. Moreover, since the natural vegetation is a guide to the type of cultivation possible, altitude clearly helps to determine the uses to which man may put the land surface of the earth.

NOTES AND QUESTIONS
ON THE PHOTOGRAPHS

1 VICTORIA FALLS. This view along the Falls was taken from an aeroplane, a wing of which is seen on the right. The Zambezi flows from right to left in the picture, and below the Falls discharges through a gorge under the bridge, a part of which is seen on the left.

2 VICTORIA FALLS. This view of the Main Falls was taken from a point near the edge of the chasm into which the Zambezi falls. In some places the spray is like heavy rain and is then sufficient to support forest growth.

3 VICTORIA FALLS. In this view the Eastern Cataract is seen through palm trees growing at the edge of the Falls, while the rocky edge of the Zambezi above the Falls is seen on the right.

Questions

These three photographs were all taken in September. Do they suggest that the volume of water was then above average or below average?

What evidence is there to suggest that the Zambezi falls into a deep cleft in an otherwise generally level area?

What vegetation would you expect to find in the vicinity of the Falls? Account for what you observe in the photographs.

How do these photographs emphasise the hindrance to communications imposed by the Falls?

How can Falls such as these be harnessed to provide a source of power?

4 NIAGARA FALLS. This view of Niagara is taken from the Canadian side of the Falls and gives an indication of the tremendous source of power available.

Question

To what extent and for what purposes has the power available in Niagara been harnessed?

5 GRAND CANYON. This particular photograph is of Duck Point, overlooking the Grand Canyon on the Colorado River, and clearly illustrates a number of the characteristics of erosion and weathering under arid conditions.

Question

Study the photograph, list the features that are characteristic of arid regions and explain how they have taken on their present form.

6 FRASER CANYON. This view of the Fraser River is in the region where the river winds through the Coast Range of British Columbia—an area opened up initially in the search for gold. Note the railroad on the ledge running along the valley side.

Question

Compare this photograph (6) with the previous one (5) and notice how the characteristic features differ. Account for the differences observed.

7 PAINTED DESERT. This is a general view of the region in the vicinity of the Grand Canyon on the Colorado River. Reddish tints predominate in a colourful landscape.
Question
What evidence does the photograph show that this area is a most inhospitable desert?

8 "OLD FAITHFUL" GEYSER. This geyser in the Yellowstone National Park is so reliable that sightseers are able to approach within a distance of 20 or 30 yards. Boards are placed in position to give a safe foothold.
Question
What are geysers? Give other examples.

9 CRATER LAKE. This lake in the Cascade Range of Oregon is known to be very deep in parts.
Question
Study the photograph carefully and comment on all the features you observe.

10 LAKE LOUISE. This lake is in the Rocky Mountains, near the Alberta and British Columbia border.
Question
Study the photograph carefully and describe the scenery.

11 SUN VALLEY. This is a view of a well-known ski-ing resort in Idaho.
12 MOUNT BAKER. This is a view of ski-ing in progress on the slopes of Mount Baker in Washington State.
Questions
What evidence is there in the photographs of sunshine?
Explain how it is that snow can lie in excellent condition for ski-ing, while sunshine can provide invigorating and comfortable conditions for people.
Describe the vegetation at these altitudes.

13 NORTHERN NIGERIA. Weathered rock-masses project above the general level of the ground in several parts of Northern Nigeria; in some areas they provide the only prominent relief.
Question
The place shown in the photograph is about 11 degrees from the equator. What are the outstanding characteristics of the climate in such a locality, and what is the effect of this type of climate on (*a*) the weathering of rocks, and (*b*) the natural vegetation? See also 24.

14 KOOTENAY RIVER. This view of the river is looking towards the foothills of the Rockies in British Columbia. The valley slopes are thickly covered with conifers, except where cleared for settlement.
15 BOW FALLS, BANFF. This is the area of the Banff National Park in Alberta.
Questions
Describe the relief of the areas shown in the photographs.
To what extent does this kind of relief influence settlement and communications? Comment on the natural vegetation.

16 ICE-FALL, BRITISH COLUMBIA. This photograph was taken along the Salmo-Creston Highway in British Columbia, near the United States border, about the end of March.

Question

What does the photograph tell you about the difficulties of keeping roads free for traffic during winter in the region of the Rockies?

17 YELLOWSTONE RIVER VALLEY. The Yellowstone River, which rises in Wyoming, flows through Montana to join the Missouri.

Question

Describe the relief features of this valley.

18 LOG-BOOMS, VANCOUVER ISLAND. The large, straight trunks of conifer trees are made up into extensive rafts, which float downstream in the rivers to the saw-mills.

Question

What are the main characteristics of a coniferous forest, and in what ways does a coniferous forest differ from a tropical forest?

19 COCONUT PALMS. This photograph was taken in the coastal belt of Ghana, which is typical of tropical areas where palms flourish.

20 BUSH, SIERRA LEONE. This photograph shows a tangle of secondary bush in the interior of Sierra Leone.

21 ANT-HILL. The prominent earthen mound, popularly called an ant-hill, is built by termites (" white ants "), which are not really ants, to enclose their nest.

22 BUSH CLEARED BY FIRE. The tangle of tropical bush is very difficult to clear by means of primitive implements, but it can be cleared quickly by fire. Before the end of the dry season it is a common sight to see bush-fires, deliberately started, clearing ground in readiness for cultivation when the rains begin. Subsistence farming is generally practised until the soil becomes exhausted, and then a fresh area is cleared, while the abandoned area is allowed to revert to bush, but an impoverished, secondary bush.

Questions

What do you observe as common characteristics of palm trees? See also 3 and 29.

Oil palms are valuable, as the name suggests, for the oil they produce. The fruit consists of a hard kernel surrounded by soft pulp. The oil in the pulp can be extracted by quite primitive methods, but the oil in the kernel can be extracted only after the kernel has been crushed. Find out all you can about the extraction, preparation and uses of palm oil and palm-kernel oil.

Compare the view in 20 with an English lane through wooded country.

Termites are numerous and widespread in the tropics. Find out all you can about their habits.

Write an essay on subsistence farming as practised in areas illustrated by 20, 21 and 22.

23 SURF COAST. The photograph illustrates part of the coast of Ghana. Fishermen become very adept in launching and landing their craft.

Question

Describe the characteristics of a surf coast.

24 CATTLE COUNTRY. Cattle are bred in the open country of Northern Nigeria, and many of them are taken to the towns in the southern part of the country, where they are slaughtered. Initially the herds were led along recognised routes, where they were able to find grass and water, but nowadays many are transported by rail. The photograph shows cattle at a veterinary control post near Zaria.

Question

To what extent are such tropical savanna lands capable of being developed as producers of prime cattle?

25 NATIVE HUT. Villages are usually located in clearings in the bush, within reasonable walking distance of the farms currently being cultivated. The walls are made of mud, pounded into and around wicker-work, which provides reinforcement. The roof is normally thatched with grass or leaves.

Question

What does the style of the hut—the steeply pitched roof, the over-hanging eaves, the absence of windows—suggest about the climate?

26 RIVER-FERRY. Where there are large seasonal variations in the depth and width of rivers, bridges may be very costly. Simple ferries, operated by men pulling on a tow-line, are still common in underdeveloped countries.

Question

To what extent do rivers assist communication, and to what extent can they hinder it?

27 THE COTTON TREE, FREETOWN. This particular giant of tropical areas has historical associations with the early settlement of Freetown, but similar specimens are to be found over wide areas. These " cotton " trees yield kapok.

28 BAOBAB TREE. This particularly fine specimen of a baobab tree stands alongside the Kano–Zaria road. The photograph was taken during the dry season, when the tree was bare.

Question

Compare the characteristics of the vegetation in the near-equatorial, rain-forest area with those of the tropical, near-desert area.

29 ORNAMENTAL PALM TREES. There are many different kinds of palms; some of great value as food producers, others purely ornamental. In parks or along avenues some varieties of palm trees can be most attractive.

30 RAIN FOREST. Rain forest in its natural state now occupies relatively small areas in West Africa, for many areas have, at some time or other, been partially cleared. Along the road shown in the photograph, which has been cut through a forest area, a number of rubber trees have been planted where they are easily accessible.

31 BANANA TREES. Many village compounds in the forest belt have bananas growing profusely. During the dry season the broad leaves split into ribbons.

32 MANGO TREES. The mango tree is widespread in the tropical belt, and as it has dense foliage it is often valued for its shade. The fruit somewhat resembles a large plum, in that a large, flat stone is surrounded by juicy pulp, and the whole by tough skin.

Questions

What evidence is there in each of the four photographs to suggest that it was taken in a hot and sunny climate?

1   VICTORIA FALLS, River Zambezi—View from an aeroplane

2   VICTORIA FALLS—Main Falls

3 VICTORIA FALLS—Eastern Cataract

4 NIAGARA FALLS—Horseshoe Falls on the Canadian side

5
GRAND CANYON
Colorado River
Arizona

6   FRASER CANYON, British Columbia

7 PAINTED DESERT, Arizona

8
'OLD FAITHFUL'
GEYSER
Yellowstone,
Wyoming

9   CRATER LAKE, Oregon

10   LAKE LOUISE, Alberta

11 SUN VALLEY, Idaho

12 MOUNT BAKER, Washington State

13   NORTHERN NIGERIA—Weathered rock masses

14   KOOTENAY RIVER, British Columbia

15 BOW FALLS
Banff, Alberta

16
ICE-FALL
British Columbia

17
YELLOWSTONE
RIVER VALLEY
Montana

18 LOG-BOOMS
Vancouver Island

19 COCONUT PALMS—Ghana coast

20 BUSH—Interior of Sierra Leone

21
ANT-HILL
Interior of
Sierra Leone

22 BUSH CLEARED BY FIRE, in readiness for cultivation—Sierra Leone

23 SURF COAST—Ghana

24 CATTLE COUNTRY—Northern Nigeria

25   NATIVE HUT—Sierra Leone

26   RIVER-FERRY—Sierra Leone

27 THE COTTON TREE—Freetown

28 BAOBAB TREE—Northern Nigeria

29
ORNAMENTAL
PALM TREES
Ghana

30
RAIN FOREST
Sierra Leone

31 BANANA TREES
in a village compound
—Sierra Leone

32
MANGO TREES
lining a road—
Sierra Leone

QUESTIONS

The sources of questions are acknowledged thus :

University of Bristol - - - - - - • • • **B.**
University of Cambridge - - - - - • - - **C.**
University of London - - - - - - - - **L.**
Joint Matriculation Board (Universities of Manchester, Liverpool,
    Leeds, Sheffield and Birmingham) - - - - - - **N.**
University of Oxford - - - - - - - - **O.**
Oxford & Cambridge Schools Examination Board - - • **O. & C.**
Central Welsh Board - - - - - - • • - **W.**

1. Explain the following terms : (a) the tropic and polar circles : (b) the International Date Line. Consider the position of each of these in relation to (i) movements of the earth and sun, (ii) the distribution of land and water. Diagrams and sketch-maps are essential. **N.**

2. With the help of diagrams, explain each of two of the following :
(a) Why, throughout the year, there is no appreciable variation in the length of day and night at the equator.
(b) Why the mean annual temperature is high in low latitudes and low in high latitudes.
(c) Why, in cool temperate latitudes, the west coasts of continents are warmer than the east coasts during the winter. **N.**

3. Outline and justify a simple classification of rocks which would be helpful to a geographer in studying a region. **L.**

4. Describe and account for differences in the scenery of plateaux composed of (a) limestones, (b) non-calcareous rocks. Refer in each case to definite regions. **N.**

5. The Earth's surface is composed partly of igneous rocks, and partly of rocks of sedimentary origin. Give an account of the main differences between these two types of rock. Describe the characteristics of the rocks you would see if you were to examine three of the following : (a) a chalk quarry, (b) a quarry in sandstone, (c) a clay pit, (d) a quarry in massive limestone. **C.**

6. Give an explanatory description of the various types of mountains. **C.**

7. Name three mountain areas which differ in mode of formation and, by the use of diagrams and notes, describe how each has been formed. **N.**

8. Give a brief account of the chief types of movement to which the crust of the earth is subject, and with the help of actual examples indicate their influence in shaping the surface. **L.**

9. What are the major land forms and structures that arise from the earth's movements? Show, with examples, how these land forms and structures affect the exploitation of mineral wealth. **L.**

10. Describe and illustrate by reference to particular examples the effects of (a) folding, (b) faulting, upon relief. L.

11. What are the characteristics of a country which has been subjected to considerable volcanic activity? O. & C.

12. Write a short essay on earthquakes, their effects, distribution, and probable causes. B.

13. With the aid of specific examples discuss the points of likeness and difference between (a) a peneplain and (b) a plain of deposition. L.

14. Distinguish between rock weathering and erosion. Show how the processes of weathering in a cool humid climate, such as that of Wales, differ from those in a hot arid region. W.

15. Describe the action of wind as a weathering agent and discuss the character and mode of occurrence of Aeolian deposits. B.

16. Give an account of the development of a river system and indicate some of the complications which may occur. B.

17. Show how river capture may affect the drainage pattern of a river system. You may take your examples from any part of the world. O.

18. What is meant by the flood plain of a river? Describe and account for the characteristic land forms generally present, illustrating your answer by diagrams and mentioning specific examples. N.

19. With reference to specific examples, (a) state the factors that may cause river floods and describe the character of a flood plain, (b) show how floods may be both favourable and unfavourable to man's activities. N.

20. Explain the main stages of development of a river-system in a simple scarpland area as in South-east England. L.

21. Describe fully the erosive action of wind, and give an account of the development of sand dunes. C.

22. Describe and account for the land forms characteristic of desert regions. B.

23. Describe the characteristic land forms of either a hot desert or a glaciated region, and show how these land forms have been produced. O. & C.

24. What are the characteristic features of regions that have been glaciated? O. & C.

25. Contrast the types of land form that are found in (a) humid and (b) desert regions, and give reasons for the differences you note. L.

26. Describe the effect of ice in moulding the land forms of a country. B.

27. Describe and explain with particular reference to Great Britain the major modifications of topography that have been produced by glaciation. B.

28. Explain, with examples and sketches, the origin of any four of the following : (a) hanging valley, (b) rock basin, (c) corrie, (d) arête, (e) esker, (f) terminal moraine, (g) ice-fall. C.

29. Write an account of either (a) Karst topography or (b) glaciated mountain topography. Illustrate your answer with suitable examples and diagrams. N.

30. Compare and contrast the nature and origin of land forms associated respectively, in middle latitudes, with normal river valleys and with glaciated mountain valleys. **N.**

31. Summarise with reference to particular areas the evidence for the occurrence of a geologically recent glacial epoch. **L.**

32. Describe the various ways in which springs are formed, illustrating your answer with sketches. **C.**

33. Propose a scheme for the classification of shore lines, giving reasons for the scheme selected. **B.**

34. Describe the characteristic relief features of coasts (and coastlines) of emergence, and outline the processes by which these features are produced. **W.**

35. Describe with contoured sketch-maps the physical characteristics of three of the following : (a) a fiord coast, (b) a ria coast, (c) a dune coast, (d) a cirque, (e) a dissected plateau. Give a suitable scale to each of your sketch-maps. **W.**

36. What are the chief features of a fiord coast? Contrast these features with those found round the Wash. Explain briefly why the natural conditions are not in either case such as to favour the growth of great ports. **O.**

37. (a) Describe the formation of two of the following : (i) deltas, (ii) fiords, (iii) inland drainage basins.
(b) Discuss the influence on human settlement of each of the land forms selected. Refer to actual examples. **N.**

38. Describe, with illustrative examples, either (a) the chief types of coastlines or (b) the relationships existing between ocean currents and the climates of the western margins of continents. **N.**

39. Sketch and describe illustrative examples of four of the following : incised meanders, escarpments, hanging valleys, concordant coasts, fiords, raised beaches. Show briefly the influence on human activities of each of the features you describe. **N.**

40. Explain the nature, and as far as possible the origin, of three of the following and illustrate their influence on human geography : Shield, Glacial drift, Inversion of temperature, Tropical cyclone, Discordant coast. **L.**

41. How far may it be maintained that favourable geographical conditions are essential for the development of ports of world importance? Support your view with precise examples. **N.**

42. Suggest a classification of lake-types on the basis of mode of origin. Give examples of each type where possible and describe the modes of origin of two different types of lakes in the British Isles. **W.**

43. Describe the agents which have been mainly responsible for the formation of any three of the following : Dead Sea, Lake Geneva, Lake Huron, Lake Windermere, Victoria Nyanza. **N.**

44. Write a concise essay on coral reefs. **B.**

45. Say what you know of the distribution of coral islands and coral reefs. To what causes do you ascribe this distribution? What do you know of the theories of the origin of coral islands and reefs? **C.**

46. The degree of salinity of sea water is not everywhere the same. Say why this is so, and give the composition of an average sample of sea water. What are the conditions which lead to the formation of salt lakes? **C.**

47. Indicate on a sketch-map the variation in the surface salinity in the North Atlantic Ocean, Mediterranean, North and Baltic Seas. Suggest reasons for the differences shown on your sketch-maps. **W.**

48. Give an explanatory account of the phenomenon of tides, and describe in more detail the tidal movements around the British Isles. **L.**

49. Describe briefly the causation of the general oceanic surface circulation of water. Illustrate from either the Pacific Ocean north of the equator or the Atlantic Ocean south of the equator, noting the more important climatic effects of the circulation described. **L.**

50. Write an explanatory account of the ocean currents of the Atlantic Ocean, noting their influence upon the climates of the adjoining land masses. **O. & C.**

51. Examine the relation between the prevalent wind systems and ocean currents in either the North Atlantic or North Pacific Oceans. **B.**

52. Explain with the aid of diagrams the meaning of the following : (a) bore, (b) spring tide, (c) ocean current, (d) race, (e) wave. **C.**

53. Describe the characters, distribution and origin of the deposits formed on the ocean floor. **C.**

54. Discuss in detail the difference between weather and climate. **O. & C.**

55. Explain why the average maximum and minimum temperatures in June and in December for places in approximately the same middle latitude may vary considerably even when the places are at the same height above sea-level. Reference should be made to actual places. **W.**

56. The average mean sea-level temperature, in January, of West Wales is above 40° F., but snow frequently remains on the slopes of Snowdon in July. Explain carefully why this is so. **W.**

57. Give some account of the data and principles on which the daily weather forecasts formulated by the Meteorological Office are made. **C.**

58. What do you understand by " dew point " ? Give an account of the different forms of cloud, illustrating your answer by sketches. **C.**

59. Describe the pressure and weather conditions associated with any two of the following : (a) a deep depression centred over Cardigan Bay, (b) a Chinook or Föhn wind, (c) a Khamsin or Santa Ana, (d) a Southerly Burster or Pampero, (e) a typhoon. **W.**

60. (a) What conditions cause rainfall in (i) the British Isles ; (ii) either the Amazon basin or the middle Congo basin?

(b) For each of the areas discussed under (a), describe (i) the seasonal variations of the rainfall through the year ; (ii) the variations in the mean annual rainfall over the area as a whole. **N.**

61. Discuss one of the following topics :

(a) The characteristic sequence of weather during the passage of a low-pressure system over the British Isles in winter.

(b) Similarities and differences in the major surface wind systems over the Atlantic Ocean south of the tropic of Cancer and the Indian Ocean. **N.**

62. Discuss the characteristics of two of the following : (a) either south polar or mountain climates ; (b) tropical revolving storms ; (c) the climate of a " rain shadow " area. **N.**

63. *Either* (a) Compare tropical revolving storms (typhoons and hurricanes) with cyclones of the west coasts of middle latitudes. *Or* (b) Discuss hot-season thunderstorms as factors of rain supply in various climates. N.

64. Give specific examples to illustrate, as fully as you can, the influence of relief on climate. N.

65. Select two of the following pressure systems : (a) a trough of low pressure in mid-winter ; (b) a ridge of high pressure in late spring ; (c) a high pressure in late summer. Describe and explain the sequence of weather conditions in various parts of Great Britain when each of the two selected systems is dominating. N.

66. Illustrate and discuss the climatic effects of cold ocean currents in (a) cool temperate and (b) warm temperate and tropical latitudes. L.

67. Describe the general distribution of pressure in the Northern Hemisphere in (a) January, (b) July. What relation, if any, can you trace between the distribution of temperature and of pressure in each of these months? L.

68. Give an explanatory account of the seasonal distribution of precipitation over the surface of the earth. L.

69. By reference to the climate of actual localities, distinguish and compare carefully those elements that are due to latitude and those that are due to relief and the distribution of land and sea. L.

70. Describe the characteristics of the destructive storm types of tropical latitudes, and show how they differ from the cyclones of middle latitudes. A theory of the causation of cyclones is not expected. W.

71. Show in what ways the climate of England differs from the climate of places in similar latitudes but situated in the centres of large continents. Point out two ways in which a knowledge of English climate based on average conditions would be misleading. O.

72. Explain the various ways in which conditions of heat and rainfall influence plant and animal life in two of the following : (a) a desert area such as the Sahara ; (b) an equatorial lowland such as Equatorial West Africa ; (c) a cold region like Greenland. O.

73. To what extent may the climate of Germany be described as " continental "? C.

74. On a rough sketch-map of the Old World, north of the equator, mark the areas of high and low pressures (mean sea-level or actual) and the prevailing wind directions in July. Explain, with the aid of your maps, the heavy July rainfall over S.E. Asia and the dry conditions over the Mediterranean Sea and its borderlands. W.

75. Analyse, in relation to latitude and other factors, the following temperature figures, given in degrees Fahrenheit :

	Mean January	Mean daily range January	Mean July	Mean daily range July
Singapore (33 feet) (Lat. 1° 18′ N.)	78·8	12·7	81·9	12·4
Wadi Halfa (421 feet) (Lat. 21° 55′ N.)	57·9	29	88·5	32
Valencia (30 feet) (Lat. 52° N.)	44·4	8·8	58·8	10·2

W.

76. Describe and account for : (a) the winter average temperature of S.W. Ireland being relatively high for the latitude ; (b) the marked seasonal distribution of rainfall in either Cape Town or Perth (West Australia) ; (c) variations in the height of the snow-line, in terms of (i) latitude, (ii) season of the year.   N.

77. *Either* (a) " Within the tropics the eastern margins of continents and within temperate latitudes the western margins generally have the heavier rainfall." Illustrate this statement by reference to the study of the rainfall regime of four widely separated areas.

Or (b) Contrast and give reasons for the difference in the temperature conditions normally experienced in winter in England during (i) the passage of a deep depression, (ii) the presence of an anticyclone.   N.

78. On maps of the northern hemisphere is shown a great belt of arid land stretching across the Old World obliquely to the lines of latitude. The factors promoting that aridity differ in different parts of the belt. Illustrate this by a survey of four large contrasted portions of the belt.
                                                                          N.

79. On the outline map of the world supplied, mark and name the main areas of (a) equatorial and (b) coniferous forests. Contrast the climatic regimes and related vegetation features characteristic of these two types of forest.   N.

80. On the outline map of the world supplied, mark and name areas with (a) maximum precipitation in winter and little or none in summer, (b) precipitation throughout the year. Select one region from (a) and one from (b) and describe and account for the main characteristics of their natural vegetation.   N.

81. Describe and explain the annual and seasonal distribution of rainfall in South America.   O. & C.

82. Write an explanatory account of the climate of the monsoon lands of Asia.   O. & C.

83. Give an account of the rainfall of the Sahara and the bordering savanna lands. By what means are the inhabitants able to overcome the difficulties of drought?   O.

84. Give an account of the climate of New Zealand.   O.

85. Account for the characteristics and the distribution of " Mediterranean " climates throughout the world.   B.

86. Write an account of the natural vegetation of the " Mediterranean regions " of the world, showing how plant life is adapted to environment.
                                                                          B.

87. Give an account of the climate, vegetation, and mode of life of the natives in *either* (a) Siberia north of the Arctic Circle, *or* (b) the Matto Grosso district of Brazil, *or* (c) any tropical island in the Pacific Ocean.
                                                                          O.

88. Describe and account for the principal characteristics of a temperate forest.   O. & C.

89. Into what vegetation regions would you divide Africa?
                                                                        O. & C.

90. Show on a sketch-map a division of any one continent or subcontinent outside your special region into vegetation regions, and contrast the climatic conditions prevailing in any two vegetation regions shown on your map.   W.

91. " The distribution of the main types of vegetation of the world is strongly influenced by climate." Discuss this statement with special reference to North America and Africa.   C.

92. Indicate the distribution of the hot desert lands of the world and discuss the physical factors that account for their regional distribution.   W.

93. Discuss the regional gradation of climate along any west coast margin from the equator to approximately either 45° N. or 45° S. The coastal lands need not be continuous.   W.

94. Describe the characteristic features and world distribution of (a) savanna, (b) coniferous forests, (c) mangrove swamps. In each case state the climatic factors on which this general distribution depends.   N.

95. What do you understand by the term savannah country? Where and under what climatic regimes does it chiefly occur?   N.

96. On the outline map of the world supplied, mark the major areas of tropical and temperate grasslands. Select one of these grassland areas and describe its main characteristics and the climatic regime under which it has developed.   N.

97. State briefly the distribution of the major types of forest in the world. Explain the predominance of soft woods over hard woods in the world's timber industry.   N.

98. What are the particular problems involved in the agricultural development of equatorial regions? Illustrate your answers by reference to specific examples.   N.

99. Carefully locate the main areas of (a) tropical savanna and (b) temperate grassland of the world. Indicate how geographical conditions help to account for the difference in their utilisation by man at the present time.   L.

100. What do you understand by the " China type " of climate? Describe the world distribution of this climatic type, comment on the applicability of the term to the several areas you mention and note the principal economic activities of each.   L.

101. Locate carefully the major areas of coniferous forest. Estimate their importance in the general world economy and show how geographical conditions favour or hinder their exploitation.   L.

102. Compare the mid-latitude grasslands of the Northern Hemisphere with those of the Southern Hemisphere under the headings (a) position, (b) climate, and (c) development.   L.

103. Bring out, and try to account for, the differences between the Warm Temperate Eastern Marginal and the Warm Temperate Western Marginal types of climate.   L.

104. Discuss the relationship between the duration of the wet season and the type of natural vegetation within the tropics.   L.

105. Confining your attention to the northern hemisphere, contrast the Cool Temperate East Marginal type of climate with the Cool Temperate West Marginal type and try to account for any similarities and differences.   L.

106. In what respects is it true to say that altitude may give rise to a temperate climate in low latitudes? Estimate the importance of such modifications in connexion with the white settlement.   L.

107. Discuss the influences of aspect of high slopes on the height of the snow-line and on land utilisation in the northern hemisphere.   N.

108. Examine the statement that, at the equator, altitude can compensate climatically for the low latitude.   L.

109. Describe and explain the essential differences between the various types of climate in latitudes 45° to 60°.   N.

110. Give a brief account of the more important factors which affect vegetation and discuss their influence on the natural vegetation of three of the following : Ceylon, Crete, Ireland, Newfoundland, Tasmania.   N.

111. Consider the problems involved in, and the advantages gained by, the development of irrigation in one of the following areas : (a) North America ; (b) Africa north of the equator ; (c) Monsoon Asia ; (d) Asiatic U.S.S.R.   N.

112. Locate carefully the chief regions of Equatorial Rain Forest. Describe and try to account for the different development of the several areas.   L.

113. Carefully describe the distribution of the rainfall, regional and seasonal, of the Guinea Coast lands from the Cameroons to the Gambia River, and use your description as the basis of a division of the area into rainfall regions.   L.

114. Describe and account for the distribution of hot deserts. To what extent and in what areas are these desert regions utilised by man? L.

115. Give a careful account of the characteristics of the Mediterranean type of climate. Show how far these characteristics vary as between the Northern and the Southern Hemispheres.   L.

116. Outline and account for the distribution of the different types of forest in temperate or middle latitudes.   L.

117. Draw simple temperature and rainfall diagrams to illustrate the climatic conditions in each of the following locations : (a) an interior continental position in temperate latitudes such as that of Minneapolis ; (b) an equatorial island such as Singapore; (c) a position between savanna and hot desert such as that of Timbuktu. Add explanatory notes.   L.

118. The tables given below show the mean monthly rainfall in inches in the Jaffna Peninsula (a low-lying area on the north of Ceylon), at Winnipeg, and at Valparaiso, respectively.

	(a) In Jaffna	(b) At Winnipeg	(c) At Valparaiso
Jan. - - -	3·55	0·9	0
Feb. - - -	1·05	0·7	0
Mar. - - -	1·29	1·2	0·9
Apr. - - -	1·77	1·4	0·1
May - - -	1·56	2·0	2·7
June - - -	0·47	3·1	6·0
July - - -	0·75	3·1	5·3
Aug. - - -	1·82	2·2	3·4
Sept. - - -	2·74	2·2	0·4
Oct. - - -	9·60	1·4	0·5
Nov. - - -	15·60	1·1	0·3
Dec. - - -	10·96	0·9	0

Comment on these figures and give a reasoned explanation of the causes of the differences shown.   C.

INDEX

Ice sheets, 62 *et seq.*
Indian monsoon, 201 *et seq.*
Inland drainage basin, 69, 95
Interior of earth, 26–8
Interior (of continents) regions, 217
International Date Line, 9–11
Islands, 100–3
Isostasy (theory), 32–3
Isobar, 139
Isohaline, 109
Isohyet, 139
Isotherm, 139

Jointing, 70, 78

Kames, 68
Kant's theory, 24
Karst, 78–9
Katabatic winds, 155, 187
Khamsim, 185

Lakes, 95 *et seq.*
Land breeze, 147, 187
Landslide (landslip), 76
Latitude (measurement), 21
Latitude (parallels), 5
Line squalls, 178
Longitude (measurement), 22
Longitude (meridians), 5
Longitude and time, 8

Marine erosion, 81 *et seq.*
Massif, 45
Meanders, 56–8
Mean solar day, 21
" Mediterranean " regions, 209 *et seq.*
Mineral springs, 75
Mistral, 186
Monsoon climate, 170–2
Monsoon regions, 200 *et seq.*
Moraines, 66
Mortlake, 57, 97
Mountains, 39 *et seq.*
Mountain breeze, 187

Nebular theory, 24

Oasis, 73
Obsequent streams, 61
Ocean currents, 111 *et seq.*
Ocean deep, 104
Ocean rise, 104
Oceanic islands, 101
Off-shore bar, 84

Orogenetic forces, **39**
Oxbow, 57, 97
Pelagic deposits, 105
Peneplain (peneplane), 48–9
Plains of denudation, 48–9
Plains of deposition, 47–8, 54–**8**
Planetary wind system, 166
Planetesimal hypothesis, **25**
Plateau, 49
Polar front, 175
Polar regions, 219
Pressure (measurement), 127
Pressure and winds, 164 *et seq.*
Pteropod ooze, 105

Radiolarian ooze, 105
Rainfall (mean annual), 136
Rainfall (mean monthly), 136
Rainfall—convectional, 160–1
Rainfall—cyclonic, 162, 174 *et seq.*
Rainfall—relief, 158–60
Rain-guage, 129
Rain shadow, 159
Red clay, 105
Residual mountains, 47
Revolution of earth, 11
Ria, 91–2
Rift valley, 43, 95
Rivers, 52 *et seq.*
Rocks, 34–8
Rotation of earth, **7**

Salinity, 106–9
Sand dunes, 69–70, 89
Savana (Savanna, Savannah), 198
Sea breeze, 146, 187
Seasons, 11
Secondary depression, 181–2
Shape of earth, 2–4
Sirocco, 185
Snow, 163
Snowline, 62, 220
Solar system, 23
Spits, 88–9
Springs, 71–3
Squall line, 178
Standard time belts, 8
Stevenson screen, 132
Subsequent streams, 61
Subsidence and uplift (theory), 32
Sunshine (measurement), 133
Swallow holes, 78
Syncline, 40
Synoptic chart, 139, 179–81

PRINTED IN GREAT BRITAIN BY ROBERT MACLEHOSE AND CO. LTD.
THE UNIVERSITY PRESS, GLASGOW

B1